W9-CMF-222

Schools in the Landscape

Schools in the Landscape

Localism, Cultural Tradition, and the
Development of Alabama's Public
Education System, 1865–1915

Edith M. Ziegler

THE UNIVERSITY OF ALABAMA PRESS

Tuscaloosa

Copyright © 2010
The University of Alabama Press
Tuscaloosa, Alabama 35487-0380
All rights reserved
Manufactured in the United States of America

Typeface: Caslon

∞

The paper on which this book is printed meets the minimum requirements of American National Standard for Information Sciences-Permanence of Paper for Printed Library Materials, ANSI Z39.48-1984.

Library of Congress Cataloging-in-Publication Data

Ziegler, Edith.
    Schools in the landscape : localism, cultural tradition, and the development of Alabama's public education system, 1865–1915 / Edith M. Ziegler.
        p. cm.
    Includes bibliographical references and index.
    ISBN 978-0-8173-1709-6 (cloth : alk. paper) — ISBN 978-0-8173-8359-6 (electronic)
    1. Public schools—Alabama—History. 2. Public schools—Social aspects—Alabama. 3. Education—Alabama—History. 4. Education—Social aspects—Alabama. I. Title.
    LA231.Z54 2010
    370.9761—dc22

                                                                            2010006493

Front Cover: Clarke County School, circa 1910. Courtesy Alabama Department of Archives and History, Montgomery, Alabama.

Contents

Illustrations

Acknowledgments

In expressing gratitude to the many organizations and people that helped me to research and write this book, I should first mention the University of New England, whose award to me of a Keith and Dorothy Mackay Postgraduate Travelling Scholarship in 2006 defrayed significantly the expenses of living for many months in Montgomery, Alabama.

In Montgomery, I spent almost all my time at the Alabama Department of Archives and History (ADAH). I was made warmly welcome by the director, Dr. Edwin Bridges, who ensured my visit was maximally effective. Similarly, Dr. Norwood Kerr helped me to make full use of ADAH's rich archival and reference material. Dr. Kerr's advice to me before I even arrived in Alabama, and his ongoing assistance after I left, were absolutely critical to my being able to undertake my research. In fact all the ADAH staff and volunteers were tremendously helpful to me in finding and accessing relevant material. Among the volunteers I must thank Jim Snider, who generously followed up missed details for me after I returned to Australia.

The professional help and kindness I received at the archives seemed to me to be typical of the warmth and generosity of Montgomery's wider community. Everyone I met in Montgomery went out of their way to ensure I had a truly happy, rich, and rewarding experience.

I must also acknowledge the assistance I received from staff at many libraries including the Birmingham Public Library; the University of New England's Dixson Library; the University of Sydney's Fisher Library; the Montgomery City-County Public Library; the New York Public Library; and the State Library of New South Wales—particularly from the ever-obliging Ms. Sudhi Gupta who managed my constant and seemingly endless requests for books, articles, documents and microfilms from overseas repositories.

I was fortunate to have had the support and encouragement of Professor

David Kent of the University of New England's School of Humanities who afforded me the benefits of his long experience and wisdom. Dr. Jennifer Clark, of the same school provided me over many years with the indispensable counsel, beneficial direction, and watchful oversight necessary to bring my project to completion. I must also thank Professor Harvey H. Jackson of Alabama's Jacksonville State University for his suggestion that my research should be published. I will always be grateful, too, for the constructive suggestions, perceptive comments, and overall guidance provided by The University of Alabama Press.

Thanks are also due to my indulgent friends and family—particularly to Libby and Alex Jones for their loving encouragement over many years.

Schools in the Landscape

Introduction

On December 14, 1819, Alabama was admitted to the Union. Between then and February 1854 when the General Assembly of Alabama passed a law establishing a statewide public schooling system, the state's educational enactments were exceedingly modest and largely restricted to the chartering of private academies. Such action was barely sufficient to give substance to the constitutional piety that "Schools and the means of education shall forever be encouraged in this State."[1] This should not, however, be taken as a sign of any particular indolence.

Before the Civil War (1861–1865) the socialization of children was regarded in most parts of the United States as a parental and community matter. In Alabama, community schools were organized and survived—or did not survive—according to the wishes and wherewithal of the people they served. Educational policy was the province of elected trustees who were also responsible for building schoolhouses, employing teachers, prescribing texts, and generally operating the schools within a local area termed a township.

In 1929, when modernization was still a work in progress, Edgar W. Knight, professor of education at the University of North Carolina, claimed this early model of schooling inspired a "persistent devotion to and confidence in localism in education." He saw this as a continuing blight and tut-tutted that localism "still commends itself to wide popular approval because of the deep democratic color it is believed to wear."[2]

Geography goes some way toward explaining the localism that was Alabama's prevailing cultural condition during the nineteenth century. The state contains an area of 52,423 square miles, which, for comparative purposes, is about the same size as England. Within its borders are a number of fairly distinct regions, which are themselves composed of varying landscapes. Prior to the arrival of railroads and the later expansion of rail networks, these regions were often practically isolated from one another because, although Alabama has an extensive river system, this did not create a connecting transport link

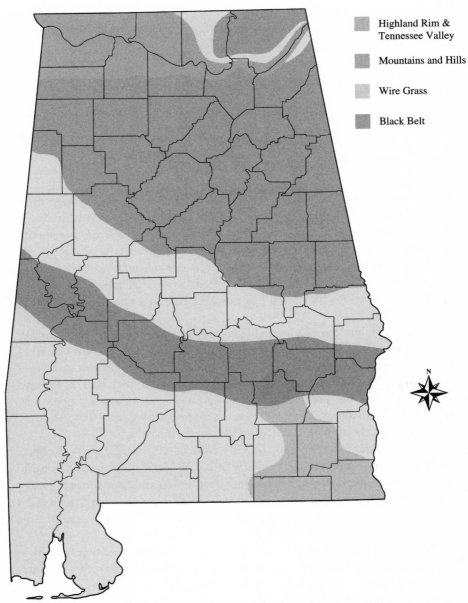

Highland Rim &
Tennessee Valley

Mountains and Hills

Wire Grass

Black Belt

N

1. Principal geographic areas of Alabama. Composite of maps produced by (i) Department of
Geography, College of Arts and Sciences, University of Alabama. Downloaded from http://
alabamamaps.ua.ed/contemporarymaps/alabama/basemaps and (ii) Robert Stroud of Auburn
University, Alabama. Stroud map included in Wayne Flynt, *Alabama in the Twentieth Century:
The Modern South* (Tuscaloosa: University of Alabama Press, 2004), opposite page 292.

between the north of the state and the south. Moreover, there were few roads, and people living in a single county could be separated by natural barriers of ridges and valleys, rivers and plateaus, or dense forests of hardwood and pine. These factors limited options for social interaction in many areas. The consequent insularity strengthened self-reliance and allowed ancient traditions to develop local expression. In the white community these traditions had their origins in what was most frequently an Anglo-Celtic ethnicity, a Protestant Christianity of an evangelical strain, a shared pioneer experience and, all too often, economic deprivation.

Apart from an early French presence in the south of the state from 1702, the European settlement of Alabama was largely undertaken in the late eighteenth and early nineteenth centuries. This was particularly after the military defeat, and later removal, of most of Alabama's Native American population. The settlers were generally either land-hungry farmers spilling south from Tennessee or moving west from Georgia or planters who had given up on the depleted soils of Virginia and the Carolinas and were looking for new opportunities for large-scale cotton production using enslaved labor. The restless movement was called "Alabama Fever." Alexis de Tocqueville, the famous French observer of early nineteenth-century American life, knew the symptoms. He called the migratory compulsion an "ardent and restless passion" for prosperity, a game of chance pursued "for the emotions it excites as much as for the gain it procures."[3]

The destination of planters with slaves and capital was Alabama's Black Belt—a twenty-five-mile wide swath of fertile clay soils (often black) bisecting the center of the state. These soils were ideal for large-scale cotton production and provided the means by which Black Belt planters became prosperous and politically powerful as Democrats and Whigs. Small farmers tended to take up land in the northern hill country of the Appalachian Ridge and Plateau area or in the southeastern Wiregrass Country. On the eve of the Civil War about 80 percent of these small farmers owned the land they tilled. They rarely possessed slaves and had neither fertilizers to make their land productive nor access to railroads that would allow them to convey their goods to market. They eked out a meager subsistence growing corn, sorghum, oats, and vegetables as well as raising goats and hogs and trapping. The similar circumstances of the inhabitants of hill country and Wiregrass counties tended to make them political allies. They were generally against secession prior to the Civil War; afterward they were more likely to be Republican Party supporters. Later still they were often the agrarian dissidents who gave strength to various populist movements and, by the 1890s, provided a serious political threat to the moneyed interests then dominant.[4]

By 1860 Alabama had eleven railroads with 744 miles of track. As well, iron foundries had been constructed and commercial cotton milling had begun. The port of Mobile was still the only city of any size but it had a growing population of 29,258. Notwithstanding these signs of change, 95 percent of Alabama's population of 964,201 lived and worked in rural areas.[5]

In the decades leading up to the Civil War, visitors to Alabama sometimes expressed surprise at its still crude and frontier nature. They adversely noted the violent behavior, intemperance, class divisions, and/or sectarian zeal of some of its inhabitants but favorably noted their generosity, frank cordiality, and boundless hospitality. One visitor was Sir Charles Lyell, F.R.S., the distinguished Scottish geologist. He described traveling through the state's pine barrens as penetrating "into regions where the schoolmaster had not been much abroad." Yet Lyell was fascinated by the entrepreneurial initiative of the urchins who were already taking advantage of the new railroads and jumped nimbly on and off the trains hawking apples, biscuits, and reading material to passengers.[6]

Another Scottish visitor—the Reverend George Lewis of Ormiston—found the state somewhat less than beguiling. The prim and censorious Presbyterian minister harrumphed that the number of adult illiterates in Alabama indicated "a very low state of education amongst the white population compared with the northern or eastern states."[7]

Philip Henry Gosse, an enquiring and perceptive English naturalist, visited in 1838 and conducted a school in a log cabin at Pleasant Hill in Dallas County. It was equipped with desks that were "merely boards *split*, not sawn, out of pine logs, unhewn and unplaned." Gosse depicted his schoolhouse as "singularly romantic" and "shut in by a dense wall of towering forest trees." His dozen or so pupils were "mostly as rude as the [school] house—real young hunters, who handle the long rifle with more ease and dexterity than the goose-quill, and who are incomparably more at home in 'twisting a rabbit,' or 'treeing a 'possum,' than in conjugating a verb."[8]

While hardly much of a sample, these and other contemporary observations provide a glimpse into the sort of existence that was the very stuff of American mythology. Gosse's real young hunters were not unlike the sorts of people upon whom writers such as, for example, James Fenimore Cooper in his Leatherstocking Tales, had built the prototypical frontier hero—the canny backwoodsman who could conquer and control nature by his own human resourcefulness and was touched only lightly by schooling if at all.[9]

In a study of cultural values in the antebellum South, the historian Grady McWhiney has extensively examined other sources to define the skills most admired then by rural people. These were not taught in school by outsiders under the guise of enlightenment and knowledge—the "book learning" necessary for trade and industry and thus associated with the dubious North. Rather, they were the skills that allowed rural people to live in accord with their environment—those of the "hunter, fisher, fighter and fiddler."[10] In 1880 the *Courier Journal,* published at Opelika in Lee County, affectionately—and implicitly approvingly—described as "presidents in embryo" the barefoot boys dressed in a hickory shirt and one suspender who were often to be seen about Troy in Pike County on trading days. The following quote suggests a hierarchy of the traits and abilities that continued to be admired in a still closely bound world: "They know but little of 'book learning,' but they can crack a whip to perfection; drive an ox team, or ride a pony as well as any other boy, Calmuck or Comanche. They are pugnacious, and always spiling. They will protect their bench-legged yellow dogs with chivalrous heroism and the inspiration of courage . . . and do you a service without hope of reward."[11]

The poorest white people of the South—particularly in the hill country and mountain counties—were often pejoratively stigmatized as "crackers," "clay-eaters," "hillbillies," or "plain people." They were not infrequently badly housed, malnourished, and beset by debt. They suffered high rates of disease and infant mortality and had a low life expectancy. Yet, because they lived close to the land, their crops and gardens, to the seasons and the weather, to the daily exchanges of church and community and, most deeply, because of the ties of blood, they had a surety about the moral quality of their simple lives. According to another historian, Anthony Harkins, the enduring appeal of the "hillbilly" in popular culture is owed to its association with the sorts of people described above—their pioneer spirit, their traditional family values and their "horse sense."[12] In Alabama such people were often fortified in their isolation by a rich oral culture and a timeless folklore of many strands that had been adapted by local conditions and was couched in a local idiom. In determining when to plant crops, kill livestock, cure meat, and/or fell timber, many farmers gave earnest consideration to the phases of the moon and other auguries. For example, a lore-wise farmer believed he should not plant "eye-crops" such as potatoes at night because then the eyes would not be able to find their way to the surface—and there was much else besides. Lore was one way in which life was understood.[13]

Along with their self-sufficiency, many poorer white Alabamians often had a contempt for authority and a spirit of rebellion.[14] They also believed that all people of African descent, who comprised 45 percent of the state's population in 1860, were irremediably inferior and that color was a nonnegotiable racial and cultural identity that stayed with one from cradle to grave. This belief was the *sine qua non* of most white Southerners' world view whether they were rich or poor.[15]

After the Civil War there was a significant change to farm ownership in Alabama. By 1880 nearly half the state's farmers, including many former slaves, were cash or share tenants—part of a trend in declining economic fortune that continued up to and through the 1930s.[16] The state's urban sector also started to grow but, even by as late as 1910, about 83 percent of the state's population was still located in rural areas.[17] While tenancy made some communities less stable, most people still had a strong association with a particular place and participated not only in its social life but often in its administrative and/or political affairs. Alexis de Tocqueville believed that such grass-roots democracy was "the life and mainspring American liberty."[18]

Until well into the twentieth century, the typical place of attachment for most Alabamians, regardless of race, was a farming neighborhood contained within an area of approximately thirty square miles and centered on a hamlet or village. This was likely to contain a store, one or more churches (usually Baptist or Methodist), a few dwelling houses and possibly a bank, a blacksmith, a gristmill, an inn, a masonic lodge, a post office, a station, or a schoolhouse. Such villages might actually have sprung up at a road or railroad junction or beside tracks. Those not near a railroad were reached by dirt roads that could become impassable after rain. The place of attachment could also be a small town with an industrial enterprise such as a cotton mill or a sawmill and/or an emerging civic identity though mostly still dependent on the surrounding district for its existence. By 1890 Alabama had one hundred incorporated towns but none of these had a population of more than 2,500.[19]

Each tiny hamlet or small town was considered to have an individualistic character given to it by its similarly individualistic inhabitants.[20] These were variously connected and comprised its community. Their interlocking relationships were those of family or kinship, friendship, cultural origin, economic interest or occupation, moral outlook or religious affiliation, shared idioms, and/or any combination of these. A community might reveal a range of internal splits along lines of class, caste, religious denomination, and/or political allegiance, and so forth, without being compromised as an entity.

Communities were always very clear about their own identity and were conscious of their actual and/or notional boundaries. They were able quickly to spot "otherness" or who belonged and who did not. A man whose family had farmed for several generations at Fayetteville in Talladega County recalled: "You could always tell when somebody was a native because, if they are, it's always called 'Fedville' and we were natives so we called it Fedville."[21]

Alabama's county structure was able to give multiple neighborhoods, even those separated by natural barriers or widely dispersed, a loose sense of cohesiveness or a larger community identity. The county was, in some ways, an expanded version of the smaller communities from which it was composed. It might be distinguished by the nature of its agriculture or other primary industry, by its secondary industry, its racial or ethnic mix, and the historical pattern of its development.[22] The county seat was the town with the courthouse from which local government was conducted. This was consequently a focus for trade, commerce, and social life. The county superintendent of education operated from the courthouse and many of the issues that could not be resolved at the school district level converged on this officer.

Newspapers with a county readership both represented and cultivated a sense of identity and cohesion. In a 1903 item about an out-of-county teacher who had been appointed to a local district school, the editor of the *Mountain Eagle* asked: "Why can't some more of Walker County boys prepare to teach and keep this money here at home?"[23] On another occasion he reported from the Jacksonville State Normal School: "There are several boys and girls here from Walker—as is usually the case. Walker is pretty well represented in all good things."[24]

~

The statute of February 1854 establishing the statewide public schooling system was the product of a new political milieu. It was sponsored by legislators who were impressed by the economic outcomes attributable to "the advancement of popular instruction" in New England, whose states had, "despite every disadvantage of climate and soil, been the most successful in all the arts, comforts, conveniences, securities, and other excellences of a social and political character." One such legislator was Alexander Beaufort Meek, who had helped to set up a public schooling system in Mobile and thought this might offer a prototype for the state.[25] The general populace—largely Jacksonian in sentiment and suspicious of book learning—may have detected the patronizing scent of *noblesse oblige* attending the law's introduction; there was little indication that, beyond the assembly, it was much appreciated.[26]

From 1854 onward, Alabama's "public schools" were those provided for by successive statutes usually entitled *An Act to organize and regulate a system of public instruction for the State of Alabama.* They were supported from public funds even if such funds might be substantially supplemented with parental tuition fees and other moneys. In accordance with the ideas of the hugely influential Massachusetts educator Horace Mann (1796–1859), the schools were conceived as "common schools"—schools whose educational purpose was common to all and could be commonly attended by anyone between the ages of

2. Alabama's counties. Map produced by the Department of Geography, College of Arts and Sciences, University of Alabama.

five and eighteen years regardless of class, religion, or gender—but not race.[27] Furthermore, the schools were to be a common resource of the communities they served and by whom they would be controlled. Their titular designation was fixed only by habit or local preference. Over time, public schools were variously described as "community schools," "county schools," "district schools," "free schools," "free public literary schools," "municipal schools," and "township schools." After 1907, when publicly funded county high schools started being established, they were increasingly delineated as "elementary schools"—but never "state schools." That term was reserved for other, generally tertiary, publicly funded institutions such as the University of Alabama, the Alabama Polytechnic Institute, or normal schools.[28] Confusingly, and not infrequently, state funds were used to underwrite the costs of private academies. Fee-charging private town schools, actually often termed the "[town] Public School" sometimes offered a free session underwritten by state funds. Over time, some of these metamorphosed into full public schools with municipal oversight or governance through representation on the school board.

Despite any indication of much general enthusiasm for the new system, the first state superintendent appointed under the 1854 act, William F. Perry, set to work to realize its objectives. In his first year in office he carried out a status review and discovered just how indelibly Alabama's frontier ethos, its rural society, and its subsistence economy was stamped on the schools then existing. Perry also discovered that unless a community happened to be blessed with public-spirited citizens or teachers with "personal magnetism" that schooling provisions in whole blocks of counties were wretched and "hundreds of districts could scarcely boast of a single pleasantly located, comfortable schoolhouse." He decided that the new system would have to be built on existing foundations rather than be imposed from above. Perry's account of what he termed "the genesis of public education in Alabama" provides an early example of the organizational plans of a knowledgeable professional in tension with an existing cultural tradition of independent, local decision making, which often rendered the reformer impotent.[29] When the Civil War broke out in 1861, Perry's successor was still trying to establish the system envisaged in 1854. After the war it was necessary to start afresh.

In the half century following the Civil War, successive state superintendents oversaw the growth of a public schooling system whose origins could be traced to the 1854 legislation. Bit by bit, but predominantly after 1898, this system accrued features such as certified teachers, a standard core curriculum, uniform textbooks, lengthened terms, and graded classrooms—all elements of an envisaged ideal of educational efficiency.

The legislative, regulatory, and fiscal changes of the early twentieth century sustained a contemporary narrative of progressive and Progressivist educational reform by officeholders and activists. Yet not all the reformers' plans came to fruition. Some plans were contested or modified; some were felt to be politically unfeasible. Reformers found themselves engaged regularly in defensive debates about the nature and purpose of education, the rights of parents, and the proper location of policy-making authority. They learned that, if they wished to succeed, they had to dispel parental skepticism, engage community interest, and garner popular and financial support.

Debates about educational reform were conducted on white terms and involved a white constituency. The aspirations of black parents and their children were not paid much heed by educational reformers. Their general indifference, if not outright hostility, to black schooling reflected the racism that then pervaded Southern life and whose pernicious influence extended into the second half of the twentieth century.

$\sim$

In the period under review, Alabama's educational system operated under conditions that were similar to those existing across much of the South. The region had a high ratio of children to adult taxpayers—only four states in the Union had a greater proportion of school-aged children than Alabama and all were in the South. In addition the region had daunting illiteracy levels, a dispersed rural population and, although decreasingly, noncompulsory school attendance owing to the need for child labor on family farms.[30] The various states also chose to maintain dual systems of racially segregated schools when their revenues were usually insufficient to support a single system.

The scope of these problems and the ways in which they were confronted has made the development of public education in the South a subject of perennial interest for historians. In 1936 the eminent university president Charles W. Dabney Jr. published *Universal Education in the South*, a two-volume, magisterial account of the expansion of public schooling systems throughout the region. By documenting the achievements of the (mostly Democratic) reformers and supportive philanthropists, Dabney's book sought to cement their legacy and to associate the South's conservative governments with progressive change. Later writers, with the benefit of a longer historical perspective, have considered the topic in a more critical and nuanced manner.

In his 1986 book *A Hard Country and a Lonely Place: Schooling, Society, and Reform in Rural Virginia, 1870–1920*, William A. Link examined Virginia's experience to discover the reformers' modernizing ethos was often rejected unless and until they harnessed the strengths of local rural communities to develop policy.[31] In 1988 James D. Anderson published *The Education of Blacks in the South, 1860–1935*, a revisionist account of the South's educational development. He provided compelling evidence to demonstrate the white reformers' support for black education was both limited and intentionally directed toward maintaining the region's caste system and white social control.[32] In his 1996 book *Schooling the New South: Pedagogy, Self, and Society in North Carolina, 1880–1920*, James Leloudis explored the complex interaction between schooling reforms and the economic and societal changes happening in North Carolina.[33]

This book is intended to complement prior state-based studies of educational reform in the South between the Civil War and World War I. Its focus is on the actual operation of Alabama's public schooling system over time and how this was influenced by localism and cultural traditions. Yet it also seeks to place Alabama's experience against a regional and national backdrop.

Some of the educational issues Alabama faced at this time were not dissimilar to those being faced in other states with dominantly agricultural economies. From the Midwest to the great plains, from the Southwest to the Pacific coast, educators grappled with matters such as wresting school governance from farmers and local communities, consolidating schools, lengthening sessions, devising a relevant curriculum, and training teachers to play a role in the revitalization of country life.[34] Also, particularly from the 1890s, the national educational environment was being fundamentally and rapidly altered by demographic, economic, and technological changes.

If Alabama's experiences in developing its public education system can be likened to those of other states in the South and, in some respects, to those of rural America overall, they were influenced by a number of factors—sociopolitical, cultural, economic, and fiscal—that were specific to the state itself. These factors had long-term, if not lasting, consequences and would prove a testing restraint for reformers and those who believed the public school was Alabama's best hope for eliminating ignorance, illiteracy, and poverty.

Reconstruction and Its Reach, 1865–1901

In the immediate wake of the Civil War—the period of so-called Presidential Reconstruction (1865–1867)—Alabama's General Assembly was primarily concerned with returning the state to a recognizable normality. This meant conservative white rule and the continued repression of its black population, which now included 439,000 former slaves or "freedmen."[1] A new constitution adopted in September 1865 reflected this goal of normalization and included a number of conditions required for Alabama to rejoin the Union. The assembly was granted authority to "enact necessary and proper laws for the encouragement of schools and the means of education" but otherwise was short on detail.[2] Implicitly the schooling to be encouraged was to be for the benefit of the white population, which was significantly illiterate and experiencing a baby boom.[3]

In this same period the freedmen were starting to seek the schooling that they had been denied by law in slavery and with which they associated power and influence.[4] Their requirements were often met by Northern schoolteachers operating under the auspices of agencies such as the American Missionary Association (AMA), and in conjunction with the Bureau for Refugees, Freedmen and Abandoned Lands—the "Freedmen's Bureau."[5]

In October 1866, against a background of ugly race riots in Tennessee and Louisiana and an emerging pattern of harsh black repression all over the South, Radical Republicans swept the congressional elections. Determined not to see the achievements of the Civil War invalidated, they used their legislative dominance to pass the first Reconstruction Act in March 1867.[6] This placed Alabama, along with Georgia and Florida, under the military rule of General John Pope, thus initiating "Congressional" or "Radical" Reconstruction in these states. The act also required the Southern states to ratify the Fourteenth Amendment to the U.S. Constitution—designed to ensure freedmen obtained all the rights and privileges of citizenship—and to prepare new state constitutions.[7] To further safeguard black civil rights, Congress passed the second Reconstruction Act, which concerned voter registration arrangements and electoral supervision.[8] The imposition of martial law and an externally prescribed political order upended all the normal interactions and customs that had long been part of Alabama's cultural fabric. Many whites furiously resented the new status of former slaves and the congressional intervention on their behalf.

It was within this sociopolitical context that the Northern teachers embarked upon their mission to assist Alabama's freedmen. Some of the teachers had been schooled in the equalitarian ideas of abolitionism and, for a number of reasons, they ignored the fact that many whites regarded them as purveyors of alien notions that breached age-old conventions and taboos.[9] The perceived threat posed by the Northern teachers was sometimes met with nothing less than terrorism. Organizations such as the Ku Klux Klan were responsible for intimidation, arson, and even murder. When a Canadian missionary, William Luke, taught his Calhoun County pupils that black and white women were equal in God's eyes, and that workers of both races should receive the same wages, he was promptly hanged by local vigilantes.[10] Luke's fate was a stark warning to those who might encourage talk of civil rights.

Although white attitudes toward black schooling did not follow a simple trajectory from resistance to acceptance, overt hostility subsided somewhat after about 1868 when some white opinion leaders grudgingly acknowledged such schooling might be necessary.[11] In some places "colored" schools seem to have been tentatively encouraged by whites—as long as they were in the reliable hands of Confederate veterans or local teachers.[12]

In November 1867 a constitutional convention elected on the extended franchise met in Montgomery to draft a state constitution. The convention's "Committee on Education and the School Fund" comprised four Carpetbaggers (allegedly opportunistic Northerners who had moved South), two Scalawags (local Republicans), and one black representative, Peyton Finley. The chairman, Gustavus Horton, had assisted in organizing Mobile's public schools in 1852 and three members of the committee—John Silsby, Benjamin Yordy, and Charles Buckley—were agents of the Freedmen's Bureau.[13]

The committee proposed an entirely new model for the public schooling system based on an Iowan precedent. Its principal feature was a "Board of Education of the State of Alabama." This board was to have legislative powers in relation to education and, in this respect, would rival the assembly. The system's principal funding source was to be an appropriation equal to one-fifth of the state's total revenue.[14]

A novel feature of the proposed system was that schooling would be free for all students between five and twenty-one years. In the antebellum period, except in cases of parental hardship, tuition fees had been payable. Thus, instead of the new provision being seen as a way of guaranteeing universal access to schooling, critics saw it as a needless expense with the potential for stigmatizing all students as paupers.[15]

Newspapers covering the convention made their opinions clear. The Montgomery *Daily Mail*'s description of the education article was a rant of racial suspicion: "*One* legislative body, not able to do all the harm to the white race, desired by the majority of the convention; an additional one, nicknamed the Board of Education, is created, and armed with the power to force all white children to go into all the free public schools upon terms of social equality with all sorts of negro children or else surrender the schools as a monopoly to the negroes."[16]

This intemperate outburst was prompted because, while Section 7 of the proposed article did not specifically rule in integrated schools, neither did it rule them out. Proposed amendments to make separate schools compulsory were defeated, allowing opponents of the new constitution to whip up fears about social equality, miscegenation, and "Negro supremacy." The education committee had not really believed in the likelihood of racially mixed schools, but knew that specifying separate schools would mean inferior schools for blacks.[17]

After a vigorous campaign by conservatives and newspapers such as the *Montgomery Advertiser* to denigrate the provisions of the new constitution and create fear about its racial implications, it was not ratified by the people. It came into effect anyway in June 1868 as a result of the fourth Reconstruction Act.[18]

≈

The white response throughout much of the state to the new education regime was often averse and even truculent. Conservatives, whose criticisms were politically based, regarded the board of education as an incubus to be borne until Reconstruction's end. While all Southern states were developing public education systems in the postbellum era, the hostility of many Alabamians to what was seen as a costly external imposition made the state's experience *sui generis*. In his first annual report to the governor in 1869, Dr. Noah B. Cloud, the state superintendent of public instruction, reported on the unpopularity of the schools with those whom they were intended to benefit. He felt this reflected antigovernment feeling and a flow-on hostility toward its agents who were organizing the schools. Cloud's report also blamed "idle politicians and certain unscrupulous disappointed newspaper editors."[19] But whoever or whatever was to blame, white communities appeared not so much interested in accessing schooling for their own children as in demonstrating their mistrust of the new system and of funds being expended on schools for black children. The experience of Coffee County's superintendent was typical: "At the time I commenced appointing trustees, the prejudice of the people was general and strong against the free public school system—so great that there was difficulty in getting people to act." He explained this prejudice as being "mostly on account of the proposed enumeration of the colored children and their prospect of the benefit of the system." The opposition he encountered initially prevented him from organizing black schools.[20] The superintendents for Dallas, Marengo, Macon, and Sanford (later Lamar) counties all reported similar antagonism. They were finding it hard to obtain teachers and/or to get men to act as trustees. They said the intense opposition to "colored" schools meant organizing them could prove dangerous.[21]

If they could not resolve matters of schooling policy for themselves, teachers and trustees generally looked for direction to the county superintendent. This official was now a political appointee of the state superintendent and, in the fractious and factional political climate of Reconstruction, could only ever be as popular as his patron.[22] Aspersions smacking of disgruntled local gossip were cast on some of the appointees: one was illiterate, another corrupt, and yet another, Dr. Ezra F. Bouchelle of Pickens County, suffered a double whammy of calumny. He was accused of being both incompetent and corrupt.[23] In Clarke County, a dispute over the commission payable for disbursing teachers' wages erupted into a bitter contest between the county superintendent, Miel S. Ezell, and the local Democratic "courthouse clique." Ezell owed his appointment to a Republican state superintendent who was thus tagged as a Radical. Ezell's supporters described him as being "from an intelligent and respectable family," and as "a man noted for his piety and devotion." His enemies claimed Ezell was a person of "repulsive temperament and manners" and a "Radical of an independent faction." As soon as the Democrats recovered the state superintendency, Ezell's enemies alleged he had been corruptly installed and—this was key—that his political positions "were against the interests of the Democratic and Conservative Party in Clarke County." Ezell was soon dumped.[24]

The difficulties of supervising the county schools were either genuinely onerous and the additional duties required by the role were overwhelming or the county superintendents had inflated ideas about their own importance. They certainly had rather ambitious expectations with regard to their annual remuneration. In 1869, the Committee of Clerks and Trustees for Bullock County's schools proposed to the state superintendent that a salary of $1,200 be paid to Columbus Cunningham, the county superintendent. The committee, probably in cahoots with Cunningham, who believed he deserved far more, said it was "reflecting the general desire that such salary should be given as will secure the services of entirely competent and reliable men in the office."[25] Perry County's committee recommended a salary of $2,000 for Louis W. Temple, because of the "large number of children and amount of labor devolving on the superintendent." When the state superintendent reduced this to $1,500, the committee's chairman, Theophilus G. Fowler, darkly alluded to "political and civil issues in the county which made the superintendent's labor arduous." He remained huffily convinced the reduced amount would be "insufficient compensation for the amount of labor needed to be done for the cause of education, particularly among the colored people, where the field is a vast one and their desires and necessities urgent."[26]

Across the rest of the state the level of recommended annual salary ranged from the not unreasonable $375 in Covington County to $2,000 in Dallas. However, it was becoming evident that the state was not in a position to fully fund the costs of the new school system as intended by the constitution. Dr. Cloud might flatter the framers of that document and assert that its education article "was the first decisive blow ever before struck in the planting states, and especially in Alabama, to clear out among all classes every vestige of ignorance with its long and attendant train of evils."[27] The reality was that money earmarked for schools was not being made fully available. This early and critical breach of "the chartered pledge of the state to furnish the means and facilities adequate to the education of all the children of the state" would be long remembered.[28]

～

In the years between the establishment of the board of education and the election of 1874, which returned conservative interests to power, the official annual reports to the governor by successive state superintendents contained both self-justifications for their own actions and broadsides against their predecessors. The stance of each report was influenced by whether the superintendent and the governor were of the same or different political stripes. Similarly, the turf wars between the board of education, where the Republicans held a majority, and the assembly where, after the 1870 election, the Democratic and Conservative Party held a majority in the lower house, meant that what was actually going on in the schools up and down the state was a matter of contested opinion. Yet the county reports appended to the state superintendent's annual report give some idea of how schools were being conducted in different parts of the state and the extent to which communities regarded schooling as part of their cultural and socioeconomic life.

In 1871 many superintendents reported their townships were often without their own schoolhouses and that pupils had to be taught in churches or Masonic lodges. The shortcomings of the buildings that did exist, and the paucity of their furnishings and equipment, were widely reported—and would continue to be for the next thirty-five years and longer. Yet parents overlooked exhortations to provide something better, citing "the hard times, the bad crops, &c." Schooling was not compulsory and money could not be wasted on what was still something children might opt to squeeze into "every spare day" when they could be excused from farm duties.[29]

The reports of 1871 show the difficulty some of the superintendents were having with the concept of universal free public schooling, still regarding assistance from the state as a last resort for children who were unable to get an education in any other way.[30] Many thought patrons should pay tuition fees to supplement the public fund as they had done before the war.[31] Blount County's superintendent said he had implemented a fee-charging regime and "made the *public* fund auxiliary only." He had had to do this he said because parents were only sending their children to school while it was free. As soon as the funds ran out, children were withdrawn. This overwhelmed the teacher in the first instance and subsequently cheated children "out of the benefits of schooling and the teacher out of employment."[32] The subscription school supplemented by state resources had the compelling appeal of the tried and true. Moreover, it allowed teachers to believe they would be paid.

In June 1870 General Oliver Otis Howard, who headed the Freedmen's Bureau, ordered its work in Alabama to be finished by July 15—a month later. After that date, the schools operated for black children by missionary societies in conjunction with the bureau, became part of the state system—though not an integrated part. The county superintendents' reports for 1871 describe black communities struggling with familiar problems—nonattendance owing to seasonal labor needs, inadequate schoolhouses, unreliable trustees, and/or insufficient private funds to buy books or supplement public allocations.[33]

The reports just described were made to Joseph Hodgson, a member of the Democratic and Conservative Party, who had been elected as state superintendent in November 1870 and would serve until 1872. During his term of office, Hodgson could never secure the appropriation promised by the constitution for school funding. The state's failure to comply with its constitutional obligations meant teachers were going unpaid. In some desperation and often fruitlessly, superintendents issued warrants for payment from local tax collectors. Others provided teachers with vouchers with which they could redeem goods from a local merchant.[34] According to Hugh W. Caffey of Lowndes County, some teachers bore "their deprivation of pay with commendable fortitude." He blamed the "financial embarrassments" on Republican Scalawags.[35]

In his annual report for the 1872 scholastic year—his last before leaving office—Joseph Hodgson wrote about education's purpose and benefits. He condemned Alabama's alarming illiteracy rate and opined that even laborers were deserving of a "pastime and a power"—such as that derived from being able to read newspapers. In Hodgson's comments there is a glimpse of the Jeffersonian ideal—access to education for the common man whose world need not be limited by occupation or location.[36]

Hodgson's ideas did not suit the hour. Not only was the financial situation of the school system in dire straits, it was deteriorating fast. The number of school warrants issued and unredeemed in 1872 very nearly equaled the annual amount of the state revenue. As tax collectors were required by law to receive these warrants in payment of taxes, little was coming into the treasury except the warrants. In December 1872, facing a free fall to bankruptcy, the board of education passed a law ordering all public schools closed from January 1, 1873, until such time as funds were available for the prompt payment of teachers.[37]

In November 1873 the next (Republican) state superintendent, Joseph Speed, addressed the board regarding this catastrophe. He justified the action taken and suggested a remedy which prompted a memorial to both houses of the assembly. This gave an itemized account of revenue shortfalls and the accumulating deficit, which he said was the fault of the treasury. He alleged constitutional breaches and the diversion of funds to defray other governmental expenses.[38] The memorial was ignored.

The closure of the schools fell most heavily on the teachers who sent off desperate letters to anyone they thought might help. A black teacher wrote to a legislator: "We the teachers of Chambers County have not got any money this hole year and now we are in debt and don't no how to get out."[39] A white teacher from Conecuh County pleaded for moneys due: "I have had to mortgage oxen and wagon—the only property I have accept for seven head of cattle and if I cannot make some arrangements in a few days, yes in less than ten days, I will lose them having been compelled to do so to get bread and meat for my family consisting of five little children."[40]

Many whose patience had been exhausted by "long delayed, incomplete or uncertain payment" took up other work. When the schools reopened nine months later, teachers were often selected for "the price they could be obtained instead of their qualifications." Ill trained and ill compensated, some found their school duties "humdrum, listless and lifeless."[41]

The records do not show the extent to which school patrons—parents and guardians—were fazed by the accumulating problems of the education system. Joseph Speed expressed astonishment at their "cold-blooded apathy." He said parents turned over their children to teachers with absolute unconcern and neither knew nor cared whether teachers were competent, whether their principles were compatible with home values or "whether their little ones were receiving proper mental food." He also slammed their indifference to the "shabby and outrageous buildings" in which their children were taught.[42]

But away from Montgomery, the demands of agriculture meant other priorities held sway. Some Talladega parents said they could not, and would not, spare children for more than three months from farm work and complained of being compelled to have a five months school or no school. The county superintendent noted resignedly: "the people of the state will have to be educated to the idea of free public schools before any system will succeed. The experiment will be expensive and tedious."[43]

It seems from both the defensive comments in the superintendents' reports of this period, as well as opinions offered in other forums, that not everyone in Alabama was even yet committed to public education and the need for the system might have to be justified all over again. In 1875 John M. McKleroy (state superintendent, 1874–1876) hoped public schooling would "not be permitted to die, either suddenly or slowly by retrograde." In Jefferson County, the largest taxpayers wanted to see the system abolished and "everyone placed upon his own resources for educating his children."[44] These people probably sent their children to private schools, as did many members of the prosperous middle class. Members of the Baptist Church believed their children should be educated in denominational schools so they would not "be subjected to the contamination of un-Christian ideas and ways of life."[45] Some people's dislike for public schooling refused to die. In April 1890 at Midway in Bullock County one of the town's oldest residents, Colonel William Jordan, addressed a teachers' institute. Without mincing his words, he said, "I'm opposed to public education; I don't think it is right and I voted against it in the legislature. I think it is an imposition on the people."[46]

⁓

The political trials of white conservatives ended in 1874 when, as one historian put it, they "struggled out of the abyss of Reconstruction."[47] In other words, internal differences within the Democratic and Conservative Party were buried sufficiently so as to be able to exploit splits opening up in the Republican Party. The Democratic nominee for governor, George Smith Houston, was elected and the party recovered both houses of the General Assembly thus restoring "home rule." Conservative Democrats, who eventually settled on being known simply as Democrats, cast themselves as "Redeemers." They were determined to implement a regime of thrift and low taxation. There was to be general retrenchment in all areas of governmental expenditure and, in their complete break with Reconstruction, the Redeemers decided the state needed a new constitution. A convention was duly arranged to draft one. The days of the board of education were numbered.[48]

The 1875 convention's committee on education brought in a report that was thoroughly in tune with the new conservative *zeitgeist*. Its recommendations would abolish the board of education; provide for an elected state superintendent of education; make separate schools for black and white children compulsory; and set aside at least $100,000 annually for educational purposes together with some other specified sources of revenue. This would reduce the annual school budget from $484,000 to $348,000 at one stroke. Another stipulation was that not more than 4 percent of the school funds could be spent on other than teachers' wages.[49]

Republicans charged that the proposed funding arrangements were too meager and that the education system would be destroyed leaving the schools "dependent on the prejudice, whim or caprice of the legislature."[50] Democrats defended the reduction in the moneys earmarked for schools by claiming the schools would actually receive more—because there would be fewer useless school officials. In any case, as they correctly pointed out, the schools had never actually received the fifth of annual state revenue provided for in the 1868 constitution.[51] Some delegates wanted to abolish the positions of state and county superintendents. There was plenty of dissenting opinion regarding the intended changes. The *Alabama State Journal* said: "a herd of voting cattle is to be created, and the herd is to be domineered over by a privileged caste of educated men."[52]

On November 16, 1875, the people ratified the constitution by a vote of 85,662 to 29,217. The Democratic and Conservative Party was now not only in power but on its way to becoming entrenched politically.[53] In 1876 the assembly met to work out a reorganization of the public schools. An overly optimistic newspaper correspondent said its goal was "to re-establish the grand old schools of primary, academic and collegiate; to restore local self-management of schools to parents, to teachers and to trustees, and to have a high rank of teachers and continuous school for the better promotion of 'popular education.'"[54]

The new constitution's recognizably familiar arrangements and the ensuing school legislation pleased county superintendents. Tallapoosa's Samuel C. Oliver believed he might now be able to entice back his best teachers who had been driven out by "the two or three months free school system."[55] Acceptance of the constitution made it easy for leaders who were barely committed to public education anyway to throttle the schools in the name of frugality—that sacred cow of the Democrats, whose members were now known as "Bourbons"— a not always kindly meant soubriquet.[56] On one occasion, LeRoy F. Box (state superintendent, 1876–1880) boasted that "for cheapness of instruction and economy of supervision" Alabama surpassed all the other Southern states.[57]

Without much power attached to the state superintendent's position nor sustained advocacy from county superintendents, trustees, and/or patrons, the assembly showed no interest in rethinking its approach to the schooling system. When surpluses started accumulating in the 1880s, few thought these should be employed to reduce illiteracy.[58] The appropriation did increase over time— in 1890 it was $350,000 or $1.34 per capita of school population. But in 1888, when the assembly considered a motion to further enhance an approved increase, this was defeated by Black Belt representatives who did not want any more expenditure on black schools.[59]

One of the reasons there was no clamor for greater educational expenditure from those who might have stood to gain from better schools was aversion to taxation. Before the Civil War a tax on slave property had generated a significant proportion of state revenues; farmers were largely exempt from land tax. During Reconstruction, Republican legislators turned to land taxes to make up for the loss in the slave tax and, between 1860 and 1870, farm taxes multiplied by almost two and a half times.[60] To meet their increased tax liabilities, farmers had to generate additional cash income and so they moved from subsistence farming to cotton production—cotton being a high-yielding cash crop even on a falling market. Raising cotton was labor-intensive and children were a valuable means of extending a family's productivity. But even large families could only farm about forty acres at most.[61] Hard-pressed farmers were unsympathetic to their taxes being spent on social welfare programs such as schooling.

White farmers were particularly averse to having their taxes spent on schools for black nontaxpayers. Although black tenants indirectly contributed to tax receipts by providing part of the income from which their white landlords paid land taxes, white farmers did not see it that way.[62] In 1871, Hale County's superintendent, Miles H. Yerby, asserted: "The public school system will ever be below par in this county so long as there remains among us so great a preponderance of the black population. The cry will ever be raised that the negro gets all the school funds and we pay the taxes."[63]

In the 1870s the notion of disbursing tax revenues for school expenditure on a racial basis started to gain currency. As new municipal school districts were established, the enabling legislation provided for poll-tax receipts to be allocated to schools according to the race of the taxpayer. Such a provision was included in the 1887 act establishing the Opelika school district in Lee County.[64] In 1891 white township schools benefited from a new law allowing trustees to apportion school funds as they saw "just and equitable"—which was intended to ensure white schools received the lion's share of the apportionment.[65] Starved of funds, the continued existence of black schools became increasingly precarious.

From the middle of the 1880s there were signs that some of the thinkers in Alabamian society were beginning to be seriously concerned about the persistent inadequacy of public schooling. They believed local taxation would provide a panacea and the federal government was also considered as a possible lifeline. During four federal Congresses between 1881 and 1889 a proposal was discussed to grant money to each state based upon its illiteracy rate. The so-called Blair Bill passed each time in the House but failed in the Senate. It was opposed vigorously by Alabama's John Tyler Morgan, who feared external interference and higher federal taxation.[66] Morgan was especially concerned that the moneys involved would double the school term. If black children were in school for six months it would ruin the cotton crop. William C. Oates, then a congressman, considered the bill unconstitutional. He said it would just add "a brick to the tower of centralization which the Republican Party is endeavoring to raise."[67] Yet there was a heavy consequence for underinvesting in education. In 1890 Alabama ranked fourth from the bottom in national school statistics, it had the shortest school session, and 41 percent of its population was illiterate. Its white illiteracy rate was 18 percent.[68]

In the early 1890s, discussions about schooling in newspapers showed an increased tempo and there was a growing sense of a "teaching profession"— promoted through teacher associations. Commencing in 1888, a legislator, Oscar Hundley, campaigned for a constitutional amendment whose intent was to enable the (optional) levying of a local school tax. Newspapers such as the *Montgomery Advertiser* were fully behind it, and teachers spoke widely in the amendment's favor at institutes and other forums.[69] Yet, when the amendment was finally put to the people it was overwhelmingly defeated—"dying of indifference in the camp of its friends."[70]

~

In 1890 Major John G. Harris was elected state superintendent; in 1893 he embarked upon an educational crusade throughout the state. He scheduled six meetings in Walker County and approximately 3,600 people—15 percent of the county's population—attended. Statewide attendance was 100,000. Harris said that "the minds of the people have been stirred as never before."[71]

In pursuing his crusade for educational reform, Harris said he had "a higher and nobler aim than politics."[72] He used methods that were quasi-religious and based on the trusted dynamics of revival meetings with which, as a Missionary Baptist, he would have been familiar. Harris employed a sequence of speakers to make exhortations to a crowd of both believers and skeptics. He offered a conditional promise of a bright future and a request for their commitment to the cause. Harris's successors would increasingly be professional educationists with more knowledge and expertise. Yet Harris's rallies in 1893 suggested that using time-honored forms of engagement to arouse interest in social objectives might be an effective stratagem.

~

Until well into the second half of the twentieth century, Reconstruction was remembered or imagined by many white Alabamians and some historians as a lurid melodrama cast richly with a stock set of villains including iniquitous Republican scalawags, rapacious Northern carpetbaggers, and illiterate black dupes.[73] The potency and resonance of the melodrama can be attributed to the Democratic and Conservative Party. After gaining power in 1874, the party persistently and self-servingly represented Reconstruction as a time of societal trauma, racial threat, and fiscal mayhem during which the state was governed recklessly and burdened with an intolerable debt. This representation helped the party to cement itself into political power and to pursue policies of white supremacy, low taxation, and minimal public expenditure.[74] Alabama's unsuccessful experiment during Reconstruction with an educational system based on a Northern design was always available to politicians as an object lesson in the risks of too much bureaucracy, centralized decision making, and unnecessary innovation. Such conservatism had perennial appeal in a state where the economy, though not static, remained dominantly agricultural and where its chiefly rural population was distrustful of contributing more to government coffers.

By the end of the 1870s, white conservatives were back in control of policy making not only in Alabama but in other Southern states as well. In 1877, Northern troops were withdrawn from the South as the price for settling the disputed 1876 election of President Rutherford B. Hayes.[75] The North had lost its enthusiasm for protecting black civil rights and, in successive rulings, the U.S. Supreme Court rolled back the legislative protections for such rights that had been enacted during Reconstruction and beyond. After the court's 1896 decision in *Plessy v. Ferguson*—the malignant "separate but equal" ruling—the complete segregation of public facilities known as "Jim Crow" rapidly accelerated. The Supreme Court further condoned discrimination with decisions made in 1898 on voter disqualification measures—*Williams v. Mississippi*—and in 1899 on racially unequal educational provisions—*Joseph W. Cumming, James S. Harper and John C. Ladeveze v. County Board of Education of Richmond County, Georgia*. The Cumming decision gave the whole South including Alabama "a green light to heighten discrimination in publicly funded activities."[76]

The Supreme Court's retrograde decisions occurred at a time of growing racial hysteria in the South. This was fomented variously by political opportunists, promoters of pseudo-scientific racial theories, rabble-rousing editors, and white supremacist demagogues. In 1898 there was a murderous race riot in Wilmington, North Carolina, and in the 1890s the number of lynchings in Alabama led the nation.[77] White politicians fastened on the black franchise as a threat to social stability, whipped up fears about black domination, and called for the repeal of the Fifteenth Amendment, which guaranteed black voting rights. Alabama's state superintendent of education, John W. Abercrombie, called these rights "a crime against civilization."[78]

In November 1901 Alabama ratified a new constitution whose principal intent and outcome was to eliminate the black vote. Most of the major innovations of the Reconstruction regime were now gone except for black public schools. However, without a black constituency, white politicians no longer had any compelling reasons to consider the needs of these schools or their black pupils. Henceforth, anyone who was interested in education and the modernization of Alabama's public schooling system would focus primarily on the ability of the system to meet the needs of the state's white population.

2
Captains and Cohorts

Following the adoption of the 1875 constitution, Alabama's General Assembly enacted new legislation relating to the public schooling system. This specified the roles and responsibilities of various office bearers and, by so doing, indicated an organizational structure that was highly decentralized and roughly pyramidal with an elected state superintendent at the peak. If it were not quite a case of *L'État c'est Moi,* the "State Superintendent of Education" and the "Department of Education" were, for all practical purposes, one and the same. As late as 1914 the entire department comprised the superintendent, an officer entitled "Chief Clerk," and five clerical or administrative staff.[1]

Under the school law of 1876, the state superintendent was legally bound to "devote his time to the care and improvement of the common schools and the improvement of public education," and to diffuse as widely as possible by "addresses and personal communication, information as to the importance of public schools."[2] He was supposed to visit each county annually to inspect schools and to encourage the holding of teachers' institutes but most of his duties were fiduciary and administrative. The statutory prescription of the role seems to have been based on some template of educational administration not modified to suit the expenditure constraints of successive Bourbon governments, the demands of the office, or the geographic reality of Alabama's huge area and sparse settlement. Most state superintendents stated emphatically in their reports that it was just not feasible to visit all counties annually and also conduct departmental business.[3] Even office business could not be conducted without resources. John O. Turner (state superintendent, 1894–1898) actually had a circular printed headed "MUST STOP," and this was mailed to anyone seeking information. It explained inquiries could not be answered—there were just too many.[4]

One of the principal roles of the state superintendent was to appoint upward of sixty county superintendents. This task was fraught with controversy owing to rambunctious local disputes and politicking. The superintendent's decision often had to be made after receiving letters of both fulsome praise and scurrilous denunciation in relation to the same candidate. In 1877 LeRoy F. Box (state superintendent, 1876–1880) faced such a dilemma when he had to choose between reappointing P. Brown Frazier, the incumbent superintendent in DeKalb County, or considering the merits of a new contender, George Lowry. Claims, counterclaims, and shifting alliances all had to be weighed. One writer described Frazier as "almost destitute of firmness of character and as little qualified to the business as anyone." Frazier was apparently involved in a dispute with a committee member's neighbor.[5]

State superintendents were rarely able to solve neighborhood quarrels but these were referred to them anyway. In 1883 Henry Clay Armstrong (state superintendent, 1880–1884) was contacted by a Mr. H. J. Martin, who was spokesperson for some angry residents of Winston County. Their superintendent was said to have "trampled upon their rights as free American citizens" owing to his decisions. Martin realized Armstrong might not wish to get involved but requested he might "cite a law that would free us from his tyranny."[6]

The county superintendent occupied the next level in the notional organizational pyramid. The position was held for two years and combined the roles of administrator, receiver of public moneys, steward for school lands, and payroll officer. In the school law of 1879 fourteen sections dealt with the role of the county superintendent. None dealt with educational policy making or school supervision, although the county superintendent was responsible for appointing and providing oversight for arguably the most important educational official—the township (school district) superintendent—whose role will be discussed below. He also had to preside over a "county educational board"—actually just himself and two teachers.[7]

Though rather a thankless role with mundane duties, few resources, and inadequate remuneration, the position of county superintendent was sought after and fought over. This was because it conferred upon its incumbent prestige and status. Although a regard for position and status might seem a contradiction in a culture shaped by frontier individualism, as the writer W. J. Cash observed in his well-regarded cultural analysis, *The Mind of the South,* "crackers and farmers" accorded such entitlements to their "captains" in the public arena because they associated the "master class, not with any diminution of their individuality but with its fullest development and expression."[8] For many years after the Civil War these "captains" were often literally so—former Confederate officers in whom a degree of local swagger was invested.

While it was seen as a disadvantage for a superintendent to have "scarcely enough education to attend to ordinary business affairs" the opposite did not hold.[9] If a potential appointee had specific skills or knowledge as an education-ist or teaching experience this might stand him in good stead but, as with other county officeholders, it was more important that he was attuned to county and neighborhood political sympathies and values.

Most county superintendents were not from the antebellum gentry. They were often businessmen—cotton and produce buyers, druggists, printers, gen-eral merchants, undertakers, dealers in wagons and furniture, or persons in-volved in other commercial activities. Others were newspaper editors, physicians, lawyers, or notaries. Some were planters and some were farmers. For some the position was just one occupation among many in a varied career. Eugene C. Williams, who was elected superintendent for Shelby County on three succes-sive occasions from 1896, was later postmaster at the town of Vincent. He fol-lowed this with a stint as nightwatchman for the Bessemer jail and ended his working life as caddy master for a golf club.[10]

The position of county superintendent did not become an elective office in all counties until early in the twentieth century and the state superintendent's appointment decisions were usually based on recommendations from the rele-vant county's Democratic and Conservative Party. Yet candidates for appoint-ment had to demonstrate their local support by arranging a substantial bond and gathering petitions.[11] In 1877 Samuel C. Oliver's reappointment as super-intendent of Tallapoosa County was supported by 138 petitioners. Individuals might send in their own recommendations asserting they knew "the senti-ments and desires of the people of the county."[12] Some candidates regarded petition gathering as demeaning and believed their known achievements and/or record of public service should be sufficient testament.[13]

An expanded set of personal characteristics and other criteria regarded as important in a county superintendent emerge from a review of the petitions and letters from members of various communities in the state superintendent's files. It did not need spelling out that any candidate would have to be both white—after 1875 this was assumed—and male.[14] Beyond this, the superinten-dent definitely had to be a local person because external appointees might de-prive one of the county's own people of a due entitlement. Thus petitioners mentioned that "his property is here and he has long been fully identified with this county," or "Pickens County can furnish citizens to fill her offices without going to Tuscaloosa for them," or, in objecting to an appointment, "he is not in touch with the teachers of the state having come from abroad."[15]

Confederate credentials were highly regarded—"he went to battle in his country's cause and made a most gallant officer"; "he is a true soldier." So illus-trious were these credentials that they were allowed inheritance by a civilian son—"his father was Col. F. R. Beck who was killed . . . during the war." The superintendent had to be a "high-toned" person of impeccable behavior—"he is industrious and temperate"; "he is a gentleman of the very best position"; "he is a man of most excellent moral character." He had preferably to be a member of one or more of the associations that were an organized expression of male camaraderie and exclusivity such as local fraternal societies or farmers' groups—"he is a good Templar"; "he is a Mason"; "it will be gratifying to the Patrons of Husbandry to know that one of their number has been made superintendent." Moreover, although the county superintendent was expected to remain nonpartisan in denominational battles, he did have to be a man of faith (and a Protestant)—"he is a strict member of the Baptist Sabbath School"; "his walk, conversation and habits are those of a Christian gentleman." In addition, his political sympathies had to be aligned unambiguously with those of his sponsors and constituency—"he is the choice of the Party"; "he is no fairweather Democrat"—or a nonsupportive view—"he is a Radical and has done all he could in opposition to the Democratic Party."[16]

Overall, county superintendents were expected to be conventionally virtuous. If superintendents did not meet community expectations in this regard, petitions flew up to the state superintendent seeking their removal from office. In 1885, the superintendent of Morgan County, Edison J. Oden, was accused of being "a whoremaster" and was thus "unsuitable to be at the head of our moral institutions." Multiple perfidies were attributed to Thomas Cowart of Winston County—allegedly of a "mean disposition"—but his use of "insulting, profane and indecent language" in the presence of a patron's family and his drawing of a knife and pistol on a township superintendent were, understandably, regarded as outrageous. The removal of James H. Ward of Dale County was urgently requested because Ward was behaving in ways that were an affront to "the dignity of the office." Ward had transgressed by compromising a young female relative and—this seemed the greater concern—by "professing to be a hypnotist." It was alleged he "gave entertainments in different places and exhibitions of his hypnotic powers and legerdemain."[17]

The extent of community investment in the office was made clear in the *Troy Enquirer* in February 1886 when the superintendent of Pike County, John T. Stephenson, attempted suicide. Stephenson had been discovered siphoning off school funds to subsidize his business losses. The paper was not in a forgiving mood: "If he could have realized the immense amount of trouble and worry in which the state, the county, the town, the poor teachers of the county, many of his fellow citizens and not a few personal friends and relatives would have been involved by his acts, perhaps he would have paused in his career ere fraud, forgery and dishonor had met their victim."[18]

County superintendents who served their constituency well were accorded honorary titles of grateful esteem. Thus William Neal, who served as Escambia County's superintendent for twenty-three years from 1886 and who was a tireless campaigner for better schools, was remembered as "The Father of Public Education in Escambia County."[19]

As the state superintendent's appointee, the county superintendent was implicitly expected to promote the cause of public education.[20] Yet, in accordance with the tradition of devising local rules for local needs, some declined to observe lines of separation between public and private schools, which were blurred anyway. Professor J. Mack Thigpen, who was Butler County's superintendent throughout the 1870s, operated at least two private schools. Those seeking to teach in Butler's public schools had to contact Thigpen at his South Alabama Female Institute instead of the courthouse. Thigpen encouraged parents to consider the institute over the county's public schools.[21]

Although dignified by its own article in the pages of the school law, the county board of education—the superintendent and two teachers—was hardly the authoritative regulator by which a county's educational standards were going to be securely established or maintained.[22] Fayette County's superintendent wrote to LeRoy F. Box in 1880 advising him that "if the local board must be composed of professional teachers, there cannot be one formed in this county according to the requirements of law. There is but one man in the county who follows teaching as a profession and he is sixteen miles from the courthouse."[23] There were licensed teachers in Fayette County, but they were either minimally qualified or were female. Women could not serve on boards of education until after 1915. Yet some boards did operate as the law intended and issued formal instructions to trustees and teachers on their responsibilities.[24]

Although the county superintendent was somewhat circumscribed by law in respect of his educational responsibilities, his licensing authority did allow him to exert a certain amount of local power. For a fee of one dollar he could hand out first-, second-, or third-grade teacher's certificates on the basis of an examination that he himself prepared, supervised, and marked. In Coffee County it was claimed a certificate would be granted if someone could spell "baker" and also that "for a fee, a well-educated person could take the test for anyone who desired a certificate."[25] At the end of the century, when the state assumed the licensing authority, John William Abercrombie (state superintendent, 1898–1902) was horrified to learn that one superintendent "in one day, without calling his examining board together, issued ninety certificates, and put ninety hard-earned (?) dollars into his pocket." In another county where horse-swapping conventions were held, the superintendent "exchanged 'critters' with a neighbor and gave a first grade certificate as 'boot.'"[26] There is a folkloric quality to these anecdotes but just the telling shows that in some places a teacher's certificate was not so much regarded as a testament to knowledge as it was a neighborly transaction or a tradeable commodity.

Some superintendents took pride in using their licensing authority to raise educational standards. In 1875 Sumter's superintendent boasted that his teachers were an "intelligent, educated, industrious and efficient corps" because he had weeded out the "ignorant, indolent and drunken."[27] Yet weeding out could be very subjective or partisan. In the 1880s an upsurge of agrarian populism across the South challenged Democratic dominance. A farmers' organization called the Agricultural Wheel was active throughout Alabama, particularly in the north. When a branch of the Franklin County Wheel decided to replace a local teacher with a "Wheeler" named Jeremiah S. Daily, the county superintendent, Asa Frederick, suspended the trustees and canceled Daily's contract. Daily's incensed supporters asked Solomon Palmer (state superintendent, 1884–1890) to remove Frederick. When Palmer attempted to sort out the brouhaha he was warned off by Franklin's probate judge: "the controversy . . . is of a purely local character growing out of neighborhood prejudices and in which the county generally has no interest whatever."[28]

County superintendents mostly operated on their own authority and had a good deal of latitude. From time to time, this gave rise to financial irregularities or embezzlement—which newspapers always reported with condemnatory zest.[29] There were also other illicit activities. On June 3, 1880, a Franklin County farmer named Isam J. Loyd, wrote to LeRoy F. Box, with a range of complaints. He was living in a township "cut off by Bull Mountain Creek from any convenient school" and wanted to transfer his children to a nearby school in adjoining Madison County. His transfer requests had been ignored by the county superintendent, Thomas Vickery. Probably as a means of payback, Loyd went on to provide a colorful tale of how Vickery notoriously operated a whiskey still. A few months earlier he had been in the middle of an oration at a schoolhouse when a revenue marshal came to arrest him. Seeing his quarry take off into the woods, the marshal sought to assuage the disappointment of those assembled by saying he would give the speech himself "if they would just tell him Mr. Vickery's topic."[30]

If the actual educational responsibilities of the county superintendent were somewhat limited by the constitution and by legislation, those of the "township superintendent"—the position at the next level down in the notional pyramid—were extensive. Prior to 1879 this role had been performed by three trustees and would be again after 1891. Old habits dying hard, township superintendents were sometimes referred to as trustees and, where there might otherwise be confusion, the position will be referred to below as "township superintendent/trustee."

The 1879 legislation specified a great number of responsibilities for the township superintendent. He had to conduct a biennial census of school-aged children to assess potential enrollments, determine the number of schools required, and decide on suitable locations. He had to consult annually and carefully with parents and guardians and assess the community's capacity and willingness to supplement the school fund. Schools were not supposed to open unless they could operate for a minimum of three scholastic months with a minimum enrollment of ten students. Perhaps most important, the township superintendent had to contract with licensed teachers, visit schools, ensure teachers were keeping proper records, and remove teachers for major disciplinary breaches. He received no remuneration for these duties other than a "social wage"—being exempted from paying poll tax, serving on juries, and undertaking the onerous chore of annual road duty.[31]

Having to be a "freeholder and householder," township superintendents/trustees were frequently yeoman farmers or storekeepers and financially well established. They might be at the high end of the social hierarchy of their immediate community but, in fulfilling the obligations of office, they had to be responsive to its wishes and interests. If a community was indifferent to the importance of schooling, the township superintendents/trustees were also likely to be indifferent. Yet if they were officious then this too was unacceptable. In February 1880, Lowndes County farmer Jesse S. Sampley requested a copy of the school law from the state superintendent. Sampley believed the local township superintendent, J. Wesley Avenger, was wrongfully construing his authority. He was said to have "a great deal of zeal for the educational caus and not much of anything els as he is a very bussy body in the matter—to much so some of us think to do the people the justise of giving them fair play."[32]

One county superintendent complained of his trustees taking little interest in their schools: "They say the matter is a farce and is no use in spending their time in such manner." Another said his were "careless and inefficient," which he attributed to their lack of "pay or emolument."

Successful township superintendents/trustees were "as punctual in the discharge of their duty as could well be desired" and valued the good opinion and approval of school patrons though these sometimes acted as willful clients who expected all their desires to be satisfied.[33] If patrons were displeased with a township superintendent's decision they might refuse to assist in acquiring the land and/or materials necessary for building and maintaining schoolhouses. As well, they might withdraw their children from school or not insist that they attend. In 1877, John J. Steele, the superintendent of Lowndes County, received a petition signed by 104 "colored" patrons who were angry at being ignored "when they had made it plain that they would not send [their children] to a certain teacher if employed."[34] Boycotts threatened a school's very survival.

Fiats from Montgomery advising county superintendents that township superintendents/trustees should not be allowed to locate schools just to suit themselves, and reminding them that patrons had no legal rights to select teachers, were largely ineffectual.[35] They failed to acknowledge that the families comprising a school community believed the school and all things relating to it was theirs to control.

Unacceptable nepotism was guaranteed to arouse the ire of patrons, particularly when superintendents favored their own children. In 1877 a DeKalb County parent complained about a township superintendent who had appointed his daughter to teach. She was too young and had no experience, and her very limited knowledge of the primary branches meant she was "wholly incompetent to properly conduct a school."[36] In 1880, petitioners from Washington County felt themselves to be "imposed upon" because they had selected a teacher and, although he had been examined and licensed, their township superintendent would not provide him with a contract. It was alleged the township superintendent wanted to employ his son—described as "totally unfit"—and apply the available school funds to establish a school near his own home.[37]

In 1884 Marengo County's superintendent, Levi Reeves, wrote to the state superintendent on behalf of a teacher involved in a local dispute. Reeves felt obliged to insist that nepotism was not a factor in his representations: "he [the teacher] is no kin—true—not connected with me *in any way*—owes me nothing."[38]

Most complaints about township superintendents concerned the imposition of an unsuitable teacher, the location of schools, and/or the consequent allocation of funding. "Is it right," asked the citizens of a Henry County township, "to deprive a large percent of the people of their public money or have them send to a school dominated by a man that is odious to them?"[39]

In adjudicating disputes and trying to withstand factional pressure, county superintendents were often faced with a dilemma. They were well aware that, along with the church, the school was one of the few social institutions regularly encountered by rural communities. The rural schoolhouse belonged to them in more than a legal sense. It was a focus for neighborhood activities such as Masonic meetings, exhibitions, spelling bees, and "box-suppers, fish fries, cake-walks, ice-cream socials and plenty of music."[40] But, though the school was often an integral element of local life, county superintendents were also responsible for seeing public funds were spent appropriately. Conscientious officeholders were at a loss to know what to do when they found township superintendents had contracted teachers who, when examined, showed they knew "scarcely anything about even the simplest elements of a very common school education."[41]

When trustees, patrons, and officeholders all saw eye-to-eye and policy determination was a consensual affair, the schools operated quite smoothly. One county superintendent purred about the long tenure of his trustees and how they consulted in a "concert of action for the interests of their schools."[42]

∽

Harmony could be disrupted by matters that, while not directly connected with the public schools, were an extension of a community's political attitudes or religious allegiances. The factionalism of contemporary politics was a case in point. From about the mid 1880s, the discontent of economically distressed farmers started to find a political voice all over the South. Members of farmer alliances and societies such as the aforementioned Agricultural Wheel and Granges as well as organized labor and Republicans grouped under various populist banners and increasingly posed a serious threat to Bourbon dominance.[43]

As county superintendents were appointees of Alabama's dominant political regime, those who dealt with them were anxious to establish their political fealty or stance on some issue in party terms. In 1875 Colonel Asberry S. Stockdale of Clay County, a member of the "Executive Committee of the Democratic and Conservative Party," expressed his dissatisfaction to the state superintendent with the incompetence of the county superintendent, Archibald J. Williamson. Stockdale wrote "Williamson claims to be a member of Our Party"— as if "incompetent Democrat" were an oxymoron. In 1875, mystified petitioners from Chilton County protested the replacement of their superintendent asserting he had been "a good superintendent and a good Democrat." During the dispute between Asa Frederick and Jeremiah S. Daily, the state superintendent was advised by a Democrat newspaper that the Agricultural Wheel was "a secret, socialistic, Republican organization in this county that is abominably obnoxious to all decency." As late as 1902, the superintendent of education for Geneva County defended himself from the allegations of school trustees that he was a drunkard by explaining the calumnies as the work of his "Populist enemies."[44] The aspersions "Pop" (Populist), "Kolbite" (Reuben F. Kolb supporter), and "Radical" (Republican) occur frequently in the state superintendent's correspondence providing a thumbnail designation of potential or actual political enemies and also class suspicions.[45]

A further factor that was important in ensuring the roles of superintendents were not compromised by conflict was the degree to which they were able to keep religious sectarianism or denominationalism out of the school-house. This was not always easy in nineteenth-century America when local-ism and denominational religiosity went hand-in-hand. Denominations fit-ted people into their own community while providing reference to the larger society; they gave people a sense of heritage and place. Furthermore, full par-ticipation in civil society anticipated membership in some denomination even when a single community might be represented by several denominations or multiple divisions of one.[46]

The public schooling system was only secular in the sense that it was con-ducted under state legislation and that it was nondenominational. All public education at this time was underpinned by the notion that the true citizen of the American republic was a moral individual rooted in a (Protestant) Chris-tian community. One superintendent wrote in his annual report, "Alabama needs that her children be educated, and her young men and women be taught correct conduct, pure morality, right living with all the sweetness and light that shed their radiance about the teachings of the gospel of Christ."[47]

Though the school day often began with a Bible reading, parents were wary of denominational dogma. In 1884, Henry Clay Armstrong was asked to rec-ommend a teacher who would "start the day with a prayer but will not ad-vocate his religious views too freely for we have several religious denomina-tions here."[48]

Denominational differences could impede the efforts of county superinten-dents trying to achieve efficiencies. In 1885, an attempt to combine two publicly funded black public schools in Troy foundered. The respective patrons were set on having their children taught solely by members of their own denomination in their own churches, which doubled as schoolhouses.[49]

In 1906, the state superintendent, who was trying to establish the full extent of educational provisions, asked each superintendent to investigate the num-bers of children attending private and denominational schools in his county. Colbert County's Josiah W. Johnson replied he would only be able to guess at the numbers attending Catholic schools because, of course, as a practicing Methodist, he would not be able to visit them.[50] In 1910, an anxious preacher from Hale County noted a "tendency on the part of teachers to teach religion more and more." As every community had various denominations—he him-self was an "Old Line Baptist"—he felt it would be "difficult for any teacher to teach religiously so as not to offend or disgust some of the patrons and sup-porters of the school."[51]

～

It was eminently reasonable that—at the very least—the public schools should not "offend and disgust" their patrons and supporters because, at least until the end of the nineteenth century, these were the people who, apart from teachers, most heavily influenced the ways in which schools actually operated.

The state constitution of 1875 stipulated that virtually all public educational funds had to be spent solely on teachers' salaries.[52] This left decisions regarding other expenditure—on land, buildings, and equipment—in the hands of township superintendents/trustees and the school patrons themselves. The authority of patrons to influence expenditure was additional to the authority they held for deciding whether to support contracted teachers, whether to subsidize tuition so as to extend the school term, whether to allow their children to attend and how frequently. Patrons largely determined or influenced when schools would be held, what would be taught, and what educational outcomes were, ideally, to be achieved. Some took particular pride in exercising this influence.[53]

Of course, when patrons were poverty stricken, and many were, particularly in black communities, their options were limited and their schoolhouses, if they had any at all, were "very poor structures." In the face of such exigency, patrons and/or trustees arranged for pupils to be taught not only in churches and Masonic Lodges but also in dwelling houses or in other public or privately owned buildings.[54] It often happened that a better off farmer and/or patron—someone with sufficient land—would donate part of his holding so a schoolhouse could be built. This might involve self-interest—his own children could be schooled close to home—and the gesture might be conditional. The title to the land might revert to the donor/owner or to his/her estate once the school was no longer needed. Schoolhouses built on a donated site were often named for the donor. For example, Blalock School near Hood's Crossing in Blount County was on land once part of Jack Blalock's farm.[55]

Location was always a crucial decision because it could make schooling accessible to one community while denying it to another. In a sparsely settled county such as Shelby or one whose whole landscape was divided by streams and mountains such as Talladega, it was difficult to place either sufficient schools or ones that were accessible to enough children to make them viable or "acceptable to all." In Perry County, which was also interlaced with waterways, one parent complained that his seven children were being deprived of an education because it was not possible for them to reach the schoolhouse. This was three or four miles south of his home and on the other side of a river that was difficult to cross.[56] A long, tiring, often barefoot walk—up to five miles was considered walking distance—that sometimes involved wading through streams or negotiating muddy roads, was not the only disadvantage of remote schoolhouses. In heavily wooded areas of wilderness, parents had to worry about their children encountering wild animals such as bears, livestock, and/or other perils. When the distance between home and schoolhouse was too great, parents might arrange for their children, even those as young as six, to board with relatives or friends who lived nearer.[57]

Besides influencing decisions regarding the location and construction of schoolhouses, patrons were able to flex their parental muscle in all sorts of other ways, too. As early as 1875 one superintendent suggested that the government should furnish aid for uniform textbooks because patrons were "too apt to buy those in which they themselves studied despite all persuasion."[58]

Patrons also influenced directly the length of the school session and the wages paid to teachers through their tuition supplements. A black man named Ned Cobb, who grew up in Tallapoosa County in the 1890s, recalled: "My daddy, when he had the opportunity, never did send me to school long enough to learn to read. If he'd sent his children he'd have to supplement the teacher's salary. But if he don't send his children, it don't cost him nothin and there's nothin said."[59]

Plenty was said about patrons who could afford to pay a tuition supplement but chose not to. In 1875, Robert B. Crawford outlined a common problem. If a competent teacher capable of earning $50 per month contracted with his trustees to teach for five months at $20 per month (the available state funds), many patrons would feel no obligation to make up the $150 difference. If only some patrons supplemented and others did not, the inevitable disputes would adversely affect the teacher, who might possibly leave.[60] Thirty-five years later, Alabama's attorney general was asked to advise whether there were legal remedies available to compel supplementation. This was owing to the unfairness involved when only some patrons were willing to supplement.[61]

⁓

Other than those whose roles have already been described and teachers, who are the subject of the next chapter, there were the students—the whole *raison d'être* for the public schooling system. These might be anywhere between the ages of five and twenty-one years but were sometimes even older.[62] In the year ending September 30, 1890, there were 292,052 students enrolled.[63] With so many students and with such a wide range of ages, their attitudes to education, their expectations of what they might learn or achieve by attending school, and their experiences were probably nearly as various as their numbers.

For many country children, schooling was actually just one noncompulsory component in an educational process by which they were prepared for a future that would probably be spent entirely on the farm. The education for this future was largely undertaken at home. Boys were taught skills such as splitting rails, land clearing, plowing, planting, sowing, harvesting, and butchering live-

3. Hickory Grove School, Lowndes County, October 1907. Courtesy Alabama Department of Archives and History, Montgomery, Alabama.

stock. Girls were taught spinning and weaving, sewing and mending, cooking and keeping house. They were also taught how to milk cows and tend chickens, how to smoke hams, how to cultivate a kitchen garden, and how to make soap and candles.[64] Students who attended school regularly—and, even by 1900–01, only 54.3 percent of the school-aged population was enrolled with fewer than half of those in average attendance—understood that at school they would learn skills needed for more than mere existence.[65]

Personal memoirs from this period suggest that unless there was a particularly harsh teacher, many children often enjoyed being in school despite its discomforts. This may have been due to the relief it offered from the physical toil of working in cotton fields from "can't see" to "can't see."[66] Pleasure was also derived from being with other children from their own familiar world. When teachers were from the same community or closely related to the students, this could cause problems for role differentiation and reputation. One student remembered, "a prophet is not without honor save in his own country."[67]

Older students might hear the lessons of younger children and, by so doing, start down their own road to becoming a teacher. During his Jackson County schooldays, James Clemens, born 1908, remembered such older children being

in the room: "There were two that I thought of as ladies there, Maude Bog-
gus and Amy Lewis, and I thought they were grown, but of course they weren't
hardly . . . They were students too."[68]

Some students approached school with a specific objective. William J. Edwards, born 1869, said his "one desire was to learn to read the Bible for my old
grandmother, who like my mother, was very religious." In some black rural
communities the post-emancipation enthusiasm for learning to read and write
waned over the years and, in the first fully free generation, literacy was regarded with ambivalence. Adults interviewed in Macon County in the 1930s
said they had attended school fitfully as children because they were needed on
the farm. They thought "reading and figuring" carried elements of danger to
established owner/tenant relations and were unneeded in everyday life.[69]

~

In the last decades of the nineteenth century, Alabama saw the foundation
and/or growth of a number of cities and towns. By 1900 Birmingham had a
population of 38,417; Mobile, 40,000; and Montgomery, 30,346. In these places
new industries were springing up together with new and specialized occupations to meet their needs. These places needed appropriate schools.

The roles of those in charge of urban schools were somewhat different from
those performed by officeholders and trustees in rural areas. City school systems preferred professional experts and bureaucratic managers rather than
teachers under community and patron control and the lay management of
schools by farmers and other unqualified people.[70] Some well-regarded city
schools—such as the Montgomery and Selma Public Schools—became city
drawcards in their own right.[71]

Birmingham's middle class, including commercial and industrial entrepre-
neurs, evangelical Protestants, German and Irish immigrants, and even the
leaders of the black community, all regarded the public schools as a device for
enhancing economic development and productivity. In 1890, expenditure on
public education represented 20 percent of Birmingham's operating budget.
Such a sizable investment was intended to yield demonstrable benefits and had
to be managed properly.[72]

Although urban citizens had a set of preferences for the governance of
their public interests, they often retained rural folkways, kinship ties, religious values, and traditions of neighborly cooperation. In Birmingham's earliest days, a group of workers appealed to a prominent citizen, Colonel John T.
Terry, to help them in providing a school for their children. Terry located a site
and this was donated by the president of the Elyton Land Company, Colonel
James R. Powell, who was also the city's mayor. Powell subscribed liberally to a

building fund and surrendered his salary to pay teachers.[73] The arrangements were not dissimilar to those worked out in rural townships—but writ larger for a larger sphere.

~

In its rapid growth in size, its increasing complexity, and its diversification, Birmingham was something of a special case. Most of the state's dozens of small towns were variously sized villages servicing their immediate surrounds. Yet many towns had their own newspaper; in 1890 there were 179 in the state.[74] Papers that were regarded as the voice of the county helped to impose a coherent identity on multiple communities and mark its boundaries. This encapsulated local world had its own *dramatis personae* including county superintendents, school principals, and teachers. Reports of their activities, concerns, and opinions over consecutive years allow an insight into the pressing issues of the day.[75] In this book, material drawn from the newspapers described below will provide some illustrative continuity on schooling matters in three areas of the state.

The *Mountain Eagle* was published at Jasper, the county seat of Walker County, a northerly area of minerals and mines as well as farming districts. This paper regularly reprinted articles of interest from the *Birmingham Age-Herald* and other major Alabamian newspapers. The *Troy Messenger* was published at Troy in southeastern Pike County, an agricultural area and trading point for the Wiregrass counties. In the 1880s a normal school was established at Troy making it something of an educational center. The *Wilcox Progress* (later the *Wilcox Progressive Era*) was published at Camden in the Black Belt. Wilcox County's main economic activity was cotton growing and its population was predominately black.[76]

In May 1888 the editor of the *Wilcox Progress* defined schools as the mark of a progressive town and necessary for realizing civic potential.[77] The *Mountain Eagle* concurred: "A well-regulated, well-disciplined and well-governed free school would add more to Jasper's growth and advancement than any other institution be it a cotton-mill, rolling-mill or anything else that would tend to build up our town."[78]

The mix of information, boosterism, and hectoring was relentless. In the 1890s Professor Douglas Allen, a man firmly in the camp of education's new men, wrote an education column for the *Mountain Eagle* in which, among other topics, he regularly promoted the benefits of regular school attendance and punctuality. Such habits would assist children to participate in the New South's industrial world—a world of hierarchy, directive power, and fixed routines.[79] These were novel concepts and very different from those in the rural world where social and economic roles overlapped and were flexible, unspecialized, and loosely organized to match seasonal rhythms.[80]

Newspapers were not only a community coach but also a mirror of societal attitudes. Female teachers were usually described with adjectives such as "beautiful," "charmingly mannered," or "neatly dressed," or might be said to have "a sweet disposition" or "grace of mind."[81] These terms suggested their incipience as candidates for what W. J. Cash called the "mystic symbol" of Southern nationality—its pure and superior womanhood. Readers would infer that Southern values were safe in their hands.[82]

Some newspapers were consistently hostile to any black aspiration, used racists epithets in their news reports, and derided or caricatured successful black people. At the turn of the century, the more malevolent editors claimed a correlation between rising crime and black education. The *Bullock County Breeze*, whose associate editor and business manager in 1905 was also the county superintendent, sustained the editorial line that black schooling should be strictly limited.[83]

~

In the last decades of the nineteenth century, Alabama's population increased rapidly—by nearly 21 percent between 1890 and 1900. However, despite the growth of a number of towns and cities and the first signs of rural exodus, the state remained predominantly rural.[84] Also, at a time when the northeastern and midwestern states were receiving literally millions of immigrants, Alabama received comparatively few except in places such as Birmingham and its surrounding mineral district. This relative sociocultural stability meant traditional folkways, local hierarchies, community-dominated institutions and the meanings derived from shared ethnicity and/or race and kinship had a particular tenacity. As voices started to be raised about the need for reform in public education they went largely unheard outside professional circles. One county superintendent opined—apparently without irony—that "the public school system we now have . . . is almost an ideal system and few changes only should be made to make it perfect."[85] In 1898, when James E. Alexander stood for election as state superintendent, he promised to maintain the *status quo* by preserving "the ideal of local self-government in educational affairs."[86]

Alexander lost to John William Abercrombie, whose intentions were very different. Abercrombie was a member of the Alabama Education Association (AEA) and its "Committee of Thirty-three"—a subgroup formed specifically in 1897 to develop and seek passage of educational reform bills. His ideas were often influenced by concepts of technological and industrial efficiency as well as by modern sociological, psychological, and educational theories. He and his successors and supporters were keen to end an era during which, except in large towns or emergent cities, Alabama's educational "system" was really just the composite of a dispersed multitude of separate community arrangements—albeit in a loose organizational structure. There was little evidence to suggest that rural communities were going to be much interested in Abercrombie's reform vision.

3
Teachers and Teaching

If students were the raison d'être of the public schooling system, then teachers—whose numbers more than doubled between 1868 and 1901 from 2,902 to 6,302—were its necessary enablers.[1] Their critical importance meant they were always vessels for the expectations and ambitions of others. To most communities teachers were instruments for achieving social and cultural reproduction but, particularly from around the turn of the twentieth century, teachers were foot soldiers in the battle for the reform and development of public schooling.

~

While the statutory reports prepared annually (or biennially) by the state superintendent showed the numbers of teachers employed in public schools, they did not provide information on the sources of these or the relative importance of each source. In the immediate aftermath of the Civil War, however, teaching positions in public schools, both black and white, were often a form of charity to the poverty stricken. General James H. Clanton, a Confederate hero who was active in postbellum conservative politics, assisted war veterans and widows to obtain teaching positions in black schools.[2] It was common newspaper opinion that such people would save the freedmen from indoctrination by Northerners.[3] County superintendents also found such placements for destitute constituents. In Sumter County, Michael C. Kinnard "induced moral, and highly respectable old men, who had taught the white children in former years, to teach colored schools." In Marengo County, Levi W. Reeves contracted an elderly white man who was very poor but had many mouths to feed. His example, Reeves claimed, would be "advantageous to the colored race."[4]

Rural schoolteaching at this time was often just another type of seasonal labor and, as such, the sorts of people willing to do it were often either unqualified or uncommitted and just "making it a stepping stone to something else."[5] Sometimes farmers taught to supplement their income. In the early 1870s the superintendent of Baker (later Chilton) County, James M. Cordirie, issued a teacher's certificate to a farmer who, having broken his leg, could not work. He was allegedly told to "go on back home and start a school in the community." The following Monday the farmer started teaching in a stable he had cleaned out for the purpose.[6] This was another example of teaching as a form of welfare when little state relief was available. The farmer's immediate needs trumped questions of suitability.

Despite its low occupational status, there were some who actually enjoyed teaching and canvassed on their own behalf for employment. In August 1873, M. H. Savage of Delevan, Wisconsin (home base to more than twenty circus companies), wrote to the state superintendent, then Joseph Speed, requesting a school he might "work up." He was currently considering the better-paying option of being an agent for P. T. Barnum's circus but "preferred teaching to any other employment."[7]

Canvassing letters were sometimes supported by testimonials. Writing on behalf of a Miss Ethel Ervin, her Baptist pastor said it gave him "very great pleasure to commend in unreserved terms a young lady of irreproachable Christian character, modest almost to a fault, full of lofty ambition and determination to succeed, self-reliant and industrious."[8]

By the late nineteenth century there were already specialist employment agencies such as the North West Teachers Agency that promised its clients they would save "all unnecessary trouble and also have the opportunity of securing the best talent possible." There was also at least one "Colored Teachers' Agency" in Alabama managed by W. T. Breeding of Montgomery.[9]

Despite the appointments that were actually made, it was generally recognized that, ideally, teachers should be appropriately qualified. As early as 1869 Dr. Noah B. Cloud, the state superintendent during Reconstruction, advised that nine teacher training or "normal" classes had been held in six locations and that three hundred pupils taught.[10] Governmental parsimony in the initial years of Bourbon rule affected the establishment and expansion of publicly funded normal schools. Nevertheless, by 1875 the state was allocating funds for normal school training for white teachers at Florence and for black teachers at Marion, Huntsville, and Sparta.[11] Further normal schools for white teachers were later opened at Troy, Livingston, and Jacksonville. The normal schools aimed "to give tone and character to the vocation of the teacher."[12]

Some of these schools, which were often more like high schools than tertiary institutions, offered a broad curriculum. In 1887 students at Florence could study botany, chemistry, geology, Greek, Latin, mathematics, philosophy, political economy, and rhetoric, as well as the basic "branches." Students were also exposed to the "theory and practice of teaching."[13] For decades after the Civil War, teachers generally practiced a pedagogy that emphasized the authority of the instructor, the need for memorization and recitation, and the importance of discipline. However, from about the 1860s, normal schools started imparting a child-centered pedagogy based on the ideas of Johann Heinrich Pestalozzi.[14] Over time, Pestalozzi's ideas, and those of Johan Friedrich Herbart, William James, and others would increasingly influence teaching methods—even those used in one-room rural schools.

While of benefit to those who could attend them, the normal schools could only prepare a tiny fraction of the students needed to maintain teacher numbers. In 1890 the state superintendent pointed out that Alabama needed two thousand trained teachers annually but "if all the graduates of the university, normal and denominational colleges, and all the high grade high schools and academies in the state were trained for teaching, it would not meet the falling off."[15] Those who did attend normal schools could not always be relied upon to honor their pledge to teach for two years after graduation, nor were they automatically recommended for employment.[16] Graduates from black normal schools might forfeit a recommendation if they were thought to be insufficiently biddable. In 1883, William B. Paterson, the white president of the Lincoln Normal University, advised the state superintendent that he would like to provide Chambers County with some "strictly first-class teachers, no politicians or mischief makers."[17]

To the communities in which teachers were going to work, although qualifications were valued, what mattered more was the ease of fit of the teacher, his or her values, and those of the community itself. The township superintendents/trustees were the gatekeepers to assess this fit. Being beholden to their patrons, having no bureaucratic protection and little sense of belonging to a profession, teachers were obliged to act in accordance with local expectations or risk future employment. Such compliance presented few difficulties when a teacher was drawn directly from his or her own community—as was frequently the case. It was common for a teacher to be in charge of instructing his or her own siblings, cousins, and other students with a less well-defined familial connection. Mitchell B. Garrett (born 1881) attended a school at Hatchet Creek in Clay County from the late 1880s. His teachers included a first cousin and a cousin by marriage.[18] A school might be taught over time by a parent and then by a son or daughter. Such intergenerational continuity of occupation was unremarkable.

If not from their own community, teachers were likely to have come from a comparable environment—some small hamlet or farm—and were familiar with rural routine and attuned to local social structures. This was beneficial not only in understanding their students, but also in adapting to a life where their every move was noted—particularly as they usually had to board locally. In the federal census of 1880, 15 percent of those listing their occupation as teacher in Chilton County were living in someone else's household. Boarding actually offered advantages to teachers because it enlarged their knowledge of their students and the patrons they served.[19] Some teachers moved from one family to another in a round-robin fashion with their board being a "payment in kind" element of their remuneration. Katharyne Perdue, who taught in Escambia County in 1899, paid eight dollars per month from her salary of twenty-five dollars to board with a local family. In Marshall County teachers "would go home with pupils to spend the night." When lodgings could not be found, teachers improvised; one teacher slept in a cloakroom attached to the schoolhouse.[20] Black teachers who needed to board had the greatest difficulties. Black families often lived in dilapidated one-room cabins that were barely adequate for their own needs let alone boarders.[21]

Local teachers had the advantage of understanding the school community, but it meant their horizons rarely extended beyond it unless they had attended a normal school. Young teachers in particular were restricted to teaching in accordance with the methods by which they had been taught themselves. They also had to respond to the demands of patrons who were anxious their children should be drilled in basic skills but did not always see the need for "advanced studies" such as geography and grammar.[22] Thus quarantined from outside ideas, teachers helped to perpetuate local traditions and attitudes. The sort of education they provided would later be castigated by influential educationists as "the main single deficiency in rural life today." Teachers were said to have "little comprehension of the rural life problem or of the possibilities of a reorganized and redirected rural school."[23]

In the years following the Civil War, women became an increasingly important source of teachers in all the states of the former Confederacy. This reflected a trend that had actually begun before the war in the northern states. The postbellum rate of feminization, however, was probably attributable to male mortality in the war itself; Alabama lost between 34,000 and 40,000 of its enlisted soldiers.[24] Male labor shortages meant young men had more occupational choices and these did not carry teaching's disadvantages—an uncertainty about the regularity and continuity of employment, a short contractual engagement of usually no more than about three months in the wintertime, and an inadequate salary of twenty dollars per month.[25] In his annual report for 1874, state superintendent Joseph H. Speed was blunt. He asked how a male teacher, who had the same needs and feelings of other men, could possibly do his duty when his salary had not been paid by the state and his dependents might be going hungry or suffering for want of medical attendance.[26]

The correspondence files of the superintendent of education for the 1870s contain many letters from indignant teachers seeking unpaid wages. Typical of these is a claim for forty dollars from T.V.R. Matthews of Etowah County. His letter has a notation from the county superintendent saying: "Matthews taught the school regular but the Trustees did not stop public school when they knew the money was exhausted." Matthews was still chasing his money six months later.[27] Some men taught "because it is easier to sit in the shade than to plow; although from education and physical culture they are better qualified for the latter."[28]

In 1884, Amory Dwight Mayo, a Unitarian minister and observer of the Southern educational scene, noted that few of the "foremost young men of the South" would work for a teacher's scanty pay. Yet Mayo, who had been influenced by Pestalozzi's ideas, believed the movement of Southern women into teaching was "almost providential." He believed they were "consecrated" and would help "to uplift the region's backward people" and "to join them to the larger nation in an enduring social bond." He offered an example of his faith.

Traveling through northern Alabama in the 1880s, Mayo had glimpsed "two or three wild-looking boys romping with the inevitable crowd of dogs that is the annex to every poor Southern family; two pairs of girls with hair in snarls and bare feet heavy with the red mud of the roads, and such strange looks in their faces, with their arms thrown over each other's shoulders, slouching in the rear." He compared other children he had seen in Wilmington, North Carolina, who "would have grown up as wild, as unkempt, as hopeless as that group I saw in Alabama had the Lord not come by in the form of a good schoolmistress and made of them such a kind of children as we might not be ashamed to call our own."[29]

Actually, for many young rural women in the South teaching was a very satisfying option—particularly as it had such a low entry threshold in respect of age and qualifications. It was a role that provided interest, a certain amount of status, and further educational opportunities both formal and informal. Also, although a young woman's wage might be used to supplement family earnings, she was not usually the breadwinner and consequently more likely to be able to exist on the paltry remuneration. Also, even if teaching took women away from their own home or neighborhood, it was an occupation consistent with traditional gendered expectations of behavior—the complex of attributes described as "true womanhood" in nineteenth-century America.[30] A female teacher's virtue, religious piety, and ability to keep house—whether at home or in the community—were traits or skills that confirmed and strengthened the *status quo*.

Around the turn of the twentieth century, the United Daughters of the Confederacy (UDC)—an organization devoted to promoting state's rights, white supremacy, and reverence for the Confederacy—saw the potential of teachers for passing on the values of the Old South and perpetuating the nar-

4. Delphine Feminear, a rural school-teacher at the turn of the twentieth century. Courtesy Alabama Department of Archives and History, Montgomery, Alabama.

rative of the Lost Cause. It thus provided scholarships for young white women to study at Southern colleges to become teachers.[31]

In 1890 female teachers represented nearly 36 percent of Alabama's public school workforce of 5,916. By the end of the 1906 scholastic year, although more than a quarter of all the counties still had more male than female teachers, women comprised nearly 60 percent of the state total.[32] The trend was similar in the schools for both races. In 1906 more than 58 percent of the state's 1,591 black teachers were female.[33] In fifteen counties the figure was more than 70 percent.

Over time, it appears that men may have started to regard teaching as women's work because the trend toward feminization accelerated. In the two years ending September 30, 1908, the female composition of the teaching workforce increased by nearly six percentage points.[34] When a male teacher was in charge of a school he was accorded the honorary title of "Professor" and regarded somewhat as the local intellectual.

The increasing feminization of the teaching workforce may have been the reason that "school discipline" was a staple topic at teachers' institutes over several decades. It may also have been the reason that teachers were given advice on expected standards of social conduct outside the school—particularly with the opposite sex. One board of education advised female teachers that walking in the woods with a young man would "overstep the line of what the board considers decent." Such inflexible restrictions must have been irksome to young people and topics such as "The Social Life of Teachers" were often discussed at teachers' institutes. Advice on personal relations was not always taken. In the 1880s in Randolph County an assistant teacher ran off with the married principal causing the patrons such moral panic they considered closing the school. Yet in some places teachers were warmly welcomed as potential brides.[35]

Although state superintendents did not give the ages of teachers in their statutory reports, information can be gained from census data, published oral histories, memoirs, scholarship announcements, and other sources. From these it can be deduced that, in the period under review, while there were many middle-aged and older teachers in the public schools, the greatest number were clustered between seventeen and twenty-five. In the 1880 census report from Chilton County, more than 28 percent of the teachers listed were twenty-five or younger though the oldest, Ezekiel W. Dunlap, was eighty-two and the youngest, Lizzie Langford, seventeen.[36] In 1889 Hattie E. Taylor was only seventeen when she obtained her teacher's license from the superintendent of Lamar County.[37] In 1892 Vincent Jones Gragg, a sixteen-year-old farm boy, was licensed to teach in Chilton County. Four years later fifteen-year-old Clara Hall was allowed to teach in a Baldwin County school.[38] Applicants for scholarships to the Peabody Normal College in Nashville had to be at least seventeen. They had to pledge in writing to teach for two years after graduation and to "express a purpose to make teaching their profession in life."[39] They would thus have taken up their positions at around the age of twenty or twenty-one and, as a condition of their bond, been teaching until they were about twenty-two or twenty-three.

In the early twentieth century nationally influential educationists such as Ellwood P. Cubberley, who had a marked antirural bias, would condescendingly describe the rural schoolteacher as "a mere slip of a girl . . . who knows little as to the nature of children or the technique of instruction and whose education is very limited and confined largely to the old traditional school-subjects."[40] Though most of these "mere slips" were young and single, other teachers were older unmarried or married women. Three years after being licensed, the now twenty-year-old Hattie Redus (née Taylor) was a farmer's wife with a baby girl. She taught a winter school of twenty-five children in a log cabin where her child slept in a cradle. The next year (1893) Redus was still teaching though her daughter was walking, talking, and sharing her day with the pupils.[41] In 1896 at Fairhope in Baldwin County, a school conducted by Clarence L. Mershon closed when he left for the North to study medicine. When he returned, both qualified and married, his wife was hired to fill his former position.[42] Alabama did not require teachers to retire upon marrying or childbearing, and those who taught after marriage were not considered in breach of appropriate female behavior.

∼

After obtaining a license from the county superintendent, teachers who were without sponsors or connections might take to the road to prospect for a school and/or directly arrange their own employment. In *The Souls of Black Folk,* the famous black intellectual W.E.B. Du Bois described his own prospecting experiences in Tennessee during the 1880s when, under a July sun, he tramped for days through a landscape sprinkled with cabins and farmhouses. At every settlement he asked, "Got a teacher?" Upon hearing "yes" he walked on and on. Eventually, he found a little school tucked away in the forests and hills.[43]

Once a district's need for a school had been established, the aspiring teacher would contact the township superintendent or trustees. In seeking to initiate a district school, it was the custom in some counties for a licensed teacher to present "Articles of Agreement" to prospective patrons stipulating employment terms. These would be discussed and amended or ratified by the township superintendent/trustees and patrons. The township's financial position was the main determinant in deciding whether to issue a contract.[44] Parents who wanted their children taught also solicited teachers directly. As already mentioned, these were often local young men or women known to everyone and toward whom there was already an inclination to employ. Parents might reach agreements with them that would later be formalized by the township superintendent/trustees. This did not always end as planned.

In March 1880 Sarah A. Marshall, a farmer's daughter living in Elmore County, wrote in consternation to the state superintendent. She described herself as "a lady schoolteacher" (she was thirty-five) who had been solicited by the parents of nineteen children to take their school. A few days after commencing she had been told by the township superintendent, a farmer named Alex Nummy, that he would neither be giving her a contract nor allowing her pupils a share of the public school funds. She could not get the county superintendent to give her a hearing though her patrons were "very displeased with Mr. Hummie's [Nummy's] proceedings." She wanted to know "is Mr. Hummie acting according to laws?" None of her patrons knew.[45]

When there was community unanimity about an appointment and the teacher was duly contracted, he or she would learn of further responsibilities beyond those associated with instruction. The teacher was expected to make the rounds of the community to seek pledges from the patrons for tuition fees to supplement public funds. Public moneys might provide as little as a quarter of the funds required to operate a school for longer than the minimum twelve weeks prescribed by law and were critical for a teacher to earn an adequate income.[46]

While having to trudge around local farms to obtain or collect subscription pledges made the teacher something of a mendicant, the experience provided him or her with a firsthand knowledge of the school neighborhood—its geography and terrain—as well as its economic circumstances. By necessarily revealing their circumstances, patrons vested substantial trust in teachers. Respect for this trust was the price of ongoing employment. It was another of the intimate reciprocities and mutual understandings comprising the web of community life.

A further way in which teachers developed a close understanding of their community was through their statutory reporting obligations. The school law required teachers of both black and white schools to complete a periodic report with information on enrollments, attendance, days taught, and so on.[47] The report had to be sworn to by the teacher completing it and approved by the township superintendent. Failure to comply meant going unpaid.[48] These reports were consolidated by the county superintendents and sent to the department of education in Montgomery where, each year, a statewide summation of educational progress was prepared. The final report tended to be a rather bland bureaucratic product but in the townships where the data originated the reports were as much a socioeconomic and seasonal snapshot as an educational audit.

From the county superintendents' overviews, some assumptions can be made regarding just what teachers knew when they completed their reports. For example, they knew erratic attendance was often due to children being needed "at home during April, May and June to make crops and during October, November and December to gather them, thus saving the expense of hired labor" or simply to "bad weather."[49] They knew which households needed "an improved social and pecuniary condition" in order for their children to develop the habit of turning up regularly.[50] They knew which parents kept children at home because of political hostility and which could not see the point of schooling—having had none themselves.[51] They also knew how many children would disappear permanently from their reports having been removed by their parents to join the wage economy via employment in the rapidly expanding cotton mills.[52] In the centers where mills and other industrial enterprises were located, teachers knew their enrollments were inflated by transient children.[53] Teachers knew too which families had moved into and which out of the neighborhood, which hamlets were growing and needed additional instructors, and where sickness was rife.[54] They knew for just how long they were likely to be able to keep their schools open owing to limited public moneys and the difficulty of procuring private supplements.[55] They were aware, too, that they could be beholden to the township superintendent for their salary. In 1901, several teachers in Jefferson County accused their township superintendent of refusing to approve their reports unless they agreed to shop at his store.[56]

In a regime where schooling was not compulsory, the report—with its enumeration of potential and actual attendees—was an instrument for measuring patron satisfaction. Teachers had to attract enrollments and then sustain the interest of those who committed to attend. As teachers were licensed, contracted, and overseen by county and township superintendents, respectively, the reports allowed these office bearers to draw some conclusions about their own performances as well.

~

Although the state normal schools survived and eventually grew "in usefulness and in popularity with all thoughtful educators," a different solution to improving teacher knowledge and competence was developed at the county level.[57] This was the in-service teachers' institute—a somewhat improvisational, largely self-supporting, and locally funded professional development activity. Teachers were supposed to attend at least one institute each year so they could gain knowledge of pedagogical ideas and instruction methods.[58]

The legal responsibility for holding teachers' institutes was actually vested in the county educational board, but, in practice, the institutes were usually organized by the county superintendent. As he was more answerable to the wants and needs of his constituency than he was to the department of education in Montgomery, the institutes were shaped with that constituency in mind and primacy was given to local conditions rather than legislative obligations. In 1891 Baldwin County's superintendent, Fred S. Bryars, reported it was impossible "to collect a sufficient number [of teachers] at one point to effect the purposes of the institutes" because many of his teachers resided outside the county and facilities for travel were inadequate. Yet, in the same year, Blount County's Samuel M. Hendricks held four institutes and pointed out that though these had been held at places "away from the railroad and very far in the interior of our mountainous country, this seemed to be a small hindrance."[59] Attendance was often subject to factors outside the superintendent's control such as heavy rain.[60]

When schools lasted only three or four months, many teachers, particularly men, took other jobs for the remainder of the year and were not free to attend institutes. Female teachers might fail to attend owing to parental responsibilities.[61] Nonattendance could be a source of great frustration to conscientious superintendents. In 1883 one suggested that it be made a legal justification for license cancellation.[62]

Besides enabling teachers to add to their theoretical and practical knowledge, county institutes were actually a sort of self-help forum. Participants were able to learn the causes of the failures experienced and the best means of achieving success in the future. Teachers effectively trained one another, provided mutual support, and aroused a "laudable spirit of emulation."[63] Their unpretentious and practical quality made the institutes attractive to local communities—perhaps even more so than the normal schools. However, some plans for institutes went unrealized because teachers were "too poor to pay their board while in attendance."[64] In his *Annual Report* for 1882 the state superintendent declared emphatically that it did not seem "right or just" that lowly paid teachers should be burdened with the expense of attending institutes.[65] This was a special concern later in the decade when, assisted with Peabody funding, two additional and longer types of institutes were offered. "Normal institutes" offered courses over a period of up to five years, enabling participants to accumulate credits for the knowledge and skills they would otherwise have had to attend normal schools to obtain. "Congressional institutes" were held in each congressional district and had intercounty participation.[66]

Institutes, along with everything else to do with public education, were organized on a racial basis. Yet in 1891 John F. Vardaman of Coosa County stated that, although he "had never held a colored teachers' institute in this county," a few "colored" teachers had attended the institutes of the whites and were "well pleased with them." Yet, in the same year, Jefferson County's superintendent explained that, despite their interest in attending institutes, his "colored" teachers had difficulty in finding a place to meet "where they could be entertained"—find accommodation.[67]

The white teachers fared better. After an institute held in July 1899 at "the flourishing little town" of Hartford in Geneva County, the county superintendent averred that "no people could surpass them [the citizens of Hartford] in hospitality or in interest manifested in educational work." The livery men had cared for their horses, the public hotels had been available gratis to all attendees, and the homes of all the prominent citizens had been thrown open for their reception.[68]

Local newspapers covered both black and white teachers' institutes in some detail, though they gave considerably more column space to white institutes.

5. Teachers attending a Pickens County teachers' institute. Courtesy Alabama Department of Archives and History, Montgomery, Alabama.

The coverage provided feedback to patrons and to the wider community generally regarding the work of the public schools and the competence of the teachers; it also demonstrated the importance of the institutes themselves as educational activities with direct relevance to "the common people" who "heartily give them their support."[69] Having their names published endowed the attendees with an importance they might never have experienced otherwise.

Reviewing the often-fulsome contemporary newspaper accounts of teachers' institutes allows an understanding of why institutes developed an economic and calendrical significance for communities in which not a great deal usually happened outside agricultural, seasonal, and religious routines. Small towns were particularly keen to be selected as the site of an institute.

When a congressional district institute was held in Camden in 1895 the *Wilcox Progress* promoted it with a chamber-of-commerce-like enthusiasm. The paper welcomed the teachers and expressed the hope "their stay may be so pleasant in our midst that when they, like other visitors, leave us, only delightful remembrances of Camden may remain." They were assured that their institute would be presided over by a Dr. E. R. Eldridge, who was not only president of the State Normal College at Troy but one of the *best* normal teachers in the South. The paper suggested that, as well as the teachers, Camden's citizens might also "enjoy the intellectual talks."[70]

The newspaper's coverage conveys the idea of teacher training as civic event and institutes as something for the whole community. In August 1886, after attending an institute at Troy, a teacher responded to the interest of the townspeople by penning an appreciative twelve-stanza poem, which was published by the *Troy Messenger*.[71]

Some of the teachers, who may or may not have attended institutes, were certainly in need of additional skills. Looking back on his Randolph County schooling in the 1880s, William Holtzclaw recalled: "Almost as soon as the Negro pupils got as far as 'baker,' and certainly when they got as far as 'abasement' in the old blue-back speller, they were made assistant teachers." They were doing "pretty good work," but the "best of them had advanced only about as far as the fourth grade."[72] Mitchell Garrett remembered that, although one of his teachers, Greenberry Jenkins, "tried hard enough, he simply could not solve the problems that lay beyond the middle of the [Robinson's *Practical Arithmetic*] book." This cost Jenkins his credibility and his older pupils stopped attending school.[73]

～

On February 10, 1899, Alabama's General Assembly, prodded by John William Abercrombie, the energetic new state superintendent elected in 1898, passed a number of new school laws including *An Act to establish a uniform system for the examination and licensing of teachers of public schools*. A precise gauge was soon available to assess the actual level of knowledge held by Alabama's teachers.

To qualify for the third-grade certificate, teachers had to achieve a mark of at least 70 percent in every subject to pass. They were examined in reading, geography, grammar, arithmetic, and physiology. For the second-grade certificate candidates had to pass all the third-grade subjects plus United States history and Alabama history. For the first-grade certificate candidates had to pass all the second-grade subjects plus algebra, physics, theory and practice of teaching, and school law.[74]

The *Mountain Eagle* reported rather breathlessly on the early state results, claiming a 76 percent failure rate, egregious individual performances, and "lamentable and ludicrous ignorance." However, the paper assured its readers, Walker County had made an "extra good showing." Only seven of its thirty-two candidates had failed to pass.[75]

In his first report to the governor, after the new certification regime commenced, Abercrombie had to admit that in its first year of operation over 39 percent of the 10,171 candidates had failed the examination.[76] Perhaps by way of defending this dreadful result, Abercrombie said that, under the old law,

6. John William Abercrombie. Charles W. Dabney, *Universal Education in the South,* vol. 1 (New York: Arno Press and the New York *Times,* 1936), 394.

each county had its own arrangements and there was "no system, no uniformity, no standard of qualification." People had been licensed who "did not know a verb from a noun, who could not solve a simple example in simple fractions—men and women destitute of moral character." Abercrombie's scorn for localism is palpable when he mentions a person's fitness for teaching had not infrequently been determined by "political affiliations." The new system, he said, would be free of "local prejudices and local influences."[77] This was all very well, but Abercrombie had to make immediate compromises just to ensure that schools across the state could actually open.

While obliged to comply with the law, some superintendents were going down fighting to protect what they saw as their own legitimate domain and rejecting centralized state prescription. The superintendent of education for Etowah County, Newton M. Gallant, was explicit: "The educators of the county know the needs of the people better than it is possible for a State Board to know and are fully competent to take care of the interest of the people in the matter of examinations. The people of Etowah County believe in the doctrine of local self-government and are not prepared to accept the suggestion as true that they need a State Board of Examiners to save them from themselves."[78]

Although all major organizational and cultural change is perplexing, Abercrombie's letter files give some indication of just how baffling the new arrangements were to teachers who had spent their lives—both as students and instructors—in a rural world well away from "system, uniformity, and standard" where they were expected to give students a basic competence in arithmetic, reading, and spelling but not much else.

Jordan J. Williams, a sixty-five-year-old white male teacher, wrote to warn Abercrombie regarding the new school laws. He established his credentials as someone who knew what he was talking about by stating he had forty-two years' experience—the imputation being that Abercrombie was an idealistic novice. He cautioned the reckless reformer that, for his own good and for the public's, he should go very slowly with the new laws: "Their application and enforcement will render all parties connected therewith most unpopular throughout the state. Good in themselves but Utopian—utterly impracticable."[79] John Jackson Mitchell, a member of Alabama's legislature, wanted Abercrombie to brief him on just how the new arrangements were going to be an improvement on those they replaced. He said they were "getting an enormous amount of cursing among our people."[80]

Questions addressed to Abercrombie and to Professor John L. Dodson, the secretary of the State Board of Examiners, indicate a level of incomprehension regarding the novel system. Henry C. Gilbert, superintendent of the Florence school system, explained that his teachers would be working "heroically" but, it being their first experience of state examinations, they were "extremely nervous about it." They wanted to know whether they would be examined "in vertical or slant writing." They were uncertain as to whether their spelling and penmanship would be judged from their papers or whether they would have to explain the rules of spelling or the principles of letter writing.[81] Autauga County's superintendent, Leander J. Sherrill, wondered whether teachers were to write their answers on both sides of the paper or only one. He pointed out it would take much less paper to write on both sides and that "if there were many applicants in such a place as Prattville, paper might run short."[82]

Ambivalence, if not outright hostility, and scornfulness about the knowledge needed for the new examinations was newspaper fodder for some years to come. In 1905 the *Florence Herald* reported a waspish teacher telling people about to take the state examination not to expect to pass unless they had "a knowledge of theosophy, sociology, agriculture, chemistry, socialism, anarchism and any old thing not pertaining to books and libraries."[83] In the same year the *Fort Payne Journal* asserted: "In another generation nobody will be able to spell 'baker' unless some old fogy insists that his children shall learn. Every child is entitled to a knowledge of spelling, reading and writing, for the public pays."[84]

Because it plays on the protective instincts of parents, the topic of "back to basics" in education has always been a hardy perennial for newspaper editors. Yet Alabama's new school laws were genuinely threatening to a society in which local people were used to deciding what was best for their own communities and managing their own affairs. As well, from the start of the scholastic year that began October 1, 1899, fourteen hundred teachers were precariously working on conditional contracts. They would not be paid for any further teaching unless they passed the examination at their next attempt. When those retained on conditional contracts were reexamined, 20 percent failed.[85] J. H. Nunnelee, the proprietor of the *Selma Times,* wrote to Abercrombie on behalf of a Captain N. N. Shephard—"one of the best Black Belt Democrats you ever saw"—a school trustee who was unable to find sufficient licensed teachers. Nunnelee said the law had "played the devil with us in big black beats," and he would take it as a personal favor if Abercrombie could "stretch the law a little bit" for Shephard.[86] Nunnelee wrote from the viewpoint of local need and a tradition of back-scratching and legal elasticity when it came to favors.

Until 1899, if a teacher's overall performance was satisfactory to his or her patrons and the township superintendent/trustees, any inadequacies in his or her knowledge or methods tended to be overlooked—specially when the teacher was kin. Abercrombie received many letters from those for whom failure to pass the examination would mean ruin for their families or themselves. One woman begged for mercy, explaining she had been teaching for years to support her siblings and invalid father and just did not know what she was now going to do.[87] George Jones, a Shelby County farmer, wrote that he had obtained a first-grade certificate in 1884. He was now too ill to farm and needed to teach again but was worried he would not pass the examination at the level now needed to obtain a first-grade certificate. He asked Abercrombie to oblige him by suggesting "a plan" by which he could procure a life certificate thus "putting him on the tracks."[88] A presumably desperate B. W. Collins of Jackson in Clarke County went beyond asking for a plan and offered Abercrombie a bribe. A furious Abercrombie threatened Collins with the prospect of jail.[89]

As soon as the new law was implemented there was widespread evidence of cheating. As early as June 1899 Abercrombie was being warned that in some parts of the state stolen examination papers were being peddled to anyone willing to pay five dollars for them. The source of the stolen papers was alleged to be Frank L. Todd, a former teacher working as a porter at the capitol. Whether from Todd or another source, stolen papers turned up in Bullock and Barbour counties and, at the time of the next round, in St. Clair.[90] In Jackson County, an administrative bungle meant teachers at Pisgah received their examination papers before other towns. The questions were soon distributed via the rural grapevine. This neighborliness at the expense of the careless superintendent, Charles L. Hackworth, was not seen in that light by Abercrombie.[91]

When the next quarterly examinations were held, Abercrombie was on his guard. He wrote to the superintendent of Barbour County warning him to avoid every appearance of irregularity. He explained that "opponents of the examination law, unsuccessful applicants and personal enemies take every opportunity to accuse county superintendents of wrongdoing."[92] Abercrombie seemed oblivious to the cause of the acrimony—that people were peevish at the central government's assumption of rural ignorance and its depriving people of their livelihood.

Under the old regime licenses could be canceled for "intemperance" or "unworthy or disgraceful conduct." But boards of education or superintendents sometimes displayed the sort of lenience they might extend to a wayward family member. Thus James Agnew, an Escambia County teacher who attended meetings under the influence of whiskey, retained his license because he was deemed a fine scholar who was trying to reform.[93]

County superintendents could exercise their own judgments, but when it came to assessing moral character, state officials had to be scrupulous in demonstrating impartiality. Thus when state examiner George W. Brock discovered he not only knew several of the teachers presenting for examination in Escambia, including Agnew, but also knew them to be overly fond of liquor, he had to achieve with paperwork what had previously been a local discretionary matter. He required each candidate to provide a character reference signed by "three or more persons in good standing within their communities." He enclosed these with the papers he sent to the State Board of Examiners.[94]

In Henry County, where the rancid politics of this period were fought out with gusto at the local level, twenty-five citizens were determined to see that a black teacher named Culver was not granted a life certificate. They testified to his "immorality." The superintendent, James B. Espy, was able to advise John Dodson that the citizens were local Populist Party members who wanted to thwart Culver's ambitions because he had helped deliver the county to the Democrats in the last election.[95] In 1901 the law was amended and candidates had to produce written references before being examined, "unless the applicant is known to the person appointed to conduct the examination (the county superintendent) to be of good moral character."[96]

If the county superintendent were also a teacher, state adjudication was necessary. In 1901 when Frank M. Justice, who was both superintendent of Geneva County and a teacher, was accused of intemperance by his Populist opponents, Abercrombie obtained legal advice on the validity of the charges. Twenty-five affidavits of support were forwarded from Justice's school community and his accusers were denounced. One "was billed at last term of court for stealing" and another "lay in jail at Montgomery and also went to coal mines for twelve months."[97]

In Abercrombie's biennial report for 1899 and 1900, he included opinions on the changes to the teacher certification and licensing law from fifty-five county superintendents. More than 70 percent supported the changes while the rest either provisionally approved of them or were totally against them.[98]

For years afterward, superintendents maintained protests about the rigidity of the examination process, claiming it was driving experienced teachers out of the profession. John N. Word complained "the state board has nearly rid Randolph County of colored teachers." Winston County's Levi T. Steele pleaded for examination leniency because "a poor school is better than no school at all."[99] In 1903 lawyers from Camden lobbied their state senator to procure a license for a Mr. Fortune Williams, "a Negro of excellent moral character and of much more than ordinary ability," though he had failed arithmetic.[100] Seven years later William M. Cook, a Camden resident, was adamant that "opinion is opposed to a too rigid enforcement of the rules."[101]

The pleas of these men showed them struggling for an outcome that mattered to their constituents. In October 1903 the legislature appeared to recognize they might have a point. It enacted a bill authorizing an annual appropriation of $5,000 to fund summer schools for white teachers at the University of Alabama. The six-week schools were essentially crammers for the teachers' examination and, in this respect they were quite successful.[102] In 1907, of those who attended the summer school, 77 percent subsequently passed.[103] From April 1911 state support was provided annually for a compulsory week-long institute led by expert instructors for each race in each county.

When William Francis Feagin became state superintendent at the end of 1913 he was astute enough to recognize the limitations of the law governing teacher accreditation. He said: "We are shutting the door in the face of many teachers who are succeeding in other states and will not make the change to Alabama so long as the grind of an examination is a condition precedent to admission here."[104] Through Feagin's influence, the law was changed in 1915 to allow Alabamian university graduates to be granted first-grade certificates upon application and to recognize qualifications gained in other states.

In 1910 Harry C. Gunnels (state superintendent, 1907–1911) issued the department of education's first comprehensive teachers' manual. This was to assist teachers in planning their work and making their instruction more effective. Some of the advice provided appears to have been influenced by contemporary theories of cognitive development and by a Herbartian pedagogy in which the teacher builds on a student's existing knowledge and aptitudes.

The manual described how to adjust a course of study for local and individual needs.[105] Three years later, Henry J. Willingham (state superintendent, 1911–1913) issued an updated version as well as a booklet specifically written for rural teachers emphasizing the significance of the school in country life.[106] These manuals were an entirely new resource for teachers. They showed the developing role of the education department as a professional bureaucracy providing statewide support for the schooling system and its teachers. They also showed a trend toward standardization and regulation, which, all over the nation, was increasingly being equated with "reform."[107]

∿

In the years leading up to 1915, professional organizations—such as the Alabama Educational Association—expanded and were able to lobby for legislative and policy changes on schooling matters. In addition there was a growth in the popularity of county teachers' associations that sought "to cultivate the social and professional spirit of the teacher and public sentiment favourable to them and their work."[108] The growth of this professional consciousness in teachers was due largely to reformer initiatives—the statewide examinations and certification based on measurable achievement, the summer schools and annual institutes conducted by expert instructors, the extension of teaching engagements, the manuals, and so on. While all these developments were encouraging to reformers, the concomitant benefits of raised status tended mainly to advantage urban teachers. They were rarely available to the teachers of one-room rural schools who also had to be "superintendent, supervisor, janitor, and community worker."[109] If these roles caused dissatisfaction, the teacher could always seek the greater challenges and experiences—and better pay—of an urban school. But, as an exodus of rural teachers to towns would just create a new dilemma, school consolidation was touted as a solution. If multiple rural schools were combined into larger units, reformers believed they would more closely resemble urban schools. Teachers would thereby have greater professional scope and opportunities.[110] But consolidation was contingent on factors such as better roads and transportation and was slow in coming. In some places it would be resisted for its potential to undermine local control of education and to dilute the influence that trustees and parents could exert on teachers and the values that the teachers were expected to impart.

4
The Schoolhouse—Inside and Out

In the nineteenth century and even later, the pedagogical methods employed in Alabama's public schools were intended to assure (almost wholly rural) parents that their children would acquire basic skills in the subjects or "branches" regarded as the essence of education.[1] These were reading, writing, and arithmetic; spelling, grammar, and composition; history and geography. Most parents, some of whom were suspicious of "book-learning," were wary of subjects beyond this core curriculum.[2] However, they did not want their children burdened with illiteracy and destined forever to survive on "mother-wit."[3]

Parents and guardians took it for granted that, if home was the place from which children would take "their conduct, morality and their mental, emotional and spiritual key," teachers would mirror and reinforce the home in their own behavior and values.[4] It was recognized in law that, even if young and/or inexperienced, the teacher was "within reasonable bounds, the substitute for the parent, exercising his delegated authority."[5] From the 1880s, a teacher's contract specified an obligation to improve the "education and the morals of his pupils."[6] Some counties went further and required a teacher to "be active in the leadership of the church and community affairs."[7] Teachers were also expected to model and uphold the cultural values and assumptions of their school community, particularly those concerning race and interracial relationships, which were clearly evident anyway from the constitutionally segregated schools.[8] All these implicit requirements formed the hidden curriculum.[9]

The successive pieces of legislation that regulated Alabama's public schools after 1875 defined the school calendar—its scholastic year, months, and days. Within this context, however, school trustees, patrons, and teachers determined their own school routine to match local needs, priorities, and resources. Schools were held from Monday to Friday and, depending on the extent to which patrons supplemented the teacher's salary, the length of the annual session was upward of three months. This was often cut in two with winter and summer sessions. By law, a school with fewer than ten pupils could not receive state funding. The maximum number of pupils one teacher was allowed to instruct was fifty.[10] The law was often ignored.

Within the schoolhouse seating was usually organized so the youngest pupils sat at the front with each "grade" a row further back. Girls and boys mostly sat on opposite sides of a central aisle—possibly divided again to ensure cleaner children from better homes sat together. The teacher occupied a desk facing the class—often on a platform.[11] As late as 1913 nearly 80 percent of rural schools had only one teacher; the elevated platform attested to his or her sole authority.[12] The schoolhouse interior was a reflection of the outside community's unambivalent ideas about race, hierarchy, gender, and class.

Schoolhouses in rural districts were commonly as unpretentious as the vernacular farm buildings that were scattered throughout the local area and from which they were barely distinguishable. Frequently they were rudimentary barn-like structures made of logs or planks—some so rudimentary that they shook when anyone entered and needed buttressing. They often had unglazed window openings with wooden shutters or oiled paper to keep out the rain. They mostly had a single entry/exit door at one end. Some were without ceilings or floorboards and infested with fleas. Those elevated on pillars might serve as a shelter for hogs, goats, and even sheep in inclement weather. Ventilated only by the cracks in the walls, they were stiflingly hot in summer and often freezing in winter. They were usually built near a spring but when no spring was nearby, a well was dug. There were rarely facilities such as privies; children "went in the woods" to areas designated by sex.[13] As state funds could only be spent on teachers' wages, the quality of the schoolhouse was a gauge of a community's economic wherewithal.

School buildings in cities and towns were altogether more suitable in every way because they were acquired or constructed with funds not generally available to farmers. Even in rural areas there were occasionally purpose-designed schoolhouses owned by individuals who might, as a matter of benevolence, make them available "for use by the free schools."[14]

The hand-crafted, improvisational nature of the rural schoolhouses extended to their equipment. Some were furnished with rough wooden desks and seats fabricated from split pine. According to one superintendent these were "low enough for a pygmy and the desk part high enough for a giant."[15] But many had old church pews or log puncheons on pegs for benches with sometimes a second elevated log, still with the bark on its underside, serving as a desk. Recently cut logs were likely to exude a resin which stuck to the children's clothes.[16] Most schoolhouses had a stove to ward off winter cold, a water pail from which students drank with a shared gourd dipper, and a container of

7. Class inside a Lawrence County schoolhouse, circa 1913. Courtesy Alabama Department of Archives and History, Montgomery, Alabama.

hickory switches. There were seldom pictures, pointers, globes, or charts of any kind, and the blackboard was merely an area of an interior wall painted with lampblack.

Unless they were actually squalid hovels, schoolhouses constructed of local materials and equipped with homemade furniture often engendered a quiet satisfaction despite their shortcomings. This was possibly because they were the products of self-reliance, human exertion, and financial sacrifice. Their unpainted exterior was not unlike a protective coloration that blended into the landscape. Their names tied them to their locality. They might be called after the farmer who donated land for the schoolhouse (King's Schoolhouse), a prominent citizen (Kelley's School), a village feature such as a turpentine still (Mill's Still School), a nearby church (Shiloh, Mount Zoar), a creek (Turkey Branch). In Greene County there were schools named for their forest setting— Beech Grove, Pine Grove, Live Oak, White Oak, Green Oak, and Gum and Oak Hill.[17]

The first session of the school day was an "opening" of about fifteen minutes during which the teacher recited a prayer and/or read from the King James version of the Bible. This ritual performance with a sacred object served to confirm the group identity of both teacher and students. It also confirmed the Christian and Protestant, if nonsectarian, ethos of the school and gave religious legitimacy to its educational agenda. At the end of each week some schools closed with hymn singing. It was said approvingly of Winston County's schools in the 1870s and 1880s that, even if they might have been "limited in academic curricula, they were strong on their endeavors to teach the principles of morals and religion."[18] Whether religious exemptions were allowed for Catholic or Jewish pupils is unclear, though such children certainly attended public schools.[19]

The principal pedagogical method employed by Alabama's schoolteachers, until after the turn of the twentieth century, was memorization and recitation—a method peculiarly suited to a world in which traditions of oral communication—spinning yarns and telling folktales—were still strong in white communities and sustained by an agrarian culture. Though deriving from a different culture plus the enforced illiteracy of slavery, oral communication was also a strong tradition in black communities.[20] A "Daily Programme for School" included in the state superintendent's report for 1889 recommended a lesson plan for a day of seven hours inclusive of breaks. This required the teacher to conduct twenty-one separate recitations.[21] Actually, teachers sometimes conducted fifty or more recitations daily.

If not particularly effective as an educational technique—though at the time it was believed that by training memory, the faculties of reason and logic were also trained—recitation did have advantages. It enabled a single teacher to manage a fairly large number of children by delegating the hearing of recitations to older pupils. When up to fifty children inside a single room were, by turns, jumping up from their benches and queuing to recite a multiplication table, to spell a list of words, or to stumble over a passage from a reader and so on, the result must have been a serial clamor—hence the origin of the pejorative term "blab schools." Teachers were told to regard the schoolroom as "a musical instrument" and themselves as performers. If the teacher was a "skillful performer," harmony would result but if unskilled, there was "discord, strife and war."[22]

Teachers were concerned to ensure that, during the hearing of recitations, the children who were not involved refrained from talking or communicating with one another. "How to Control Whispering" was sometimes a topic at teachers' institutes.[23] Yet whispering was the least of a teacher's problems. Seasonal swings in attendance, absenteeism, and tardiness played havoc with any attempts to classify children and their progressive, if self-paced, acquisition of skills and knowledge.

Because students lived at varying distance from the schoolhouse, not all arrived at the same time. Even the children of a single family did not always set out together, having been delayed by chores such as milking. Katharyne Perdue, who taught public schools in Escambia County during the 1890s, recalled: "The children came to school at all hours of the day and cared not for 'tardy marks."[24] Sporadic attendance was not just the result of indifference to "book learning" or the attitude that school was something to be fitted in between competing priorities. Nor was it due entirely to an undeveloped sense of regularity. All these factors may have been contributory but children were a major part of Alabama's rural workforce. Some families risked destitution without the contribution that even the youngest children made to subsistence.

Variable weather and sickness affected the attendance of those who were enrolled. In 1880 Randolph County's superintendent reported that two of his schools had "failed to continue for sixty days owing to whooping cough and measles."[25] Other scourges were malaria, typhoid, tuberculosis, yellow fever, and/or a debilitating lassitude caused by the hookworm parasite. Disease was rife around creeks and rivers.

The enrollment figures compiled each year for the state superintendent's annual report show that for the scholastic year ending September 30, 1880, just 46.3 percent of the school-aged population was actually enrolled in public schools and 65.7 percent of those were in average attendance. For the scholastic year ending September 30, 1910, although 59.3 percent of the school-aged population was enrolled, only 62.8 percent of those were in average attendance.[26] These figures suggest that, while parental intentions regarding schooling may have improved over this thirty-year period, actual rates of attendance had not.

Data for a number of different years show a clearly discernible correlation between low black daily attendance as a percentage of enrollments in the Black Belt counties and low white daily attendance in the "white counties" of the Appalachian hills and valleys or the piedmont. For example, in the scholastic year ending September 30, 1890, the number of enrolled black students in Bullock, a Black Belt county, was 4,347 but the actual average daily attendance was only 224 (5.15 percent).[27] In 1896, William C. Bledsoe, the superintendent of Chambers County, audited that county's public schools. Despite the enrolled students numbering 7,155 students, nearly 9 percent of these attended for fewer than ten days each year. More than a hundred students over sixteen were illiterate.[28]

Student misbehavior presented more difficulties for teachers—particularly young women—than any other factor. In the one-teacher school there was no one of higher authority whose name might be invoked to instill fear or to whom they might send an unruly student. Some dealt with discipline problems by absenting themselves until the trustees could persuade them to return. Others threatened beatings without following through—as did Mattie Lou Williams, a Bullock County teacher, whose pupils deliberately scared her by placing a small snake under her hand bell.[29]

Male teachers seem to have had no difficulties in meting out corporal pun-ishment and, when they took on grown adolescents, the results could be nasty. In 1889 at China Grove in Pike County, Benjamin Boyd, aged twenty-five, ran out of patience with an eighteen-year-old pupil named Lee Crowder, who was "subverting the good order of the school." Boyd struck the farmer's son so violently he sustained an eye injury. When Crowder brought charges against Boyd for battery, the Pike County Criminal Court found in the plaintiff's favor. Boyd's appeal to the Supreme Court of Alabama *(Boyd v. State)* was dis-missed. In a rather arch-sounding judgment by Justice Henderson M. Somer-ville, Boyd's conduct was found "unseemly on the part of one whose duty it was to set a good example of self-restraint and gentlemanly deportment to his pupil."[30]

Not many assaults reached as far as Alabama's Supreme Court but school-room beatings were by no means rare. Mitchell Garrett recalled one of his teachers viciously thrashing two boys who tried to ward off the blows with their arms. Garrett "hoped never to see such a thing again" but he hoped in vain. Half the teachers he was taught by at his Clay County school employed corporal punishment.[31] Students who experienced violence at home feared school would offer more of the same. During the 1930s a black man look-ing back on his Macon County childhood recalled: "My folks wanted me to go to school but I was scared of whuppings so I never would go. I uster hide behind the pines 'stid of going to school. . . . When my mother found out I wasn't going she whupped me till I like to had spasms. She knocked a hole in my head."[32]

It may be unlikely that most children experienced incidents quite as ugly as the ones described above but these were hardly alien to the local communities in which they took place. Corporal punishment by teachers was an approved aspect of nineteenth-century schooling all over the United States and the ul-timate authority of the Bible could be cited to give the practice legitimacy.[33] Parental acceptance may have been religiously based but it was not in conflict with frontier traditions of summary justice and ritualized violence in the face of perceived threats. Black teachers could draw on a legacy of the inherent vio-lence of slavery and the remembered practices of plantation overseers for mod-els of discipline.

Yet it would be misleading to imply that corporal punishment was purely a rural phenomenon—part of a continuum that began with "paddlings" and ended with lynchings. At an 1884 meeting of the Alabama Educational Association—a largely urban white teachers' association begun in 1882—some of the foremost citizens of the state were present including the state superintendent of education, Major Solomon Palmer; a former governor, Robert M. Patton; and a judge, William B. Wood. A lengthy session concerned the topic "Can a School in which Corporal Punishment is Prohibited be Successfully Taught?" Six speakers believed "no" was the proper answer. Judge Wood said he was "in favor of flogging. Moral suasion was a humbug."[34]

Besides unruly behavior and pranks, teachers could experience other kinds of intimidation. Some actions carried the implication that a teacher must conform to community mores. In the late 1880s, Sally Roberts was employed to teach a school at Bon Secour in Baldwin County. Roberts was known to be a member of the Episcopalian Church, which, owing to its liturgical rites of worship, was sometimes regarded by rural Southerners as a veiled form of Roman Catholicism and aroused a similar suspicion. With a touch of Breughelian rustic heartiness, the lumpen element of Bon Secour expressed its disapproval of Roberts by placing a dead hog on the schoolhouse step with a label "for the teacher's lunch."[35]

Their *in loco parentis* status permitted teachers not only to beat children but also to kiss and pat them affectionately—at least in the 1870s. In March 1874 at Troy in Pike County an eleven-year-old girl was sexually molested by her teacher. Her parents had ignored earlier complaints because "it is an almost common practice for teachers to kiss their pupils." The *Troy Messenger* commented: "Although the habit of kissing schoolgirls—indulged in by male teachers both North and South—is, as a general thing, prompted by a pure regard for their pupils . . . the custom is calculated to lead to sad and disastrous results when practiced by men of impure desires."[36]

~

Teachers had few disciplinary problems when they were able to engage fully their students' interests. This was difficult in one-room schools where teachers had many students and had to manage simultaneously such variables as age, learning stage, motivation, and capability—all factors underpinning the notion of grading. In 1854, William F. Perry, the first state superintendent, had suggested a school grading structure and relevant grade-related textbooks.[37] Similarly, in December 1869 the board of education set up under the Reconstruction constitution of 1868 legislated for four grades and also considered the benefits of having uniform textbooks throughout the state. Just two grammars had been selected before the board's pressing financial problems overtook further inquiries.[38]

Being so ill trained, teachers depended almost entirely on textbooks for what and how to teach.[39] The textbook for any subject and the curriculum for the same subject were as one. An increasing focus on textbook uniformity by educational officeholders was prompted by a desire to use textbooks as a tool to support grading and to see students taught a common curriculum in all parts of Alabama. Many parents were not in favor of uniformity and, as will be shown below, demonstrated a mix of attitudes, some highly antagonistic, when it was proposed.

As parents had to provide the textbooks and this involved a cash outlay from their scant resources, any texts acquired had to last a long time. Some of the books children brought to school had the attributes of a family heirloom passed down from one generation to the next—more a talismanic artifact testifying to a family member's literacy rather than a learning aid to a contemporary curriculum. In some cases textbooks were a family's only reading material besides a Bible and perhaps an almanac. Katharyne Perdue remembered: "And as for books—a blue-back speller, perhaps a reader and an arithmetic that 'Pa' or 'Buddie' had studied—and very few of these books of the same grade were by the same author—were the only things which the teacher had with which 'to rear the tender thought.'"[40]

The "blue-back speller" was Noah Webster's *The Elementary Spelling Book*—its name derived from its binding. In 1854, when Alabama's education system was first established, Webster's speller and William Holmes McGuffey's series of readers were already in use. They were still in use more than forty years later. But in 1903, when Alabama's Textbook Commission finally mandated statewide textbook uniformity, neither was adopted.[41] A sense of cultural loss may have contributed to the hostility to uniformity that was expressed in other ways. The reasons for these books' perennial appeal in Alabama is worth reviewing.

During much of the nineteenth century, Webster's speller and the McGuffey readers were popular across the whole of the United States, including the South, and both books sold in their millions, creating a degree of universality in the national common school experience of learning to spell and to read. Numerous writers have examined the multiple reasons for this popularity. For example, E. Jennifer Monaghan has demonstrated that Noah Webster's genuine innovations, scrupulous editing, and unflagging promotion led to his spelling book's early success and this was able to be sustained by later publishers.[42] Henry Steele Commager noted that Webster's commercial acuity was combined with a conviction that American nationalism could be strengthened by education with textbooks as the vehicle. Early editions of the speller contained such items as the Declaration of Independence and George Washington's farewell to his army. Webster felt these contained "such *noble, just and independent sentiments*" that he could not "help wishing to transfer them into the breasts of the rising generation."[43] The Civil War created new military heroes for the South such as Robert E. Lee but did not erase its reverence for earlier heroes such as Washington, who remained the iconic "Founding Father."

The McGuffey readers were a direct expression of the deeply held religious beliefs long associated with communities on the American frontier. Elliott Gorn has shown that, throughout all their editions and revisions, the McGuffey readers were written within a religious and rural frame of reference. They sustained an emphasis on individual choice in the matter of salvation, on leading a Christian life, and on taking personal responsibility for sin—all messages consistent with the values and Protestant religious beliefs dominant in Alabama. Later editions of the McGuffey readers, particularly the 1879 edition, reflected the nation's changing social and economic life. They emphasized the values of an urban-industrial culture such as steadiness, thrift, responsibility, piety, self-restraint, and sobriety. As the temperance movement in Alabama gained strength, the readers would have reinforced its mission.[44]

Richard Mosier has also examined the McGuffey readers, pointing out their highly conservative attitudes to political, social, and economic matters; their rationalization of class and wealth; their anti-Jacksonian distrust of popular participation in government; and their depiction of women as symbols of virtue and charity but of limited capabilities.[45] While such content may have jarred with the beliefs of some Alabamian parents and teachers, the books were regarded as having a beneficial effect on "shaping character."[46]

Students were not oblivious to the moral didacticism of the McGuffey readers but enjoyed their "interesting" stories and pictures and their underpinning belief that country life with its closeness to Nature was superior. The readers were well produced, were relevant to an oral culture—because they emphasized the importance of reading aloud—and provided concrete rather than abstract examples of moral philosophy. In addition, they included material from writers of the first rank such as Dickens, Longfellow, Scott, Shakespeare, and many others.[47]

Other readers were also used in Alabama's public schools. In 1896 a teachers' institute in Walker County discussed "How to teach the first three lessons in Holmes's First Reader."[48] Holmes's readers were a series written by George Frederick Holmes of the University of Virginia, who also wrote grammars and histories. Before the Civil War, Holmes had staunchly defended slavery and had also been responsible for fear-ridden attacks on critics of conventional Christianity. He believed the modern economy had eaten away at the bases of traditional society. In Alabama the Southern authorship of the Holmes's readers would have been greatly in their favor.[49]

Learning to spell and to read was an insistent process of rote learning and drill with progress checked by recitation to the teacher. Spelling developed an importance beyond its educational purpose and became a much-enjoyed competitive social activity such as an end-of-week game or for holiday fun.[50] There could not have been much other purpose for farm children knowing how to spell "peripateticism," "provincialism," or "scholasticism"—all words on page 132 of Webster's speller.[51]

In spite of the important pedagogical function of textbooks, their general scarcity meant that when a student finished one reader the more advanced version might not be available. Leola Tidwell, who attended school at the beginning of the twentieth century near Logan in Cullman County, recalled that "often as not when we had finished a reader, the teacher would decide we might as well go through it again." Sometimes students would go through each reader up to three times.[52] When students had worked through their own textbooks they might borrow from other boys and girls.[53] Once all the books in the neighborhood had been shared and exhausted, parents might decide their children had had enough schooling. In Coffee County in the 1870s when a child "had conquered the blue-back speller, he was considered pretty well educated."[54] In Clay County's rural schools in the 1880s "few pupils ever studied the Fourth [McGuffey's] Reader."[55]

Public school students received their instruction in the other branches—arithmetic, grammar, geography, and so on—in much the same way as they learned to spell and to read—by the memorization and recitation of textbook material and by rule-based exercises. Geographic and historical facts were learned by heart and then the teacher would test this knowledge by asking a question to which there would be a catechismal response. Studying arithmetic involved memorizing rules and then applying these to problems that were worked out on a slate. Slates were also used to practice "penmanship" with special slate pencils or chalk, which students often wiped off with their sleeves.[56]

The instruction described above achieved its objectives insofar as basic skills were taught, rules memorized, routine and repetition accepted, and moral precepts absorbed. The din of the schoolhouse, rather than being a hindrance to learning, was consistent with oral cultural traditions and helped to reaffirm the everyday connections of neighbors. This was schooling as social reproduction in communities that might variously be conformist and conservative, religious and reactionary, self-protective and self-aware. White communities were particularly protective of their cultural tenets, especially those to do with race and Southern identity.

In his 1912 book *Civil War and Reconstruction in Alabama*, Walter Lynwood Fleming alleged that, during Reconstruction, the first superintendent of public instruction, Dr. Noah B. Cloud, recommended history books for use in Alabama's public schools that "were insulting in their accounts of southern leaders and southern questions." Fleming also alleged that Cloud secured a donation of several thousand copies of history books that gave a Northern view of American history and "these he distributed among the teachers and the schools." Other material "objectionable to the whites" came from the Freedmen's Bureau and "was used in the schools for blacks."[57] Some of this was material from the American Missionary Association and included *The Freedmen's Book* by Lydia Maria Child, which was full of selections from Abolitionist writers such as William Lloyd Garrison and Wendell Phillips and described the daring deeds of black insurrectionists.[58] Freedmen's books generally aimed to "communicate religious and moral truths" and provide "instruction in civil and social duties as are needed by them [the freedmen] in their new circumstances."[59] As many white Alabamians in the postbellum period did not yet accept the change in the civil status of former slaves, textbooks with such avowed intentions were destined to provoke their outrage.

The school legislation enacted after the adoption of the 1875 constitution was silent on textbooks, meaning their selection was to be a matter for local school communities. Yet this did not mean the end of anxiety about the representation of the South in textbooks or the belief that there was a need for an Alabamian—or more generally—a Southern curriculum.

In the years following the Civil War, John B. Gordon, a famous Confederate general, had become an agent for the University Publishing Company of Virginia. One of the goals of this company was "to create non-partisan school literature" that would help rid the nation, and the South in particular, of sectional hate. It also sought to promote Southern self-respect. General Gordon regularly addressed audiences all over the South, including Alabama. "Do the schoolbooks illustrate Southern life, Southern habits, and Southern history?" he would ask rhetorically. He would then answer his own question: "I have been unable to find in a solitary school-book used in the South, where justice is done to her people in the late trouble in which we have been engaged."[60] This was, of course, a not disinterested sales pitch from a publisher's representative—albeit someone with impeccable credentials. However, as with all successful product-marketing strategies, it was based on the recognition of a real and perennial customer anxiety. In 1889, during a discussion on textbooks at a white teachers' institute held in Wilcox County, the teachers resolved: "Children must not be taught their fathers were traitors and rebels." Teachers' institutes debated "The Need of Southern Histories."[61]

On September 11, 1891, Major John G. Harris, state superintendent, issued a circular advising county and municipal superintendents: "No book should be taught in any public school that reflected on the character, patriotism, chivalry and honesty of those who supported and defended the Confederacy, or in any way took part on the Southern side."[62]

Even before the Civil War there had been calls in Southern legislatures to address the need for textbooks written from a Southern point of view. There was a conviction that Abolitionist sentiment pervaded the textbooks sent South from Northern publishers and this was decried.[63] During the war itself, several textbooks were written locally in Alabama. These included readers and spellers—"carefully prepared for family and school use"—by Mme. Adelaide De Vendel Chaudron of Mobile. Standard texts, such as Warren Colburn's 1840 *Mental Arithmetic,* were given a makeover, printed in Mobile, and advertised as "prepared expressly for use in Southern schools."[64]

Textbooks—specifically history and civics textbooks—have always been, and continue to be, critically important "sites of public memory." They transmit ideas about an idealized past and a promised future. The adoption of a particular textbook gives it an official imprimatur that allows it to be seen as a canonical narrative.[65] Its purpose is thus to institutionalize a particular set of cultural beliefs, to define and spread a particular version of patriotism and thus set the terms of citizenship for the future. Because these terms are themselves contested, textbook content is often bitterly contested as well. This type of contest was behind the ongoing determination by white officeholders, teachers, and parents to ensure Alabama's textbooks reflected an orthodoxy in respect of all the tropes of white Southern identity. For example, the Confederate Veterans Association kept a close eye on history text content.[66]

Attitudes toward textbook selection were not solely to do with the cultural suitability of their content; there was the question of local and parental prerogatives. An early article in the *Alabama Educational Magazine* was forthright: "In the past administration of the school system of this country, there has been the wise recognition that the state should assume no power which can be safely left to the people in their local capacity."[67] The article went on to describe the proposed adoption of a state series of textbooks as a "mischievous innovation" and the promotion of the benefits of uniformity as a "specious plea." The issue rumbled on for years.

The *Montgomery Advertiser* was an unswerving opponent of the state adopting uniform textbooks. In November 1888 it claimed publishing houses would be the only beneficiaries of such a policy and their financial interest in gaining a monopoly would create scope for corruption. By 1892 the paper was strident. Any compulsion with regard to state uniformity in textbooks would, it claimed, "be condemned by the educational sentiment and experience of age." It would be indefensible as a political principle and could never be enforced "except by the most arbitrary legislation and the unjustifiable interference with the domestic rights of the people." Because such legislation had actually been proposed, the newspaper went on the offensive. Such a prescription would be "paternalism of the rankest kind" and a declaration "that the people are unfit to manage the affairs of their local schools." In essence, it said, uniformity would be "wrong in principle and injurious to the public weal in practice."[68] The *Montgomery Advertiser*'s position was consistent with a number of interests including parents, teachers, and book publishers or the "book trust." The strength of this opposition was recognised in discussions at teachers' institutes and seemed a comforting bulwark against change.[69]

Around the turn of the century the textbooks being used in the schools were no longer just those either owned or preferred by school patrons. The teachers, who had to be familiar with certain texts in order to pass their examination, were prescribing their own preferences. Patrons were asked to buy new books—arrangements they found "costly and burdensome."[70] Elmore County's William C. Cousins described the book system as chaotic and driven by the "caprice of the teachers."[71]

Publishers were thought to influence educational associations. They were certainly assiduous in lobbying the legislature against state uniformity and it is likely their agents paid commissions to teachers who chose books from their list. In his report for 1901–02, William W. Hinton of Autauga County said the practice had "a disintegrating effect rather than a tendency to organize" and tantalizingly alluded to there being "many other reasons but I cannot mention here why we should have uniformity of books in the county." Sanders J. Griffin, who was a member of Alabama's house of representatives and also on Cullman County's book selection board, complained to John William Abercrombie that Thomas C. King, the county superintendent, "has 'kinda' kicked out because he could not get two certain books on the list."[72] King's attitude was attributed to his having been "got at" by Griffin's Populist political enemies. It is more likely he had made some commitment to a publisher.

Yet the cause of uniformity was gaining by stealth. The special school districts created to serve the needs of municipal areas or large towns were making considerable progress in the development of their own schooling systems. These were supported by a rising middle class and funded by municipal appropriations and special bonds. Their boards of education adopted uniform texts and some seventeen counties had followed suit by the end of the century.[73] For example, on December 9, 1896, Alabama's General Assembly approved *An Act to establish a County School Book Board to select a uniform series of text-books for use in the public schools in the County of Winston.* A similar act in 1898 for Lamar County established a book board comprising the probate judge, the circuit clerk, the county superintendent, and three teachers. It was this board that chose the books to be used in Lamar's schools.[74] Some of those who were, in principle, supportive of county uniformity did not believe it required state legislation and were skeptical this could be enforced.[75]

County uniformity still allowed local inclinations to be embedded in the legislation. The act authorizing the uniform adoption of textbooks for Winston contained the injunction that no book proposed by any publisher must contain "anything partisan, prejudicial or inimical to the interest of the people of the State, or cast a reflection on their past history."[76]

Just how rigorously such uniform textbook laws were enforced can only be a matter for speculation but, as the county superintendent was the compliance officer, some leeway was no doubt given when school patrons were not keen on prescription—particularly as neither the county nor the state were actually paying for the books. In Winston there was a long-standing fear of educational materials that "were all too modern for the spiritual and moral safety of the students"[77] and the new law only provided for a penalty when teachers were guilty of "persistent neglect" in using the prescribed books.[78]

In the state superintendent's biennial report for the 1901 and 1902 scholastic years, twenty-six of the reports from county superintendents commented on textbooks. Of these, fourteen declared that uniformity was working well at the county level while twelve said they were seeking or would like to have county uniformity. Only five superintendents (7.5 percent of the total number) volunteered the once unthinkable opinion that state uniformity might be beneficial.[79] A bill to achieve state uniformity had been introduced into the assembly in 1900 but rejected. Senator Ariosto A. Wiley of Montgomery claimed such prescription would "invade the home of parents and dictate to them what school books their children should use."[80]

Yet on March 4, 1903, the state legislature was successful in passing an act to create a Text-Book Commission, and to procure for use in the public schools in this state a uniform series of textbooks.[81] The adopted booklist was intended to be in use by September 1903 and to remain unchanged for five years. The act specified that no textbook "was to contain anything of a partisan or sectarian character."[82] The exquisite irony implicit in this goal would almost certainly have been lost on the contemporary legislators who, owing to black disenfranchisement in 1901, no longer had a black constituency of electors to consider—even if only perfunctorily. Had any of the books prescribed by the commission been unacceptable to the beliefs of Alabama's white community—specifically its racial and caste attitudes—textbook uniformity would have been a lost cause.

One of the selections made by the commission was *Elementary Geography* by Matthew Fontaine Maury.[83] Maury was a historically important oceanographer as well as a scientist whose interests embraced astronomy, astrophysics, cartography, geology, and meteorology. He had also been a respected Confederate naval commander in the Civil War. The stature of his reputation guaranteed his opinions would be regarded as authoritative.

In Lesson XVIII of Maury's *Elementary Geography,* Alabama's children would be taught there were five races of man—white, yellow, red, black, and brown. Maury explained the white man was "master of the world" because he was *enlightened.* This apparently meant having technological advantages and arrangements for social welfare. African Negroes were described as "ignorant savages." Red men (Native Americans) were also "savages" because they lived in tents and had no books or schools.[84]

"The Best Methods of Teaching Geography" was sometimes a topic at black teachers' institutes but there is no record of how the matter was decided.[85] Nor are there records to show how Alabama's Cherokee and Choctaw people regarded their categorization as "savages" or the information that they were "dying out."

The ideas in Maury's *Elementary Geography* were not his alone. Ever since the Civil War Americans had been grappling with issues regarding the place of African Americans, indigenous Americans, and immigrants in their society. All over the United States children learned: "Nature has formed the different degrees of genius and the characters of nations which are seldom known to change." Racial concepts were mostly set out in geographies but were latent elsewhere—even in arithmetic problems.[86]

The immutable racial inferiority of nonwhites was a prevalent idea at the time. Even the influential Dr. Jabez L. M. Curry believed "behind the Caucasian lay centuries of uplifting influences; behind the Negro were centuries of ignorance, superstition, idolatry and fetishism."[87] John William Abercrombie had the effrontery to tell black attendees at Tuskegee Institute's silver jubilee celebrations that slavery had benefited the slaves more than their masters. He also said that because educational funds were meager, it was "best for the Negro, that for a season, the advantages should go to the dominant race."[88]

The Alabamian history books chosen by the first Textbook Commission complemented the ethnographic position of Maury's geography. Yet, despite reaffirming that "whites in all ages have been the dominant race of the world and will continue to lead all others" and that blacks and whites "should be kept separate from childhood and work out their destiny on parallel lines,"[89] the history books presented the state's racial order as one of kindly white paternalism on the one hand and deferential black obeisance on the other. The principal Alabamian history adopted was William Garrott Brown's *History of Alabama,* which, in a chapter entitled "Life on the Plantation" supplied an idealized ro-

8. Sunday afternoon on a Southern plantation. Included in Joel Campbell DuBose, *Alabama History* (Atlanta: B. F. Johnson Publishing Company, 1908), 215.

mance of: "Lavish hospitality, easy cordial manners, good-natured, saucy house servants, the black 'mammy,' the masterful planter—a king within his own domain—and the gracious women and sweet-voiced children."[90]

The 1908 Textbook Commission adopted a different history text—Joel Du-Bose's *Alabama History*. Like Brown's *History of Alabama*, the DuBose book contains material written with a rosy view of a mythical past. A chapter entitled "The Negroes" is illustrated with the picture shown above. The iconography here is that of maternal kindliness, of the obligations of the rich to the poor, of the parent to the child and of the plantation as an idealized pastoral landscape.[91] The children of white farmers may have been beguiled by this tender depiction of a legendary antebellum civilization but it is hard to imagine how it would have been regarded by the children of black sharecroppers (if indeed they read DuBose's history). The book was, theoretically, for use in black schools as well as white.

There were some mutterings of discontent when statewide textbook uniformity was first introduced in 1903. However, two years before the second Textbook Commission convened, objections were heard from a very powerful quarter. In April 1906 the AEA met in Birmingham and resolved to "make a determined fight to do away with the uniform text book law in the state." The new books were claimed to be of poor quality and expensive.[92] Some parents and guardians were still mystified as to why they had to incur the cost of new books at all when they still had perfectly adequate old ones in their possession. The cost of books had always been a genuine cause for concern—"at the present prices, a proper supply is a heavy tax upon our people," cautioned A. S. Stockdale of Clay County in 1891.[93] In Birmingham, tuition and book fees often deterred workingmen from sending their children to school at all. Eventually, the powerful advocacy of the Trades Council convinced the City Commission to provide free textbooks to some grades.[94] Not having such an advocate, rural parents sometimes demonstrated hostile resistance. When a young Marengo County teacher suggested to a parent that he buy textbooks, he said, "Ma'am, if you can't teach 'em what they need to know, you don't b'long here."[95]

The turn of the twentieth century has been described as a time when "the new America came in as on a floodtide."[96] Every field of knowledge was under revision from science in general and Darwinism in particular. Research discoveries from the new fields of sociology and psychology were finding their way into pedagogical theory. Teachers everywhere began to be entrusted with delivering an expanded curriculum based on fresh ideas.[97]

Alabama was still some way from the mainstream but it could not help being affected by the tide. Even before the turn of the century, new branches started being added to the core curriculum of Alabama's public schools. From the beginning of the 1892 scholastic year, schools were required by law to teach "physiology and hygiene as regularly as other branches are taught" and "with special reference to the effect of alcoholic drinks, stimulants and narcotics upon the human system." From the beginning of 1904 the subject of "Agriculture" was also made compulsory in all public schools except those in towns with more than five hundred inhabitants.[98] Additionally, children had to be taught "the constitution of the United States and of Alabama."[99]

During their terms of office, Alabama's reforming state superintendents, particularly John William Abercrombie, Isaac W. Hill, and William Francis Feagin, were very much preoccupied with system building, policy standardization, and the widening of educational revenue sources. Yet, implicit in all their reports, speeches, and pamphlets was a belief that schooling should not just prepare students for roles defined locally but prepare them to participate in a modernizing Alabama and a New South economy. The expansion of the branches was predicated on this idea.[100]

Perhaps it was inevitable that not everyone was pleased with the expanded curriculum. In June 1905 the *Fort Payne Journal* published in DeKalb County covered a just-held meeting of the AEA in Montgomery. The topics discussed had included better schoolhouses, higher pay for teachers, local taxation, and "the various fads and fashions which infest the popular idea of education." But, the paper complained with sarcasm: "Nowhere is it set down that anybody proposes to tell how the average pupil should be taught to read and spell and the best methods of imparting this best of all branches of education. Maybe these simple studies have fallen beneath the notice of the advanced teachers of the present day."[101]

The *Fort Payne Journal* was addressing a white readership and its concern was for white children. The *Opelika Daily News* was also concerned for white education. In its account of the same meeting the paper noted approvingly that proceedings were "marked by an expressed determination on the part of the Alabama educators to do the duty of the white people of Alabama toward the white boys and girls of the rural districts of the state."[102]

In the Black Belt, the *Bullock County Breeze* regularly offered its readership opinions on black education. Nothing, it asserted, "further than the elementary branches—the ability to read and write and the learning of some useful trade" was appropriate for the Negro. Anything additional would take him "out of the fields of labor for which he is best fitted by nature and would create within him an unwholesome discontent."[103]

$\sim$

The protests regarding textbooks and curriculum can be seen within the wider context of the public schooling modernization process that gathered pace all over the South and across rural America during the first decade of the twentieth century. This process was led by educationists, lay activists, and philanthropists and included plenty of legislative prescriptions. Textbook uniformity and the expansion of the branches provided a focus for interest groups to express their dislike of such governmental prescription, particularly where this involved unnecessary expenditure. Teachers, parents, and other community members were hesitant and sometimes angry in the face of too many innovations. These struck at their sense of identity, questioned their capacities, and interfered with their prerogatives. These anxieties had to be accommodated.[104]

Making agriculture a compulsory branch of the rural school curriculum was an early indication that rural schooling would become increasingly vocational. In 1910 the department of education published the first comprehensive *State Manual of the Course of Study for the Public Elementary Schools of Alabama*. The content of this and later manuals was mainly directed toward the rural school and the knowledge needs and extracurricular activities of farm children.[105] In 1911 the department received a grant from the philanthropic General Education Board. This made available $3,000 per annum with which to appoint a

"State Supervisor of Elementary Rural Schools." The first person to hold the position was Professor Norman R. Baker. Two years later James L. Sibley became "State Supervisor of Elementary Rural Colored Schools."

Professor Baker's appointment was another indication of the state superintendent and other modernizers recognizing that traditionalist suspicions of educational change were not just a reflexive reaction to the new but arose from different conceptions of the purpose of schooling and parental authority. Baker's first annual report showed he was keen to address such concerns. He was sensitive to issues of local control and believed he could help to revitalize rural schools in ways that respected the wishes of parents and the influence of other stakeholders. In his first report he wrote that "everyone" was taking kindly to his close attention to the needs of rural schools.[106] Baker came to his task at a time when there was a growing national focus on the economic importance of agriculture and the limitations of rural social institutions.[107] Country life was undergoing a revalidation. This would have a major impact on what was taught in rural schools.

5
Funding and Survival

From 1865 onward, Alabama's public schools were chronically underfunded. Near the end of the nineteenth century the state was spending less per pupil ($0.38 per annum) than any other state in the Union.[1] This underinvestment can be attributed most readily to the long-term Bourbon hegemony but the problem had other and older antecedents as well.

In 1785, at the behest of the United States Congress, a survey was undertaken of practically all lands north of the Ohio River and west of the Mississippi River plus Florida, Mississippi, and Alabama. The survey imposed upon the landscape a grid pattern of "townships" that were numbered and described in relation to survey bearings. Each township was an area of approximately thirty-six square miles comprising thirty-six numbered "sections" of 640 acres each. Congress stipulated that the sixteenth section of each township be reserved for the "maintenance" of public schools, and this provision became part of all subsequent legislation admitting states to the Union. Thus, when Alabama was admitted to the Union on December 14, 1819, the sixteenth section of each of its 1,572 townships was granted to the inhabitants of those townships for schooling purposes. In recognition of the disparities in township values across the state—some were under water or otherwise worthless—Congress granted Alabama 100,000 acres of indemnity lands. In 1836 it also allocated to the state some $669,086.78 of "surplus revenue" and this too became part of the school fund.[2]

Alabama's General Assembly started early to regulate the use of funds derived from the sale or lease of school lands. From 1828 such funds had to be deposited with Alabama's state bank and the earned interest of 6 percent went back to the township. The U.S. surplus revenue fund was also deposited with the bank, which, for a time, was so prosperous that its earnings paid all the expenses of government and taxation was suspended. In 1839 the assembly directed the bank to pay a dividend of $150,000 per annum for school support and $200,000 in 1840. However, as the state system would not be orga-

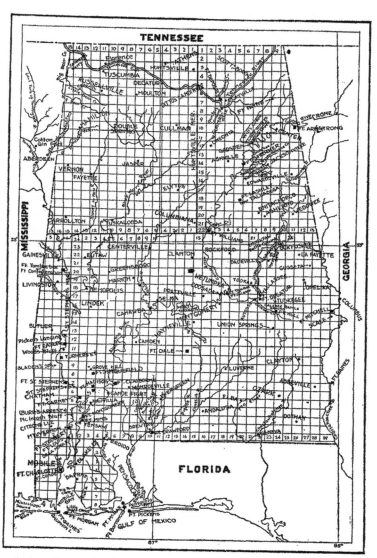

9. Alabama's township (and initial school district) grid. Joel Campbell
DuBose, *Alabama History* (Atlanta: B. F. Johnson Publishing Company,
1908), 30.

nized until 1854, the funds were expended largely on private and denominational schools.

In 1843, after a period of financial instability, the state bank could not meet its statutory obligations. In January 1846 action was begun to liquidate the bank and its accumulated funds were effectively lost.[3] In 1848 and 1851–52 the assembly enacted a number of measures by which the townships would receive interest from a paper fund with a notional capital equivalent to the sums lost through the bank's failure. This interest was to be funded from taxation. Thus the people of Alabama assumed the burden of providing the annual interest on a paper fund whose principal had been lost through governmental action. As new funds were received from sixteenth section sales, these were used for miscellaneous public purposes, and interest-bearing certificates in the perpetual fund took their place.

In February 1854 when the legislation establishing the statewide education system was enacted, the new state superintendent of education was made responsible for the management of an "educational fund." This chiefly comprised interest on the paper fund plus interest on any additional funds that had accrued from sixteenth section lands, or might do so, and various other specified taxes. The legislation provided for a special annual appropriation from the treasury whose purpose was to smooth the disparities between townships arising from sixteenth section values and to ensure a minimum level of spending per pupil.[4]

What was left of the actual sixteenth section and indemnity lands would remain a matter of contention and confusion, but successive state superintendents had neither the staff nor funds to resolve this situation and recovery efforts were never sufficient to make an appreciable difference to the educational fund.[5] The lease or sale of school lands and/or the evaluation of their timber or other assets were adversely affected by the inexperience of trustees, poor administration, disputed ownership, lost deeds, expenses exceeding proceeds, and other factors. In 1880 William D. Wilson, a farmer and township superintendent, wrote to the state superintendent inquiring: "Is it lawful to sell the 16th Sections in Winston County at this time? There is a good chance to make a good sale of the 16th Section in T12, R7 at this time and there is a dispute as to whether it is lawful to sell or not."[6] Satisfactory outcomes were unlikely when trustees were so vague about their duties.

The first postbellum constitution of 1865 was silent on school funding, but the constitutions of 1868, 1875, and 1901 all maintained what was, in some respects, a ruse with respect to interest-bearing "entrusted" funds. Each constitution required the principal of these funds to be preserved "inviolate and undiminished," but the interest was mostly derived from taxation not investment.

Besides the "trust fund" income, each constitution also provided for an annual appropriation of state revenue derived from property taxes. The constitution adopted in 1901 assigned a fixed proportion of this revenue to education.
A long-term legacy from the early sixteenth section endowment was that some
communities believed the school fund was "not a bounty of the State, but was
a fund belonging to the people of the Township to dispose of as they might
think best."[7]

In the years following the adoption of the constitution of 1875, its article on
education was given shape by several pieces of school legislation which implicitly acknowledged the Bourbon goal of reducing governmental expenditure.[8]
Public schooling might not have survived without a willingness by communities to donate land for school purposes, erect schoolhouses, provide equipment,
supplement teachers wages, and develop a multiplicity of improvised solutions
for ameliorating funding deficiencies.[9] Also important was the philanthropy
of individuals, foundations, and corporations; the willingness of teachers to
work for meager wages on seasonal contracts; and the conditional use of public
moneys to underwrite the costs of private academies.

~

In the 1880s Benjamin Frank Weathers owned a sawmill in the Roanoke
area of Randolph County. He employed a large number of mill-hands including members of the local black community. Wishing to assist his workers, he
established a small school near his mill, contracted a teacher, and urged his
workers to have their children attend. When Weathers moved his mill elsewhere, the black community decided to make its own schooling arrangements.
Accordingly, the men "went to the forest and cut pine poles about eight inches
in diameter, split them in halves and carried them on their shoulders to a nice
shady spot and there erected a little schoolhouse. The benches were made of
the same material and there was no floor nor chimney."[10]

Similarly, in the early twentieth century when four white families—the
Evans, Meriwethers, Pughs, and Rutlands—of Mitchell Station in Bullock
County decided that they wanted a nearby school for their children: "Mr Pugh
donated a lot and the four families got together and built a one-room schoolhouse. The county wouldn't pay a teacher for just eight children, but they
agreed to pay half if the families would pay the other half."[11]

Both the above accounts show how neighbors with a common need relied
on one another and their shared know-how to find ways by which their children could continue to receive schooling when state funding was glaringly inadequate. The accounts display an insouciant optimism in the benefits of joint
enterprise unshackled by any consideration for statutory compliance or official prescription. Such enterprise created feelings of connectedness to others

within the community and strengthened commitment to the schoolhouse as a symbol of that connectedness.

This overprovision meant that already scant resources had to be spread even more thinly. Thus term lengths were often shaved and, in turn, this made it more difficult to attract teachers or to pay them adequate wages.

While the school law of 1879 stated that teachers should not be engaged for less than three scholastic months and should receive a monthly wage of not more than one-third of the amount allocated for their school, it did not set minimum pay rates.[12] As late as 1899 the average monthly pay of schoolteachers was only $25.05 for teachers of white schools and $17.06 for teachers of black schools. Mobile County paid the highest overall average salaries at $48.39 for white teachers and $39.36 for black. Macon County paid the lowest white salaries at $10.00 and Crenshaw County paid the lowest black salaries at $9.29.[13]

Devising ways to open public schools with scant resources was not just a challenge for rural parents. In 1876, after completing his term as state superintendent, John McKleroy went back to Eufala in Barbour County and to private life as a lawyer. Shortly thereafter, with the intention of improving Eufala's public schools, he became a member of the local school board. In August 1877 McKleroy wrote to his successor as state superintendent, LeRoy F. Box, advising him that the Eufala board had anticipated being able to obtain municipal support but discovered there were constitutional limits on municipal taxes and this "cut off all hope of aid from the corporate authorities." Though opening a school on the assumption of subscriptions was "too uncertain and indefinite" the board was not giving up: "One idea is to start with the fund we get from the state including the poll-tax and what we can get from the Peabody Fund and establish a school with a limited number of grades—say 4 or 6 with a single teacher for two grades." McKleroy asked Box if he knew of a suitable young man who might organize the school and be its principal teacher. He expressed confidence that once properly established the school would grow. Time would prove him correct. Twelve years later the Eufala board erected a handsome school building for the city (fig. 10) at a cost of $15,000.[14]

McKleroy's deliberations about Eufala's schools were not untypical. The members or trustees of school boards operated their institutions in a constant climate of financial precariousness. Yet, like undaunted Micawbers in the face of near insuperable difficulties, they seemed ever confident of something turning up that would enable their doors to stay open.

⁓

As the nineteenth century progressed, there was an accelerating trend toward carving off from townships special school districts centered on towns or municipal areas with coterminous boundaries. The legislation establishing

10. City school building, Eufala, Barbour County. Erected 1889. Courtesy Alabama Department of Archives and History, Montgomery, Alabama.

these districts sometimes specified that their schools might receive public funds—distributed via the mayor and aldermen—on the condition that city commissioners were represented on the board of trustees. For example, this was the case with the city of Florence in Lauderdale County, whose school district was created in 1890. The mayor was the *ex officio* chairman of the school board, one of whose members was elected annually by the city commissioners at the Florence City Council's November meeting.[15]

There was no bureaucracy to help draft the bills that created these special school districts, but this did not seem to cause any difficulty. In Alabama's legislative session of 1898–99 there were 136 local bills setting up or regulating separate school districts.[16] The generation of these bills was wholly an exercise in local democracy as the following example shows.

On November 7, 1894, the *Mountain Eagle* advertised the date of a "mass meeting" to be held the following Saturday at Jasper "to adopt some plan to maintain and promote the interest of our school." The meeting was chaired by the probate judge, James W. Shepherd, and the city's mayor and aldermen were in attendance.[17] Many speeches were made about the benefits that would accrue to the city by having a good system of public schools. By the end of the

meeting a committee of six had been formed, which included the county superintendent, a physician, and two lawyers. Its task was to draft a bill that could
be presented to the assembly with the aim of creating a special school district
for Jasper.[18]

Just ten days later the committee had two draft bills ready for consideration.
One bill would extend the corporate limits of Jasper and allow up to 50 percent
of the gross revenue of the town to be set aside for school purposes. The other
would create a separate school district for the city of Jasper.

The bills were debated thoroughly at another courthouse meeting at which
those attending asked questions, raised concerns, and expressed opinions about
their implications. Eventually there was agreement and Colonel Thomas L.
Sowell, a lawyer, was appointed "a committee of one" with the responsibility
for presenting the proposed bills to the assembly immediately.[19] The bills were
enacted just under three months later on February 8, 1895.

The creation of a special school district for Jasper did not realize all the
benefits anticipated by the town's community. On September 9, 1896, the "Jasper Male and Female Academy"—which actually operated as the white public
school (it was later called the "Jasper Graded School")—opened for its annual
session. A month later the *Mountain Eagle* advised "students are still coming
in" and "those who want public money during the next scholastic year should
patronize the school during the next three months." By November the enrollments had reached 225 and the paper bragged "we now have a school second
to none."[20]

To be viable, the Jasper Graded School had to attract pupils from beyond
the city limits. In August 1897 it advertised: "Our next session opens Tuesday,
September 14, 1897. Tuition $1.00 to $3.50 per month. Public fund deducted.
No half tuition allowed. Board in good families $7.00 per month and upward,
etc."[21] Only two weeks before the school's opening date, its principal was still
out and about trying to drum up business. Although he was "receiving much
encouragement with considerable boarding patronage promised," he could not
actually be sure of how many students would turn up to enroll and then attend
regularly.[22]

The very survival of the Jasper Graded School was a matter of seemingly
constant tenuousness, and it was rescued on several occasions by direct citizen
action. In June 1908 following the resignation of the then principal, Professor
W. E. Turnipseed, plus all but one of the members of Jasper's board of education, a new board was appointed. On July 1, 1908, the *Mountain Eagle* revealed
that this new board estimated "it would take $6,500 to run the Jasper school
for five months but there was scarcely $3,000 of public money from all sources
available." What to do? A committee was appointed to solicit subscriptions

and to extend the area in which enrollments might be sought. By the end of the month the *Mountain Eagle* reported relief all round: "Jasper will have a free school the coming session. . . . The members of the city school board deserve praise for this happy solution of the school question in Jasper which looked very gloomy a few weeks ago. . . . They took hold of the question like men, however, and succeeded in raising the deficient amount of money required by volunteer subscription."[23]

But just twelve months later there was an identical crisis and an identical response. In April 1909 the *Mountain Eagle* had to advise its readers once again that members of Jasper's board of education were doing everything in their power to see that the public school ran its full length but, if the citizens of Jasper failed to come to its aid, the school would have to close. A week later the paper's headline was "*No, Our School Will Not Close*—Patrons Patriotically Come To The Rescue With Necessary Funds." But the same patrons were "urgently requested to pay the school's treasurer by Friday of this week." It seems that not all were flush with cash. When the new term opened in October, patrons were being referred helpfully to moneylenders.[24]

Pledges and subscriptions were an unreliable source of contingent funds and a clumsy mechanism for remedying inadequate financial forecasting or overspending. Yet the usual forum by which a deficit crisis was communicated and the necessary funds sought—a town meeting of citizens—was a social legacy from the earliest days of American democracy. It reflected the Jeffersonian idea that people should be free to conduct their own business however they might see fit—that they should "reserve to themselves personally the exercise of all rightful powers to which they are competent and to delegate those to which they are not competent to deputies named, and removable for unfaithful conduct, by themselves immediately."[25]

In Alabama, the frequent resort to the time-honored town meeting for the purpose of discussing and resolving educational issues helped to weave public schools into the conscious concern of the whole community—not just parents. Contemporary newspapers from all over the state show that questions of school survival and continuance—and the funding on which such continuance depended—were regularly decided at such meetings.[26]

In 1887 when the public school at Camden in Wilcox County was running short of funds the response to this recurrent problem was almost identical to Jasper's. The *Wilcox Progress* reported regularly on the efforts by local citizens to save the school. On July 5, 1887, "quite a large and enthusiastic crowd of the best citizens of Camden" assembled at the courthouse to "discuss school matters and elect a new Board of Education." This board's first duty was to appoint a school principal whose immediate priorities would be fiscal. Professor W. C.

Jones was duly employed "to seek patronage for the school." The *Wilcox Progress* was optimistic that "with the next session of the Camden Public School will dawn a new era of education in the history of Wilcox County."[27] After a meeting in Gadsden in Etowah County in 1877 the trustees hoped the town's newly inaugurated schooling system was "the beginning of a new era for good and that sufficient funds would be found."[28] Public schooling was ever on the cusp of a "new era"; the actual transition was elusive.

The town meetings described above had a loose equivalent in black communities though these were not held as the result of a call to educational conscience and "citizen enterprise" by local newspapers. Ned Cobb, a black activist in the Great Depression, had several children who attended school in Alabama in the early years of the century. But he recalled unsatisfactory outcomes: "We'd hold meetings and we knowed what we had to do. We just had to supplement our school money to a greater extent if we cared to carry our schools on. Well, there was so many patrons disagreed—and there's some false-hearted folks amongst every race of folk God got on this earth. My children could have got a good education even under supplement if some of my own color had abided by their race."[29]

Exhortations to a community's conscience and town meetings were perennial mechanisms for resolving school funding shortages because the underfunding was perennial. Yet, because the circumstances of the state did not remain static, the measures adopted to secure educational funds varied over time.

≈

All levels of government were hamstrung by constitutional restrictions on property taxes—which were generally conservative in their assessment and inefficiently collected. However, they could raise additional revenue from business, professional, and/or special license fees. Counties and municipal corporations could also issue bonds, subject to legislative approval. All these options were exploited for educational benefit. The school law of 1879 stipulated that school revenue could include "Licenses to be paid into the school fund of any county, the same to be expended for the benefit of the public schools in such county: and all such license tax shall be promptly paid by the probate judge, or such person collecting such tax to the county superintendent of education."[30]

Laws creating special school districts often stipulated the license collections that would form part of school revenues.[31] In 1881 the governing ordinance for the city of Troy scheduled no fewer than thirty-seven different types of license. The highest license fee ($150.00 per annum) applied to "retail dealers in spirituous, vinous or malt liquors in any quantity less than one quart." For each "theatrical, dramatic or operatic performance or entertainment" the license fee was $10.00 per performance but for circuses the fee was more than double at

$25.00 per performance. Dancing masters had to pay $10.00 per annum for a license but cotton weighbridge operators and "transient dealers in horses or mules" only had to pay $5.00 per annum. These fees are a sort of index to the Troy City Council's regard for the desirability or utility of different sorts of businesses or occupations as well as a willingness to cash in on the passing parade of popular diversions.[32]

The extent to which license fees were used as a source of school funds differed by county and town or municipal area and from year to year. In 1893, when a school district was established at Dadeville in Tallapoosa County, the enabling act required that a third of the city's license and special tax revenue must be used exclusively for Dadeville's public schools. In later years the figure was to be one half of such revenues.[33]

Because the requirement to have a certain type of license (as well as the fines for license violations) could be matters of state legislation or of county/municipal ordinances there was inevitably much local variation, which gave rise to confusion. In August 1899 Frank L. McCoy, the superintendent for Eufala's schools, had to ask the state superintendent, John William Abercrombie, whether whiskey license moneys collected from the city's saloonkeepers should be paid into the school fund.[34]

As with those issued by the city of Troy, licenses and also special-purpose taxes levied by the state can be seen as a guide to contemporary community concerns and attitudes as well as being an indicator of a resourceful opportunism. Some of the fees and charges had a distinctly local character.

On February 10, 1883, when the Peabody School District was established at Girard in Russell County, the enabling act provided for the president of its board of trustees to have police powers that were to be used to provide funds for the public schools. If anyone damaged school property or was "disorderly" in the school precinct, the president/constable was entitled to issue a fine of up to fifty dollars, which went to the school fund. Similarly, the act authorized the trustees to assess the "moral fitness" of liquor license applicants and to issue these to suitable retailers. License fees plus violation fines also went to the school fund. Defaulters could be sentenced by the president and committed to "a house of detention"—a school jail. The trustees were accredited as marshals and could oversee defaulters sentenced to "hard labor on the public roads."[35]

The potential conflict of interest in these peculiar arrangements does not appear to have fazed unduly the community they were intended to benefit. On the contrary, when the Russell County's grand jury made its "Presentment" in May 1883 it stated Girard had recently "been organized for educational purposes within its limits with full power to preserve the peace and suppress local disturbances" and this would lead to "a rapid increase in prosperity in that district."[36] The grand jury's confidence was justified. The following month the *Russell Register* proclaimed: "The schools of Girard's Peabody School District are booming ... and will have enough money to safely and successfully run the schools until the first of October next when the school funds from taxation fall due."[37]

In the closing decades of the nineteenth century, newspapers often excited their readers with tales of wild and hydrophobic dogs—"roving curs." For example, in 1881 the *Union Springs Herald* related how Mr. Joe Knowles of Bruceville had been savagely attacked by "a crazed animal" whose "jaws were covered in froth and whose eyes were a blood-shotten green." The rabid brute was only downed when shot twice at point-blank.[38] In 1885 the *Wetumpka Times* carried an account of the preemptive killing of twenty-eight dogs in Elmore County that had been bitten.[39] Perhaps to slake community alarm while at the same time discouraging the random killing of dogs on the mere suspicion of their being diseased, *An Act for the Protection of Dogs* was passed in 1887. Dog owners could register their ownership with the county probate judge by paying fees and taxes amounting to $1.25. The revenue derived was allocated to the county's school fund thus establishing a nexus between a community concern, a legislative response, and a local benefit.[40]

During the 1890s some of Alabama's politicians thought the large quantities of fertilizer sold in the chiefly agricultural state might make a "guano tag tax" a productive source of school revenue. In 1907 the legislature approved *An Act to improve the quality of rural schoolhouses.* This stipulated that $67,000 be appropriated annually from the proceeds of fertilizer sales "for the purpose of aiding in the erection or the repairing of (rural) schoolhouses."[41] A school district wanting the aid had first to raise not less than $100, which would then be matched by the county up to a maximum of $200. This was consistent with the tradition of communities developing their own solutions to problems of school funding and not relying on state largesse—though private largesse was applauded.[42]

⁓

The rather punitive level of license fees charged to retailers and wholesalers of liquor was justified by the public benefit supposedly to be derived from the revenue. Initially the license moneys generated local optimism and seemed to offer a win-win situation for communities and schools—but the bargain was Faustian. High license fees merely concentrated control of the liquor trade in the hands of a few politically powerful dealers. Moreover, the certainty of a revenue stream for schools predicated upon liquor licenses and other alcohol derived charges was often chimerical or short term. It could also divide communities and patrons such as those of Carrollton in Pickens County who, until 1904, had operated in "perfect harmony."[43]

In the last decade of the nineteenth century, a South Carolinian experiment with a new type of liquor control—a state monopoly of the liquor trade via "dispensaries" (stringently regulated bottle-shops) caught the attention of Alabama's temperance advocates who were dismayed at the influence of saloons and their contribution to drunkenness, violence, and high crime rates. In 1897 Frank S. Moody of Tuscaloosa introduced a bill in the state senate that was enacted the next year. This permitted seventeen counties to establish dispensaries.[44]

A percentage of the fees generated from the dispensaries was to be allocated to education. For example, in 1902 the dispensary at Troy turned over $500.00 per month to each of the city's two public schools and the *Troy Messenger* confidently asserted that "the moral condition of Troy has been improved since the dispensary was established."[45] In 1904, 40 percent of the net profits from liquor sales in Walker County's four dispensaries went straight to education. This added 75 cents to the per capita expenditure for each school-aged child and extended the free school session by an extra month.[46]

In May 1906 the *Cherokee Harmonizer* published a letter from Dr. George Sharp, a candidate for election to the legislature. He explained that although he was committed to better schools and roads these were expensive. However, "by having a Dispensary we can not only secure the additional revenue without adding to the burdens of taxation but we can and will improve the moral tone of the county." He felt that, via the dispensary, the vicious and the idle of the county would contribute to its expenses.[47]

Twenty-five counties eventually had dispensaries.[48] In others, such as Escambia County, electors were suspicious that revenue from dispensaries would prove to be fool's gold, and voted against them being established.[49] Walker County's experience (at least as reflected in the pages of the *Mountain Eagle*) provides an example of the dispensary experiment. In just five years, enthusiastic support changed to disillusioned rejection.

Before Walker County's dispensaries could be established, there had to be citizen approval gained via a referendum. The editor of the *Mountain Eagle* sought to influence a favorable outcome by soliciting testimonials from counties where dispensaries had already been established. In July 1903 he published three columns of glowing letters; the referendum passed.[50] As already mentioned, in the first year of operation (1904) dispensary revenue was of significant benefit to Walker County's schools but the *Mountain Eagle* predicted even better results for 1905. The start-up costs being out of the way, the schools stood to receive "fully $10,000 or as much as the county gets from the state appropriation, about $1.00 per child."[51]

Over the next couple of years the *Mountain Eagle* continued to gloat over the benefits flowing to Walker County's schools but by the end of 1906, the editor began to change his tune. Alabama's temperance movement had been regrouping and by 1907 a campaign against the dispensary and for prohibition was well under way. In October 1907, in a rather tortured piece of logic, the editor claimed that, although abolishing saloons and establishing dispensaries had led to increased school attendance (implying the restrictions on liquor sales had left families more disposable income for schooling), prohibition would increase it further. He claimed all readers would know of children who had "been deprived of the privilege of attending school because the father is a slave to the curse of drink." He said taking $2.25 from the drunken father was "a poor way to place the child in school even if 40 cents of the money is applied to school purpose."[52]

The campaign against the dispensary was successful.[53] In September 1908 the paper related that Professor Letson was building up the Jasper Graded School and "succeeding without any whiskey money—without blood money obtained at the expense of some hungry child."[54] But with the loss of the dispensary revenue the school struggled, leading to the desperate pleas for citizen support described earlier in this chapter.

The benefits of dispensary revenue were as elusive in Houston County as they proved to be in Walker. In July 1905 the *Columbia Breeze* favorably mentioned that, in the previous scholastic year, the local school had experienced its highest enrollments and best results owing to revenue from the town's dispensary. However, because this was about to be closed pending the outcome of a "wet or dry" election, neither the school principal nor the teachers would accept contracts for the upcoming year being unsure of their salaries. The editor carped that "those who were chiefly instrumental in ousting the dispensary do not have to face the problem of raising revenue for carrying on the affairs of the city, the schools, etc."[55]

A more benign source of revenue was available to the Pleasant Grove school district in Jackson County. A ferry plying across the Tennessee River docked on school lands, and the legislation establishing the school district authorized the school board to rent or lease the lands "in any way that will be most profitable or beneficial to the district." The board was further authorized to operate a farm on their township's sixteenth section. Farm and ferry contributed substantially to Pleasant Grove's school fund plus another township's as well.[56]

The paths to new sources of school financing mostly ended in blind alleys. A growing school population just could not depend indefinitely on inadequate state allocations supplemented by revenue from miscellaneous license fees. Other states raised education revenue through local taxation and Alabama's reformers increasingly believed it was high time Alabama followed suit.[57]

~

The acts that were passed at an ever-increasing rate after 1875 to create special school districts and systems for cities, towns, and municipal areas initially followed precedents set by cities such as Montgomery. There was no template other than the clause stating the new district would receive a pro-rata share of school funds as they were apportioned for township schools and that schools would be racially separate. As at Jasper, these bills were generally developed locally and then taken to the legislature to be initiated by the appropriate representative.

In February 1877 Alabama's assembly passed a bill creating a special school district for Oxmoor in Jefferson County. This contained the novel provision that "the trustees and their successors in office, shall have the power to levy a tax on all property, both real and personal, within the bounds of such school district."[58] Over the next ten years, similar tax provisions were included in a number of other acts passed to create special school districts. But were these provisions constitutional? Some disgruntled Cullman County taxpayers thought not. In 1887 they mounted a test case *(Schultz v. Eberly)* in the Alabama Supreme Court. The court confirmed that only municipal corporations including counties had taxing power and this could not be delegated.[59] In 1895 Birmingham secured legislation for a school tax to be additional to other municipal taxes, on which there was a constitutional cap. It was to be levied and collected as a state tax and then paid to the city's board of education. In 1897 this tax-shifting attempt was also tested and disallowed *(State of Alabama v. Southern Railway).*[60] When all attempts to levy school taxes directly were stymied, municipal corporations found they could allocate to the schools an "appropriation" from their own revenues even to the detriment of other essential services. Such funds allowed city and town schools to employ good teachers, extend sessions, and achieve high scholastic standards.

In February 1899 upon the urgent request of the new state superintendent, John William Abercrombie, the assembly increased the annual direct appropriation for public schools by $100,000. It also passed, against the governor's wishes, a bill to earmark a further and fixed component of the state's property taxes for the exclusive use of public schools.[61] Abercrombie had strong centralizing inclinations—even a corporate view of the education system for which he was responsible. Besides his implementation of the statewide examination for teacher certification and licensing, Abercrombie influenced many other standardizing measures that were implemented by his successors. Yet he was also an adept politician and understood that "local self-government is a principle for which the Southern people, and especially the people of Alabama, have always contended."[62]

The education article of the new state constitution adopted by Alabama in 1901 allowed counties the option of levying a one-mill tax for public school support. Before a county could do so, it had to inform its by-now almost entirely white electorate of the rate, duration, and purpose of the tax and put the proposal to a county referendum.[63] An enabling act was passed in October 1903 and most counties held elections over the next three years.

In April 1904, at the Conference for Education in the South, Professor Hopson O. Murfee of Marion in Perry County spoke in favor of local taxation. He said public schools had come to be regarded "as eleemosynary institutions . . . which are never held in high esteem among a free and independent people." He attributed this to education having been delegated to the state—"an authority too obscure and a power too remote."[64]

Newspapers were generally supportive of the tax. On June 15, 1904, the *Mountain Eagle,* which had urged a yes vote, was able to boast: "Walker County took the lead in all the counties of the state in voting for the special school tax. Walker leads in many things and she is going to be found in the lead from now on in educational matters."[65] This optimism was partly predicated upon the anticipated dispensary profits, which were to be additive, but he had a good grasp on the dynamics of identity.

In the Black Belt and counties with large black populations, a very different kind of identity was in play. In June 1905 the *Opelika Daily News* in Lee County told its readers that foolish Lauderdale County had voted against the school tax thus refusing "to have more and better schools at a slight cost."[66] Yet only a short time later the editor had revised his position. He asserted the constitutional provision was not put there at the behest of those who would have to pay the tax. He told his readers: "A vote for the tax is a vote to raise the salaries of three officers and for more white folks' money to be expended on Negro education. Will free white caucasian Lee County men cast such a ballot.—NO."[67] When Lee County's election was held in September 1905 the tax proposal failed. The newspaper recorded the vote without comment.[68] State superintendent Harry Gunnels told Edgar Gardner Murphy of the Southern Education Board: "Lee voted it down on account of pure 'cussedness.' If you know anything of the politics of Lee County, you will remember that things usually go the other way."[69]

By 1907, forty-six counties had voted in favor of the local tax, four counties had voted against it and seventeen had not voted on it at all.[70] In the Black Belt

counties the tax was not even on the agenda owing to the apportionment provisions of the school law of 1891 that had already benefited white schools.[71]

Roughly a decade later when citizen approval for the school tax had to be
sought once again, Henry Jones Willingham, the state superintendent, started
giving advice to county superintendents including those of the Black Belt. In
August 1912 Willingham wrote to William M. Cook, the superintendent of
Wilcox, suggesting "it would be well to have an election on the one-mill tax
in Wilcox this Fall." He hoped the people of Wilcox "might be in a frame of
mind at this time to vote for the tax." Willingham's tentativeness suggests he
did not want to appear to be interfering.[72] Cook hedged. On September 5,
1912, he told Willingham the matter was "inopportune." He explained: "Our
people have just faced a raise in the value of property for taxation and, with a
$140,000 bond issue to be voted on in November, our people turn a deaf ear
to any further taxation." A year later the matter was followed up. The response
was brusque: "Wilcox has enough school money and our people do not wish to
be taxed any higher."[73]

Although state superintendents felt it was their role to urge school taxes and
to offer "cooperation in securing elections," county superintendents were more
closely attuned to local wishes. In August 1912 Willingham wrote to the superintendent of Perry County, Charles C. Johnson, to offer assistance but was
again rebuffed. Johnson's reply perfectly illustrates rural priorities: "At one time
we had decided to ask for an election but with the weather such as we have
had this spring, with no crops started, with a large part of the best lands of the
county now under water or still too wet to plough and no certainty of sunshine
for more than two days at a time it would be foolishness to do anything now."
He said he would "feel the pulse of the people. I want to warm them up a little
after all this wet weather. We do not wish to fail at this matter so it had best be
gone at carefully."[74]

The "foolishness" of raising the question of taxes when farmers were deal-
ing with the vicissitudes of weather and crop planting would have been exac-
erbated by general resentment at the state's inequitable taxation regime. The
vast majority of taxpayers were farmers whose only asset was land. The rich,
whose representatives decided tax rates, objected to paying taxes commensu-
rate with their wealth and ensured that they did not do so. Black Belt planters
whose fertile lands were a source of high tax yields also felt they made a dis-
proportionate contribution to state coffers.[75] When resentment at taxation was
coupled with a sense of white entitlement, black communities were bound to
be the losers in school funding and they most certainly were. White taxpayers
saw themselves as "productive" people who paid excessive taxes of which un-

deserving black citizens were the beneficiaries.[76] That tax moneys might make a difference to the state's commonweal was not a consideration.

The taxation and education sections of both the 1875 and 1901 state constitutions specified a poll tax on adult males living within each county. The poll tax was $1.50 and the proceeds went to the county school fund. The superintendent of education for each county was responsible for seeing that poll taxes were racially allocated and had to report annually on poll-tax receipts for each race in each school district. In 1901, payment of the poll tax was made a condition of being able to vote. If unpaid in one election, the arrears had to be met before a voter could cast a ballot in the next. Unless a male adult was determined to vote, he had little incentive to pay the tax.[77]

In April 1905 the *Bullock County Breeze* printed a list of 441 people who had paid poll taxes. Only fifteen of these were black. The paper commented: "This money is used for public schools, and these figures show what a small percent is paid by the colored population, yet it is divided in proportion to the number of children of school age in each district without regard to who pays it."[78] This was malicious mischief. The tiny number of black people still enfranchised after 1901 meant Bullock's forty-four black schools would have shared just $22.50 in poll-tax moneys.

By 1910 Birmingham was becoming a major metropolis. According to the census for that year its population had reached 132,685. Its educational system, led by John Herbert Phillips, was centrally directed and its white schools had qualified teachers, handsome buildings, and plentiful equipment financed from the wealth of its industrial base. Although Birmingham's black schools were separate and vastly inferior, they were still the best black schools in Alabama.[79] Other cities were also building modern school systems, and it was urban schoolmen who would drive campaigns for educational investment by the state. But, at the turn of the century, nearly 70 percent of all children aged nine and over were directly involved in agriculture.[80] If they attended school at all, they did so in schools that continued to operate in much the same way as they had always done. Black children got the worst deal "only half a loaf where others get a whole one, but in some cases practically nothing."[81]

The educational improvements of the early twentieth century were important. Moreover, following the adoption of the 1901 constitution, Alabama was allocating nearly half of the state's revenue to education. Yet if Alabama was moving forward, other states were moving forward more rapidly. In a 1912 survey of U.S. public schooling conducted by the Russell Sage Foundation, Alabama's "general rank" against ten tests of educational efficiency was at the bottom of the forty-eight states.[82]

11. John Herbert Phillips, superintendent of Birmingham's city school system, 1883–1921. Charles W. Dabney, *Universal Education in the South,* vol. 1 (New York: Arno Press and the New York *Times,* 1936), 394.

Reformers, particularly those running city school systems, were perennially frustrated by constitutional limits on taxation. They were convinced that adequate school funding would only ever be achieved by a constitutional amendment allowing not only county but school district taxes as well. Yet in 1908 when the question of local taxes was being canvassed, Charles W. Simmons, who was Coffee County's superintendent and a lawyer, said school district taxation "could be a dangerous thing in some respects." He said that if centers of wealth and population voted for it and sparsely settled communities refused or favored a tax that was completely inadequate, then many people would leave their school and move to town. He said the tax should be a county tax.[83] When the district tax provision was finally approved after a constitutional amendment in 1916, the outcome was as the prescient Simmons had foreseen. The tax led to greater disparities in school funding with long-term consequences. Structural funding problems and the overall adequacy of support continued to dog the education system for the rest of the twentieth century.

6
The Progressive Urge

Around the turn of the twentieth century, Alabama's public schools came under the purview of social activists who were becoming involved with reform not only in education but in matters as various as temperance and prohibition, female suffrage, child labor restrictions, race relations, convict welfare, reformatories, public health, and child protection. This was "Southern Progressivism" and was derived largely from Protestant humanitarianism and "a mixture of paternalism and *noblesse oblige.*"[1] In the period from 1898 to 1915 various Progressive interest groups, organizations, and individuals, in a sort of symbiosis with state-paid educational officeholders and teacher organizations, sought to reshape Alabama's rural and small-town schools. Urban schools were not ignored by these reforming modernizers, but the vast majority of Alabama's children attended rural schools and it was evident that these were lagging against objective measures of educational effectiveness. Moreover, rural schools were regarded as being a key success factor in the "renewal of country life"—a nationwide focus of various influential professionals in the first two decades of the twentieth century.[2]

The concerns of Progressives for rural education were often predicated upon a condescending and elitist assumption that, owing to their isolation and meager circumstances, rural people were backward and apathetic about effecting social improvement for themselves.[3] The extent to which the Progressive agenda was successful in helping to modernize Alabama's public schooling system was usually linked to the congruence of reform initiatives with an existing rural culture and its ideas about class, gender, race, social hierarchy, and other factors. Where reforms did not match the needs and inclinations of the communities at which they were aimed, there was resentment and/or resistance and, consequently, a lesser achievement.

∼

The activists who took it upon themselves to assist with the modernization of Alabama's public schooling were often outsiders to the communities whose schools they wished to improve. They were frequently members of a newly prominent social class with industrial and/or commercial interests. They tended to approach reform as if it were simply a matter of applying good business practices or the nostrums of middle-class housekeeping to the organization and management of civic and social life. For urban women this "municipal housekeeping" meant their "household" now included "the marketplace and city hall."[4] Implicitly, the household also included the farm and the school. These women valued efficiency, expertise, and sound management but not the antithesis offered by rural cultural traditions of many strands. This attitude did not serve them well at the outset and they had to learn to proceed carefully.

The Alabama Federation of Women's Clubs (AFWC) was formed on April 17, 1895, in Birmingham. It joined together six literary clubs previously unconnected in an organizational sense. Its total initial membership was 150 women. By 1915 it comprised 153 clubs with a total membership of 4,250 women.[5] Its early aims were cultural—for example, to promote Southern literature. At its second convention, Ella Gaines Parker Going, the president, told delegates that the work of women was largely altruistic but it was becoming necessary to make this altruism less abstract. She made a plea for "isolated neighborhoods—their imperfect educational facilities, the poverty of their social life."[6] The objectives of the AFWC evolved further when Mrs. George B. Eager told the club women "that they could accomplish great things by influencing legislation." This was to be achieved by urging their menfolk to "cast their ballots in the interests of reforms which we feel to be necessary."[7]

Between its second and third annual convention—held in 1898 at Selma in Dallas County—the AFWC created a committee on education chaired by Kate Hutcheson Morrisette of Montgomery. At the Selma convention Morrisette made a speech about the deplorable state of public schooling in Alabama. She was described as "having enthusiasm like a flame and an energy that was tireless in any cause she espoused." She told several hundred delegates that Alabama's illiteracy level was a bar to civil, moral, and religious progress as well as retarding the industrial and commercial potential of the state. Because education was an issue of such importance she said it behooved "the mothers of Alabama, the Press, businessmen and commercial bodies, the clergy of all denominations and every known factor in the state" to enlist their energies in an effort "to create public sentiment strong enough to demand for the children of the state adequate educational facilities."[8]

Reporting on the AFWC convention the *Selma Times* said Mrs. Morrisette strongly advocated a new constitution claiming many educational needs were irremediable because of constitutional funding limitations. Her speech ended with a battle cry as she evoked "Robert E. Lee and his thin line of Gray defending the land we love" and called on delegates "to emulate him in defense of the children of Alabama."[9] For the AFWC, education was to be "the central thought, the pivot upon which all other reform should turn."[10] Mrs. Morrisette was soon working in alliance with John William Abercrombie, and the AEA's "Committee of Thirty-three" formed in 1897 to lobby for legislative and constitutional change. At its annual conference in 1901, the AFWC passed resolutions in favor of local taxation for public schools, a school year of at least five months, compulsory attendance, adequate school buildings, and trained educators as county superintendents instead of politicians.[11]

Not all AFWC members had the same priorities as the AEA. Around the turn of the twentieth century it was widely believed that well-planned and beautified towns and villages could help achieve a harmonious social order, improve health, and act as an antidote to the ill effects of urbanization. The chair of the AFWC's art committee, Mrs. Charles A. Cary, reflected these Progressive concerns when she told delegates at the 1903 convention that the school should be the starting point for promoting "a more wholesome and beautiful public life in America."[12] She had already made a start on rectifying schoolhouse dreariness by offering each county a "beautiful historical picture" for one of its public schools. Thirty-one had already expressed interest but "the silent, unresponsive" counties were to be written to "again and again" until the right person could be found to "awaken children to the beauty of art." Mrs. Cary seemed quite oblivious to the condescension implicit in her endeavors to administer doses of cultural uplift and the reaction to her badgering is not recorded. By 1913 the AFWC was at least suggesting that schools be given prints of paintings "emphasizing the dignity of [rural] labor such as those by Jean-François Millet and Jules Dupré."[13]

Yet AFWC members were sincere in their concerns about public schooling and wanted a more direct role in achieving reforms. Without being able to vote, they had little idea of how to achieve their goals apart from writing letters and addressing memorials to the assembly.[14] An opportunity to work in a more hands-on manner with "the people" came about in 1905 when a past president of the AFWC and Mobile resident, Lura H. Craighead, invited to dinner Isaac W. Hill (state superintendent, 1903–1907). Other guests included AFWC members who were in Mobile to attend its annual convention.[15] During the table talk, Hill told Mrs. Craighead of work going on in Massachusetts and elsewhere that might appeal to clubwomen.[16]

Craighead listened intently as Hill explained his idea for the organization of local school improvement associations that would interest communities in the betterment of their schools and bring together school and home. Much taken with the idea of a fresh project, Craighead decided the AFWC should take on responsibility for the creation of such associations throughout the state. A resolution to this effect was adopted the very next day at the convention's morning session.[17]

In April 1905 the *Mountain Eagle* carried an item on the AFWC's intentions: "They propose to perfect an organization in every school district, the members to consist of the women of the communities to be benefited." The paper believed "the women of Alabama will assuredly sprinkle the state with better schoolhouses if their plans are carried out."[18] In this extract some of the elements of the eventual success of the school improvement associations can be detected. Though coordinated externally, the associations would be organized by "women of the communities to be benefited" who were interested in the welfare of their own children—their normal concern. The bettering of schoolhouses was just a variant of that most womanly responsibility—the bettering of the home through good housekeeping. Proud communities would not be being told what to do by condescending outsiders nor receiving charity. Poverty among Southern whites was "an acceptable if not desirable condition as long as it was not attended by dependency." Every white Southerner knew this was what separated them from "the black people under them." Even if they might not feel dependent, black people could be forced to feign dependent behaviors owing to the racial caste system.[19]

Although there had been earlier instances of women organizing school aid societies for individual school districts, the AFWC brought together the parents and the teachers and created a base of support for the public school system that did not previously exist on a statewide basis.[20] Its work was so successful that in 1907 a separate organization—the Alabama School Improvement Association—was created. This operated under the aegis of the state superintendent of education and had as its constitutional objective "to create and foster a general sentiment in favor of education in the improvement of public schools and the advancement of all cultural influences."[21] By 1911 associations existed in all but four counties. In 1912 Monroe County had an association in each one of its eighty-four districts.[22]

The women of the AFWC, while progressive in respect of a wide range of social concerns, were not so in matters of race.[23] When the chair of the AFWC's education committee, Kate Morrisette (she of the flame-like enthusiasm and evocations of Robert E. Lee) decided in 1899 to enroll her daughter at the Oread Institute in Massachusetts, she made discreet enquiries to ensure her daughter would not be schooled with "negresses."[24] Some members of the AFWC were often also members of the UDC, whose policies strongly supported white supremacy. The racial attitudes of its members meant the AFWC would not permit the affiliation of even the small number of black women's

12. Margaret Murray Washington. Courtesy Alabama Department of Archives and History, Montgomery, Alabama.

clubs then existing in the state.[25] Yet, while excluded from the AFWC, these clubs had similar goals.

The State Federation of Colored Women's Clubs was formed in Montgomery in December 1899. By July 1908 it comprised more than forty affiliated clubs.[26] In 1895 Margaret Murray Washington organized the Tuskegee Women's Club, whose goal was "to improve the intellectual, moral and spiritual qualities of its members," who were all either teachers or the wives of teachers at the Tuskegee Institute in Macon County. The club arranged extension classes in vocational and academic subjects, established an elementary school, and organized the Tuskegee Mothers' Club to help black women improve their child-rearing and domestic skills. Mothers' clubs were set up in many other parts of the state as well and operated as school improvement associations.[27]

School improvement associations, whether black or white, successfully harnessed to the cause of educational modernization the traditions of small communities seen in other cooperative pursuits such as road mending, barn raisings, log rollings, and quilting parties.[28] No better illustration of this could be found than in a report of "Clean-Up and School Improvement Day," which was organized by the Department of Education and held in October 1914. In fact, the following description of processional village gaiety at Prattville in

Autauga County, inescapably suggests a depiction of country life as seen in the paintings of Winslow Homer or the lithographs of Currier and Ives: "A line was formed and the two hundred children with their teachers and the ladies marched merrily through the streets with hoes, rakes, shovels and axes over their shoulders preparatory to making war on the weeds and rubbish of the town."[29] The department believed that such cooperation meant "better schools, better churches, better homes and a better people."[30]

All over the state, children, teachers, patrons, and other local community members took part in blacking stoves, building sanitary toilets, clearing grounds, glazing windows, installing equipment, marking out courts for games, painting buildings, scrubbing floors, and repairing and enhancing facilities overall.[31] Mrs. Thomas L. Head, the president of the school improvement association at Grove Hill in Clarke County, noted the neighborly connectedness. She felt that "a great deal more than the material things was accomplished." She disclosed that members of the town's warring factions who "had been afflicted with an old school fuss for a number of years" worked in complete harmony and "she was unable to detect a selfish spirit behind a suggestion."[32]

The impact of school improvement associations, though positive, sometimes had unintended effects. Better-equipped and beautified schoolhouses increased the potency of their actual and symbolic value to school patrons; their loss through relocation or consolidation was keenly felt. Yet they could also prompt a new interest in schooling thus making patrons more supportive of reform measures such as school taxes.

In June 1905 the *Opelika Daily News* covered the proceedings of the twenty-fourth annual convention of the AEA being held in Montgomery. The newspaper noted that Isaac W. Hill and his associates had been very busy over the last year "in this class of service" and that "more than twenty counties have voted the special [school] tax." It also noted there had been "an uprising of interest in the schoolhouse question" and that many communities had gone to work to achieve better accommodation. The aroused interest was attributed to a "committee of ladies."[33] These "ladies" had no intention of resting on their laurels. They next turned their attention to reading.

How to stimulate habits of private reading was sometimes a topic at teachers' institutes with attendees reporting their patrons either wanted "libraries"—a set of books for recreational reading—but could not afford them, or were simply indifferent. At one institute, Miss Jennie Lee Reese told participants they should become "hustlers" and organize ice-cream suppers to raise funds for books. If this were not possible she recommended they buy with their own money "fifty cent editions of Washington Irving's *Sketchbook* and Daniel Defoe's *Robinson Crusoe*."[34] As a tale of the isolated, self-sufficient man who found he still needed society, Miss Reese's last suggestion was an apposite parable for the purpose.

On April 13, 1911, Alabama's legislature enacted the Rural School Library Bill establishing the funding arrangements by which school libraries could be purchased annually by rural school districts.[35] Shortly afterward Henry Jones Willingham, the state superintendent, informed the AFWC that its members could "inspire local communities to take advantage of this Act."[36] But inspiring rural communities to part with scarce funds to acquire books was an uphill battle. Private reading was regarded as a middle-class pastime that smacked of self-indulgence. When undertaken at all, reading did not stray much beyond the Bible, an almanac, or occasionally a newspaper.[37]

At the AFWC's annual conference in 1912, Mrs. Leopold M. Bashinsky of Troy told delegates her education committee had exerted every effort "to spread the news of the Rural School Library Law." Two years later the conference heard that only six out of sixty-seven counties had availed themselves to the fullest extent of the appropriation.[38] When the county presidents of school improvement associations met annually they shared similar frustrations. They were disappointed at the less than wholehearted commitment by school districts in taking the steps to acquire libraries and also at the laggardness of county officers in fulfilling their part in the funding process. There was even talk of repealing the act.[39]

In December 1914 when the county presidents met in Montgomery, they discussed how they might "secure legislation for schools." A Miss Strickland gave an inspiring talk and urged everyone present to "do something for their state so that we need not be embarrassed by seeing her at the bottom of the list."[40] The "list" she referred to was the Russell Sage Foundation's survey showing Alabama with the lowest ranking of all the states in educational efficiency.[41]

The AFWC's 1914 conference was told by its education committee that it had recently asked affiliated clubs for suggestions for school legislation. While there had been "wonderful unanimity on compulsory education and increased local taxation" there was also a plethora of other suggestions. The measures the AFWC was asking its members to adopt seemed very close to prescribing methods for teacher supervision and for curriculum design.[42]

The educational activism of the club women—in concert with local communities—was political. The women had become influential lobbyists without seeming to unsettle cultural traditions or challenge the *status quo*. Their efforts supported and complemented those of professional schoolmen, educational philanthropists, and politicians. Although they had experienced some setbacks, they helped to create a congenial social context within which the professionals were more likely to be successful.[43] In 1909 Professor Charles B. Glenn, the assistant superintendent of schools for Birmingham, spoke admiringly of school improvement associations, stating they connected home and school and that the "central thought of their constitutions is cooperation and not interference."[44]

∾

In 1898 the first of what were to become annual meetings of the Conference for Christian Education in the South was held at Capon Springs, West Virginia. The few attendees focused on a missionary agenda of Christian education for illiterate black people and poor mountain whites. The next year (1899) Dr. Jabez L. M. Curry—doyen of Southern educators and general agent for the philanthropic Peabody Education Fund and also the John F. Slater Foundation—was elected to the presidency, thus arguably initiating "the Southern education movement." This was a collective name for an organized intersectional coalition of Northern industrial philanthropists and Southern middle-class school modernizers who were set upon improving the quality of Southern public schools, the lives of Southern people, and the prosperity of the South overall. After Curry's appointment the conference dropped "Christian" from its title in order to widen its scope and encourage attendance by as many (white) people as possible with educational interests. At a third meeting in Capon Springs in 1900, Robert Curtis Ogden was elected to the presidency, a position he retained until his death in 1913.[45]

Ogden was a wealthy New York department store magnate and president of the board of trustees of the Hampton Institute in Virginia, a pioneering vocational school for black students and early model for Alabama's Tuskegee Institute. Ogden saw himself as a "businessman of ideals" and was not only a philanthropist in his own right but a consummate organizer and promoter. He wanted to interest other Northern industrialists in the cause of Southern education, to heal any residual bitterness from the Civil War, and to bring Southern economic development up to parity with the North. He became the guiding influence on the future direction of the conference. This was apparent the following year when the conference moved from the rather remote location of Capon Springs to Winston-Salem in North Carolina. Thereafter it was held in a different Southern city each year. In 1904 it was held in Birmingham.

The Winston-Salem conference received national attention because Ogden hired a plush train to transport more than seventy Northerners to the Southern town. These included influential academics, bankers, clerics, editors, financiers, industrialists, and publishers. Among their number were John D. Rockefeller Jr., George Foster Peabody, and Walter Hines Page. In 1897 Page had coined the notion of "the forgotten man"—the poor white who had been overlooked by progress, ill served by unsuitable education, and misled by Populist agitators and racial demagogues. Page believed that white educational progress would lead to nothing less than a social transformation in which the pathological aspects of poor white society would be eliminated. One board member claimed, in a singular piece of calculus, that educating one ignorant white person was "worth more to the black man himself than the education of ten negroes."[46] From 1901 onward the Southern education movement would be concerned with suitable schooling for the forgotten man. In an awful betrayal of the goals of the first conference, there would be no further consideration of the needs of black children for many years to come.[47]

One of the speakers at the Winston-Salem conference was Charles W. Dabney, president of the University of Tennessee. He gave an uncompromising address on the deficiencies of Southern education. He insisted that, if the South were ever to have an efficient system of public schools, educational legislation and methods of taxation had to be completely turned around. He emphasized the need for a central propaganda agency to "campaign for free public education" and urged those present "to take steps to establish such an agency."[48]

By February 1902 just such an agency—the Southern Education Board (SEB)—had been established comprising both Northerners and Southerners. Its president was Ogden and its executive secretary was Edgar Gardner Murphy, an Episcopalian clergyman, Progressive activist, and tireless campaigner for the abolition of child labor. Because this board lacked a permanent source of funding, another organization, the General Education Board (GEB), was incorporated by an act of Congress in January 1903. This was richly endowed by the oil tycoon John D. Rockefeller. By 1909 Rockefeller's gifts to the board totaled fifty-three million dollars.[49] The GEB served as a type of holding company for vast philanthropic interests.[50]

Writers and historians have examined extensively the Southern education movement and the reform process it stimulated. The agencies of the movement and their principals have received particular attention. The most significant texts in this historiography include the accounts of the original founders who fought a heroic and Jeffersonian "crusade against ignorance."[51] They also include highly critical examinations by modern historians—particularly black historians—of the evolution of a movement initially concerned with black schooling to one that decided consciously to make the education of poor white children its primary concern.[52] The consequence of this evolution was to corral most black students into schools teaching only the skills needed for servitude and menial manual labor. As the Southern education movement was an intersectional coalition of nationally important people with a wide regional perspective and somewhat imperial goals, these are the aspects that have invited most attention. But regional histories leave interstices within which the experiences of one state such as Alabama can be explored.

The Southern education movement's activities in Alabama were well served by the fact that both Murphy and Jabez L. M. Curry, who was one of the first members of the SEB, were Southerners and had significant associations with Alabama. As far back as 1854, Curry had helped draft the first legislation for Alabama's state public schooling system and, though near the end of his life, he still wielded enormous educational influence. Despite their scorn for the deficiencies of Alabama's localism, the officeholders of the Southern education movement's agencies harnessed some of its strengths to achieve their goals.

From its inception the SEB decided that none of the funds at its disposal would be used to assist schools and institutions *per se*. Instead, funds would go to raise awareness in order to create an environment in which legislative reforms were more likely to be sought and local taxation more likely to be approved. Propaganda work would be carried out through conventions, summer schools, local associations, and field agents who would spread the message.[53]

In May 1902 Edgar Gardner Murphy appointed Joseph B. Graham as Alabama's field agent. Graham was a one-time superintendent of education for Talladega County and had chaired the 1901 constitutional convention's committee on education. In the eleven months following his appointment, Graham visited twenty-two counties delivering up to four addresses in each. He started his first campaign by utilizing an existing opportunity—the first day of the circuit court. This was a regular occasion when people from all sections of a county came to the county seat. Some were jurors, litigants, or witnesses but others just came to swap horses, greet friends, talk politics, and/or exchange the news. Such gatherings had always been a captive audience for politicians and office seekers and, similarly, Graham used them to speak about "good schools, sounder morals and higher and purer aims."[54]

In July 1902 when Alabama was in the grip of a drought that had "almost destroyed the cotton and corn crops," Joseph Graham arranged an all-day rally in a mountain county. The site chosen was twenty-five miles from the railroad but "the people came in great numbers from the surrounding country. Many walked, some rode in good buggies and surreys; but many families of from three to twelve persons came in plain farm wagons with straw-covered beds, chairs from the fireside as seats, drawn by a yoke of oxen. Many of those attending were clad in home-woven jeans and cotton; most of them wore shoes, but some, even adults were bare-footed; but all were happy and cheerful and welcomed visiting speakers most cordially."[55]

Such meetings resembled summer religious revivals and there were instances of educational rallies and revivals being one and the same. Graham attended such a gathering where the "protracted meeting" had begun in the morning with a service at eleven o'clock. A further sermon was delivered at 6:30 P.M. and at 8:00 P.M. Graham and two other speakers began their talks, which went on for two hours. These were "pitched along the line of close relation of home, school and church, and of intelligence, morals and religion." Afterward the preacher declared to his congregation that they had just heard "the best sermons of the revival." Three years later when the crusade for educational converts was still being fought, some rallies had moved inside. In July 1905 the *Florence Herald* notified its readers of an all-day event to be held in the New Hope Church. They were invited to bring well-filled baskets and enjoy the prominent educational speakers and "pleasant, profitable program."[56]

In 1893, John G. Harris (state superintendent, 1890–1894) had utilized revival-like meetings to raise public awareness about educational reform, but the SEB was able to go much further. It was able to subsidize campaigning with advertising, literature, professional advice, and field agents such as Graham. Its influence allowed it to summon gatherings of state educational officeholders as well as legislators—and be reasonably sure of their attendance.

In January 1903, with funding from the GEB, Edgar Gardner Murphy convened a conference of Alabama's county superintendents at Montgomery. Both Murphy and Ogden felt this had to be successful if the Southern education movement itself was to sustain momentum.[57] The conference was scheduled to coincide with a legislative sitting and almost every representative attended two evening sessions that were open to the public. Describing the meeting Joseph B. Graham wrote: "For power and widespread influence among educators, citizens and legislators, it was beyond anything in the history of the state and it brought our best citizenship into thorough sympathy with the work of the two great Education Boards."[58] But Graham was not entirely impartial and there seems to have been some skittishness on the part of the SEB as to how the public might regard talk of "power and influence." An SEB press release pointedly emphasized the boards were "conducting their work only through the accepted methods and the appointed authorities of the state."[59]

Newspapers reported on the conference with a post-revival religiosity. The proceedings were said to have been "characterized by a spirit of deep earnestness and patriotic consecration to the cause." The removal of limits on local taxation was felt to be the necessary first step toward school improvement.[60]

~

Whether it was the campaigning of the SEB or just the culmination of many years of lobbying by state superintendents, the AFWC, and the AEA, 1903 saw multiple pieces of new and important school legislation passed. Some of the most significant laws concerned textbook uniformity, school redistricting, summer schools, local taxation, and the teaching of agriculture in the public schools.[61] Like most changes, the new laws were regarded cautiously by those they were intended to benefit—particularly those that struck against local decision making and parental control of schools. The teaching of agriculture was different. It had the potential for allowing some convergence between educational theory and the lives and daily occupations of rural people.

In the last two decades of the nineteenth century, Alabama's poorer farmers, frequently tenants, were regularly beset by problems including agricultural recessions, low crop yields, soil exhaustion, and subsistence poverty. Hoping for a political solution to their vicissitudes, in the early 1890s farmers had been part of an unsuccessful agrarian populist challenge to Alabama's ruling Democratic and Conservative Party. But Alabama was not alone in its rural difficulties. Thomas Jefferson's Arcadian ideal of the superior yeoman, the primacy of agriculture and the link between farming and democracy, was under threat all over the United States. Despite their all-too-frequent squalor and corruption, America's cities were attracting droves of young people fleeing rural hardship and this was causing serious alarm. In the decade between 1900 and 1910 Alabama's urban population grew by 5.4 percentage points.[62] In 1900, Thomas A. Craven, Bullock County's superintendent, wrote: "It would be better for the future of our fair land that the state do all that is possible, to improve the country schools than to have the country homes abandoned and the songs of children in the country schools hushed."[63]

Somebody who was keen to reverse the national rural exodus was Dr. Liberty Hyde Bailey of Cornell University. For many years Bailey had preached that "agriculture is not only the rock foundation of democracy, it is the very basis of humanity, morality and justice." He promoted "Nature Study" so children would develop a deep love of the outdoors and the countryside but his overarching goal was the regeneration of country life through a complete redirection of rural education.[64]

Liberty Hyde Bailey attended the Conference for Education in the South for three consecutive years from 1901. At the Richmond conference in 1903 he gave an address on "Education through Agriculture."[65] Bailey and Walter Hines Page, who was an original member of the SEB and later a member of the GEB, were of a similar educational mind and, in 1908, would both serve together on President Theodore Roosevelt's "Commission on Country Life."

This was set up to investigate the deficiencies of country life and possible remedies so that "the most precious part of the state," as Jefferson had called small landholders, would remain in the country and their children also.[66]

Around the turn of the century, an articulate minority of farmers was also beginning to have a clearer idea of what it wanted from elementary schools and this was not merely nature study. The farmers' organization—the Patrons of Husbandry (National Grange)—resolved in 1902 that, although it might be "better for a six-year-old to make friends of robins, squirrels, and lady-bugs than to pore over primers and the first book in numbers," the Grange it-self was asking "for the teaching of the elements of agriculture in the country schools."[67] Alabama's own Grange had always been interested in education and urged schools to devote more attention to the practical side of farming.[68] It was against this backdrop that Alabama's 1903 legislation regarding the teaching of agriculture was passed. Immediately teachers were wary at having to give in-struction in an entirely new "branch."

Walker County's superintendent Riley D. Argo, tried to provide reassur-ance about the prescribed textbook. He explained that although it was too dif-ficult for the very elementary grades, so long as pupils took up the book they would be complying "at least with the spirit of the law." Argo urged every par-ent, especially farmers, to read the text, which, he said, "treats not only the care and cultivation of crops but everything pertaining to home life in the country, the garden, poultry, domestic animals, etc."[69]

In 1910 the intent of the legislation regarding the teaching of agriculture was made very explicit in the manual issued to elementary schools. The manual stated that, because 90 percent of Alabama's people were living in the country and about 70 percent were engaged in farming, the state's schools had to be "the outgrowth of the leading community interest and the exponent of the ac-tivities of the people." To fulfill this role "agriculture in some form should be the main work of the schools. It should be vitally interwoven into the course in all of the grades." There was the implication that "predestined rural youth must be trained in the tasks of his future occupation" and that country children must be "ruralized beyond the seductive call of the city."[70]

The manual provided a course outline for teachers in "Nature Study and Agriculture." By the seventh grade, pupils were expected to be studying such matters as the value and care of barnyard manure; fertilizers; crop rotation; plant and crop diseases; trees and fruits; bees and insects; livestock, poultry, and dairying; farm machinery and buildings; and country roads. A huge list of *Farmers' Bulletins* issued by the Department of Agriculture in Washington was suggested as learning material.[71]

13. Corn club exhibit, Birmingham Fair. Courtesy Alabama Department of Archives and History, Montgomery, Alabama.

Knowledge gained in the schoolroom could be supplemented by practical experience gained through boys' and girls' agricultural clubs, which operated closely with the public schools. Though originating in the North the club movement grew quickly throughout the whole country. Luther N. Duncan of the Auburn agricultural experiment station is credited for organizing clubs in Alabama. Boys were given seeds, growing instructions, and a chance to win prizes. In 1909–10 fewer than three hundred boys in just two counties were participating. By 1912 every county in the state had corn clubs and 10,894 boys were involved. Many exhibited at state fairs.[72]

Girls' clubs were conceived as a way of bringing "a new interest into the home and cooperation in domestic tasks between mother and daughter." Girls were encouraged to add to family income by cultivating kitchen gardens, learning canning skills, and selling produce. Tomato clubs were just the first of other agricultural, animal husbandry, and educational extension clubs concerned with raising poultry, providing better food at lower cost, improving health, and acquiring domestic skills.[73] School improvement associations helped girls buy canning and other equipment.[74]

In 1911, Professor Norman B. Baker was appointed as Alabama's first (white) rural schools supervisor. His duties required him to travel all over Alabama visiting as many white rural schools as possible.[75] Baker's duties also involved him in grading schools, improving their supervision, and suggesting vitalizing programs. "Vitalizing" and "vivifying" were vogue words with educationists at this time and associated with the idea that rural schools—and rural life itself—were stagnant and disintegrating. Teachers and/or patrons and trustees were expected to get involved in organizing agricultural clubs, scheduling school fairs, arranging lyceums (instructional lectures), acquiring libraries, forming reading circles, and improving school sanitary arrangements. In the course of his travels Baker seems to have developed an understanding of the risks of condescension from outsiders and the need for local trust. In 1912 he advised teachers that, when arranging lyceums, they should use tact so the residents of a district would not gain the impression "that the speaker or entertainer was coming in the spirit of a missionary."[76]

While rural schools were fitting children with vocational skills so they could both perform traditional roles and participate in the market economy, the GEB was turning its attention to their parents whom it believed would support school improvement if they simply had the financial wherewithal. As this could only be acquired through increased farm productivity, the GEB decided to underwrite demonstrations of a method of improving cotton and other crop yields developed by Dr. Seaman A. Knapp, a nationally influential agriculturalist.

Knapp had striven for years to bring "scientific farming" ideas to primary producers whose ideas were still often shaped by folklore.[77] Yet Knapp's science was well served by that persistent and unscientific narrative of American culture—the belief that transformation may always be possible in even the humblest life—an idea of sufficient strength to conquer suspicion of outsider interference. In fact, all the conventions of twenty-first-century television makeover quests were present in the GEB's account of the demonstration work in Alabama.

In 1906, one of Knapp's agents visited and reconnoitred a rural district in the south of the state. He next sought out "a poor one-mule farmer" who was described as being in debt, without hope, and initially reluctant to cooperate. The farmer was persuaded to cooperate with the promise that, if he planted his fields with special seed and followed explicit cultivation rules, his crop yield and income would markedly improve within a single season.

After complying diligently with "the ten commandments of agriculture" devised by Knapp, the promise held out to the farmer was fulfilled and his achievements "revealed" to admiring neighbors at a field meeting. The farmer then became the local demonstration agent himself and assisted others to emulate his achievements. In his made-over self he discovered initiative and took pride in making his farm a showplace.[78]

Farm demonstrations, like agricultural clubs, were about redefining the cultural and economic setting for education and doing so within a familiar context. In 1908, Cherokee County's superintendent was gleeful: "Our farmers are making crops with less labor and drudgery than ever before, by the use of machinery and the intelligence by which they select their fertilizers and till their soil; such conditions have been a wonderful impetus in the building of school houses and repairing and making them comfortable."[79]

When Northern philanthropists seemed to challenge the *status quo*—especially the racial *status quo*—there was, in some counties, a stridently defensive outcry. Some of this was directed explicitly at Robert C. Ogden as SEB president. In June 1905 the *Opelika Daily News* reprinted an item from a New Orleans paper. This said, in part: "There are many reasons why Mr. Robert C. Ogden's so-called 'educational movement' has not appealed to the favor of the southern people and one of them is his exuberant enthusiasm for the negro. . . . Mr. Ogden is a negro-worshipper pure and simple. His interest in the poor white man is merely a means to an end."[80]

The alleged "end" implied by the *Opelika Daily News* was that Ogden supposedly believed black men would be fit teachers for any school in the South. This was patently untrue but part of a sustained campaign of denigration. Ogden was criticized for being overfriendly with Booker T. Washington, the black principal of the Tuskegee Institute, and his annual trips to the Conference for Education in the South were portrayed as condescending junkets. One newspaper described these as "invasions," a word evoking the Civil War and Reconstruction. Ogden may also have been the recipient of a redirected hostility at Edgar Gardner Murphy, whose efforts to control child labor in Alabama's cotton mills had attracted the fury of manufacturers.[81] Ogden ignored all hostility believing it would dissipate when the positive aspects of the Southern education movement became known.[82] But, as recounted in the last chapter, in Lee County where the *Opelika Daily News* was published, the taxation election was lost. Voters preferred caution rather than risk money going to black schools.[83]

The local taxation measure was lost not only in Lee but in a number of other counties, too. Despite vigorous campaigning by Murphy and others, some counties did not even vote on the measure. The results of the tax elections were a salutary reminder to modernizers that they could only achieve so much by moral suasion, propaganda, and evangelical campaigning. At the point where heightened community awareness had to be translated into raising funds and agreeing to a reordering of the educational polity, objections to taxation, centralized bureaucratic power, and/or externally imposed decisions often resurfaced. Also, educational modernization did not occur in a vacuum. Progressives were working on a number of fronts at this time as they tried to effect changes to social policies such as limiting the availability of liquor, securing female suffrage, restricting child labor, and so forth. These reforms, though laudable, all had the capacity to upset the everyday lives and/or long-standing traditions of ordinary people. The defeat of taxation proposals—even when the tax would mean better schools—may plausibly have been the *vox populi* of protest about changes that had little to do with schooling.

~

A long-standing objective of educational progressives—the rationalization of rural school districts—was achieved in September 1903 with the passing of an act that abolished the township as basis for the school district, made the county the principal point for educational administration—including the allocation of funds—and required counties to lay out new districts based rationally on population centers and geography.

In May 1904 Walker County's superintendent advised citizens of that county that the only way the redistricting board could "do its work to the convenience and satisfaction of all the people" was if people got together to map out the boundary lines themselves and then sent these to the board to assist its decision making.[84] But consultation could not assuage anxiety about the diminution of autonomy.

Until about 1910, the annual reports prepared for the Department of Education by county superintendents differed significantly in consistency, length, and content because no format was specified. A sort of boilerplate of reassuring comments was offered up year after year: "Our people are seemingly aroused in the interest of education as never before"; "pupils, school officials and teachers are more wide awake and enthused on educational work than ever known before."[85] But in the reports for 1903–1904, about a third of superintendents related that their constituents were negative or skeptical about redistricting or were angry about the "exercising of undue authority."[86] Monroe County's John D. Forte thought his people's attachment to the township system would have to be "drilled" out of their minds—a two-year undertaking.[87]

A similar tale was told many times over in a hostile discourse. A typical comment was that of Chambers County's William G. Jarrell, who asserted that "in many communities confusion and dissatisfaction prevails."[88] When Henry County's superintendent disclosed that the law seemed "to be very unpopular, and in some districts the people are badly frustrated on account of the removal of their school" or the superintendent of Coosa County divulged that "there are some who would prefer a small school at their own door than send to a large and interesting one at some distance," the anger at inconvenience and the angst of cultural loss can both be detected.[89]

Isaac W. Hill expressed his own opinion rather defiantly: "As soon as the new plan is understood, the people will endorse it without question."[90] But Hill was completely mistaken that a lack of understanding was the problem. In fact, "the people" understood the implications of the reform all too well. Hill seemed not to appreciate that, though decentralization and localism were problems for systematization, standards, and consistency, they allowed people to conduct their own business as they saw fit. The complaints relayed by the county superintendents suggested their constituents were suffering inchoate anxiety about a creeping loss of control and their ability to influence what their children were taught.

In the early years of the twentieth century the cause of educational reform was aided by Governor Braxton Bragg Comer (1907–1911). Comer believed education was "the most successful foundation for the future of the state." This was not just rhetoric. Comer believed state power should be used as a vehicle for change and owing to the quantity of educational legislation approved during Comer's tenure, he was tagged Alabama's "Education Governor."[91] Yet even in a more responsive political climate, without an authoritative county superintendency supported by a strong central bureaucracy, reformers could only do so much. Many schooling decisions continued to be in the hands of local trustees who, even after redistricting, could be subject to all sorts of patron pressures.

Progressive initiatives worked best where school communities could discern an immediate and/or obvious benefit or where local cooperative enterprise was involved. The participatory potential of school improvement associations, the highly practical agricultural curriculum designed to make rural schooling vocational and thus seem more relevant, and the re-valuing of country life were all measures that met the benefit criteria and assisted the shaping of Alabama's educational system in a more contemporary guise. Where reform was harder to achieve—for example, in matters such as district taxation, compulsory attendance, and school consolidation—it was because the people who were expected to gain from such reforms perceived them to be inimical to their own interests. By objecting to such changes or insisting on some accommodation of their wishes, rural communities demonstrated the enduring strength of neighborhood democracy.

7
Special Days and Festivals, Rites and Rituals

From the very beginning of Alabama's state educational system, its public schools were, and continued to be, part of their community's cultural fabric— a fabric woven from a skein of meanings that informed daily life and were encoded into the community's calendar, its social etiquette, its regard for its artifacts, and its ceremonies, rites, and rituals.[1] The school morning usually began with prayers and/or a reading from the Bible and the school week ended with hymn singing, thus demonstrating the common religious ethos of patrons, teachers, and students. School formalities such as openings, closings, and commencements offered opportunities for the celebration of rites of passage. School holidays, both sacred and secular, were decided by trustees and patrons but their observance conformed to time-honored practices. Even school-yard games—though of ancient lineage—reflected sufficient variants to make them, collectively, a folkway with their own rules and rites. All these activities helped to consolidate a sense of "belonging."

During the Progressive Era, Alabama's department of education initiated a plethora of special occasions, novel ceremonies, and contrived rituals to produce in students a heightened awareness of their identity as Southerners, to socialize them as citizens, and to confirm their membership of an "expanded community."[2]

Alabama was not unique in its enthusiasm for celebratory inventions. Between the Civil War and World War I, when factors such as mass immigration, ethnic and racial diversity, and working-class militancy appeared to be unsettling ideas about national unity, popular pageants dramatized the lives of famous Americans such as George Washington and important historical events such as the landing of the Pilgrims. As well, large numbers of holidays and celebrations were created or revived all over the country as a means of instructing participants in patriotism and citizenship. The civic elites who sponsored official celebrations often involved children and schools as a way of institutionalizing their own vision of America.[3]

⁓

Alabama's school calendar was shaped by the agricultural cycle and the need for child labor on farms. In late February or early March, fields had to be weeded and readied for spring plowing. Planting began in late April and continued into June. Cultivation could go on until the end of July. Wheat and oats were sown in the fall and reaped in early summer. Cotton was picked from early September. Other crops might be gathered as late as November. In winter fences had to be mended, land cleared, drains dug, and repairs undertaken.

Although the formal scholastic year was specified in legislation, actual session dates and all other matters relating to the time of a school's opening or the observance of holidays were matters for the determination of the township superintendent in consultation with school patrons or the city/county board of education. Until the twentieth century, school sessions were generally held in winter and only lasted for twelve weeks unless extended by private tuition. Attendance started falling off in March when pupils were needed for planting. In 1888 Virginia Adams, a black teacher at Tallahassee, opened her school just after Christmas with one hundred pupils; by May only twenty-five were attending.[4] With the completion of reaping at the end of July, some schools opened again for a short summer session. They then closed again in September in time to pick cotton, which took about six weeks. The extent to which the already short sessions were interrupted by holidays varied from place to place. Thanksgiving, Christmas, and New Year's Day were widely recognized holidays but the observance of religious days (such as Good Friday) were matters for individual communities.[5]

From the close of the Civil War onward there was a trend across the whole of the United States to reconstruct the religious and civic calendar to serve the needs of an expanding consumer market.[6] However, in the late nineteenth century, the holidays observed by Alabama's public schools were a matter of long-standing custom or were devised by parents and teachers. At Christmastime, decorated trees and gifts were commonplace but not universal. In 1910 Emmett Burch, the teacher of a Lawrence County school, gave his pupils a booklet containing all their names and a selection of biblical verses.[7] The pupils of Stewart's Chapel School in Blount County did not have a tree but had a spelling competition. At Easter they hunted for eggs that had been colored by boiling them with crayons.[8]

Besides any holidays that may have been observed, the ritual calendar of the school was shaped by its openings and closings, which, with differing degrees of formality, marked both the beginning and the ending of the scholastic year or the major session. Openings usually included a meeting of patrons and students at which new teachers were introduced. Speeches typically stressed the reciprocal duties of parents and children and made pleas for "cooperation."[9] Openings in small towns or cities were opportunities for local worthies to talk about the importance of education and to boost the town's "Graded School."[10] Such speeches were often informed by anxiety over enrollments and served as a pitch to potential patrons. Newspapers helpfully provided a running score of enrollments with the subtext that people might miss out if they did not act quickly.[11]

Closing ceremonies, including exhibitions and commencements for graduating students, were significant to the cultural life of small communities in a number of ways. They were calendrical markers and for some children, rites of passage. These ceremonies enabled social interaction and they were an assurance to the community that its school was imparting its values as well as knowledge.

Exhibitions were a group ritual in which children, watched by parents and neighbors, recited poems, delivered orations, read compositions, sang songs, and took part in tableaux.[12] Even the poorest parents wanted their children not only to perform well but to earn favorable notice from their neighbors. When William Holtzclaw was a young child at a black rural school in Randolph County, his teacher "ordered all the pupils to appear dressed in white" to deliver their exhibition pieces. Without money to buy new white clothes, his mother made suits for William and his two brothers from a white petticoat. He "supposed we looked as well as the others," and "there was no mother who was prouder of her children than ours."[13]

Closing events and ceremonies were often covered in local newspapers in great detail so their enjoyment could be prolonged and the roles of participants remembered. In 1887, when Katie McDaniel, "a queenly young lady," and Hattie Ratcliff, "graceful, tall, and stately," graduated from the Camden Public School, the *Wilcox Progress* was able to wring from their commencement ceremony enough material to fill half a column and inflate it with a civic gravity normally associated with much larger events. The paper described the rush for seats, the entrance of the graduates to marching music, the dignitaries following in their wake, the essays charmingly read, and the speeches given by Colonel S. W. John and Professor W. C. Jones.[14] The item showed Camden's admiration for oratorical skills, female refinement, youthful optimism, masculine authority, and military bearing. The ceremonial investment in just *two* students also showed Camden attached much value to this rite of passage.

~

Besides calendrical fixtures such as openings and closings, the smaller rituals of school life such as the games children played at recess provide further examples of the ways in which a localized culture operated. Before the encroachment of organized sports, manufactured toys, or the advent of the physical education teacher, there was huge diversity in children's play. In 1914, a survey of conditions affecting schooling in Covington, Morgan, and Macon counties identified about a hundred different games that were played by the children there.[15]

Many of the games played in Alabama's schoolyards were universal—hide and seek, jumping rope, hopscotch, marbles, and those involving catching, chasing, and tagging—but these had infinite local variations and rules. In Clay County the rules for ball games played in the 1880s such as "paddle cat," "prisoner's base," and "town ball" (a precursor to baseball) were different from those reported in Pike County.[16] Black children had their own forms of play or made traditional games their own. These included the ring games "Little Sallie Walker, sittin' in a saucer" and "Stooping on the Window, Wind the Ball."[17] Having one's own games or rules was clannish and a claim on identity, including racial identity. Children in one part of a single county might play games not known to children in another part. Games were thus territory markers. Girls usually played their own games but in small schools the boys needed the girls, and sometimes the teacher, to make up teams.

As late as 1918 play equipment in public schoolyards was "so meager and so infrequently found as to be non-existent."[18] In their play country children were expected to improvise from materials at hand. In Bullock County, Elma Lee Hall (born 1895) recalled "the girls played what the boys played—marbles and ball and sich like. We made our balls out of old socks. Our bat was a hickory tree limb."[19] In Jackson County, Sue Mae Freeman Powell (born 1903) said the boys at her school "would go up and cut some of the long grapevines, remove all the leaves and knots and we would jump rope over the vines."[20] In Cullman County discarded lumber served as springboards or see-saws.[21] These makeshifts by children imitated those of adults who, without financial resources, made do. The above recollections display an engagingly sly pride in the country child's self-sufficiency.

$\sim$

The first foray by Alabama's department of education into mandating a "Special Day" for statewide observance was in 1887 when the then state superintendent, Solomon Palmer, requested: "All schools of the state to observe the 22nd February, George Washington's birthday, as Arbor Day, by planting shade trees and shrubbery on the school grounds and dedicating them with appropriate ceremonies to the memory of those they love." Palmer earnestly invoked the aid of "the state press and the hearty, active cooperation of superintendents of counties, cities and townships, and separate school districts as well as every teacher" in order to make the day a success. He hoped that Arbor Day would be observed until "every schoolhouse in the state is surrounded by shade trees and environed with bowers of shrubs and vines bearing beautiful and sweet scented flowers."[22]

Arbor Day had been initiated in 1872 by J. Sterling Morton, a Nebraskan. Over the next two decades, schools across the nation adopted the celebration. Arbor Day speakers everywhere spoke of trees as embodiments of rural virtues and attachments that would "evoke commitment to place and community." They hoped this would deter the young's "hankering for city diversions and excitements."[23]

Being also the birthday of George Washington, Arbor Day did double duty. As well as planting trees, children celebrated "the memory of one of the country's most illustrious sons" with recitations, readings, patriotic songs, and appropriate talks. The observation of Arbor Day on Washington's birthday became an annual fixture. In later years teachers developed their own celebratory activities. In 1906 Professor and Mrs. W. E. Turnipseed of the Jasper Graded School entertained pupils with "delicious refreshments" in rooms "artistically decorated with flags, cherries, hatchets and the national colors."[24] The decorative combination of cherries and hatchets was presumably derived from the Reverend Mason Locke Weems's invented myth of Washington's spotless boyhood during which he allegedly cut down a cherry tree with a hatchet but later confessed his misdeed. The tale had some ambiguity for Arbor Day.

In 1903 state superintendent Isaac W. Hill acted on a suggestion by the AEA that schools should celebrate annually on December 14 the anniversary of Alabama's admission to the Union. Whereas Arbor Day originated outside the state, "Alabama Day" was home-grown. The pogram of activities suggested for its observance was prepared by a committee comprising members of the AEA, the department of archives and history and the department of education. The occasion was to be a means of "bringing together patrons, neighbors, and friends" so they could "partake of the interest, enthusiasm and fraternal feelings which always come from the mingling of people at such meetings."

But the program for Alabama Day was not that of an ordinary school meeting. It provided for the reading of a message from the state governor regarding Alabama and its future potential. Following a salute to the state flag, selected children were then to read both the Resolution upon which Alabama was admitted to the Union in 1819 as well as an extract from the address of William L. Yancey at the Secession Convention of 1861. Songs were to be sung, including "Away Down South in Dixie" or "Dixie's Land." "A Ballad of Emma Sansom" was suggested for recitation. This concerned a famous Civil War incident when a plucky Alabamian girl assisted General Nathan Bedford Forrest to evade the Union army. The anthem "America" completed the proceedings.[25]

The program recognized the strength of an implicitly rural localism; it engendered a reverence for ritual objects such as Alabama's admission document and the state flag; it linked Alabama to its Confederate history and the part children played in that history, but also to a broader (white) Southern or sectional identity. Ultimately, however, it encouraged children to recognize their fealty to the United States.

~

During the 1890s, Alabama's Southern identity was something that a formidable organization of white middle-class women was increasingly keen to impress upon the state's children. The "Lost Cause"—that prolonged lament for the Old South—enjoyed its high noon in the period between 1896 and about 1918. This was partly a result of the efforts of the United Confederate Veterans but, perhaps even more important, the efforts of the United Daughters of the Confederacy.[26] From 1896, when Miss Sallie Jones, a "well known and socially loved" schoolteacher of Camden in Wilcox County obtained a charter to establish a chapter of the UDC in Alabama, the organization grew rapidly.[27]

The UDC actively pursued a goal of educating white "Anglo-Saxon" children in the tenets of the Lost Cause and rooting out any apostasy in respect of "our heritage."[28] It sponsored essay competitions, influenced the choice of "unbiased" history textbooks, provided teaching scholarships to "aid the lineal descendants of veterans" and, most visibly, provided white schools with Confederate flags and portraits of Robert E. Lee, who was central to Lost Cause mythology, as well as Jefferson Davis and Stonewall Jackson.[29] In 1907 and 1908 the organization was particularly active in portrait distribution since those years marked the centennials of the births of Lee and Davis, respectively. In 1909 Mrs. John A. Gravlee, who was president of both the UDC chapter in Jasper and the school improvement association, presented "a beautiful picture of Jefferson Davis, the *only* President of the Confederacy" to the Jasper Graded School. The *Mountain Eagle* reported on the "appropriate and impressive" presentation at which there were flags and flowers in profusion. A speech was made by Miss Mabel Loveland, "a daughter of a soldier who wore the blue."[30] In Jasper at least, obsequies associated with the Lost Cause did not include a sustained rancor for the North.

The birthday of Robert E. Lee (January 19) was a state holiday in Alabama as well as five other states in the South. As the centenary of Lee's birthday neared, Governor William D. Jelks requested all schools to celebrate the anniversary. Isaac W. Hill responded to the governor's suggestion with "hearty concurrence" and prepared a program that was then promulgated so that "the children of Alabama may learn to emulate the hero of the Southern Confederacy. True to himself, true to his country, true to his God, no man of the nineteenth century is more worthy of our love and admiration." Hill recommended that as many children as possible take part in exercises that included songs, recited testaments to "The Character and Achievements of General Lee," and an address, preferably from a Confederate veteran. Lee's moral and Christian credentials and his dignity in adversity—the indicators of a real hero and exemplar—were the attributes stressed rather than Lee's association with war and defeat.[31]

The celebrations for Robert E. Lee's birthday showed the department of education (in loose partnership with the UDC and also the United Confederate Veterans) subscribing to a specific patriotic tradition born out of "the sting of defeat, the unhealed wounds of oppression and the proud memory of ancestral valor."[32] The rituals associated with the Lost Cause were all devised to celebrate a mythical past in which a pantheon of heroes—the highest products of Old South civilization—appeared to battle the forces of darkness as represented by the Yankees.[33] But the bonding that takes place when people participate in rituals—that which defines what it is to be "us"—members of a certain group—also creates feelings of separateness from those who are "not us"—those who are a special group within the whole.[34]

The assertiveness of the UDC in promoting the Lost Cause and the state's white cultural heritage was consistent with the views of the legislature. It was probably no accident that Alabama's state government began prescribing observance procedures for the South's Confederate heroes shortly after it had consolidated white supremacy as a political doctrine and constitutional fact. Just as black education hardly featured in the early twentieth century's reform campaigns, the likely sensitivity of African American schoolchildren to Confederate symbols, ceremonies, rites, and rituals never seems to have been taken into account. In 1906 there were 1,548 black public schools in Alabama and these had 131,121 enrolled pupils. The inclusion in the Alabama Day program of songs originating in blackface minstrelsy with lyrics in a derogatory "darkie" idiom implies either an official indifference to these pupils or their invisibility in the segregated Jim Crow environment of the time.[35] However, although there was no departmental involvement, black schools may have celebrated their own very different history. The January 1 anniversary of the effective date of the Emancipation Declaration was always scrupulously observed at the State Normal School in Montgomery and many of its graduates went on to teach in black public schools.[36] Similarly, the Alabama Federation of Colored Women's Clubs sponsored celebrations of Frederick Douglass's birthday in some black schools.[37]

In 1909 another bulletin was issued by the department of education providing a program for the celebration of Thomas Jefferson's birthday on April

13. In the bulletin, Harry Cunningham Gunnels addressed "The Teachers of Alabama." He claimed the Sage of Monticello as a Southern hero whose "work for the cause of education, for the uplift of the masses, his statesmanship, his patriotism and prophetic vision have made the South, especially, what it is in an education way."[38] In view of the shortcomings of the South's schools this statement was somewhat perplexing. Yet, while the South had clearly not fulfilled Jefferson's educational vision, he was a figure of such towering importance that celebrating his birthday could only help to associate Alabama with Jefferson's educational ambitions—his "crusade against ignorance"—and also his patriotism and belief in the American enterprise.

~

Just seven months after the formal celebrations for Jefferson's birthday, another bulletin was issued to public schools for the observance of "Alabama Library Day" on November 4, 1909. The date chosen was that upon which the Alabama Library Association had been formed and the celebration can be seen as an accompaniment to the contemporary efforts being made by teachers and the AFWC to develop the private reading habits of schoolchildren. These efforts culminated in the passing of the Rural School Library Bill in April 1911. The Library Day program included songs, testimonials, recitations, poems, declamations, tableaux, and a roll call. When students heard their name they were to respond with the name of a favorite book. The day finished with hymn singing.

The special days designed to honor and celebrate the great men of Southern history or the saints of the Lost Cause had elements of propaganda but Alabama Library Day was pure educational advocacy. It was specifically intended to exert pressure on trustees and school boards to "bring about the introduction of library facilities."[39] Library Day was an example of the state using its authority to make school fund-raising by trustees an obligation in the service of a progressive crusade.

Just six months after Alabama Library Day, schools were sent handsome, illustrated Bird Day Books and asked to observe May 4, 1910, as Alabama Bird Day. Superintendent Gunnels explained to teachers that, in order to appreciate God's gifts, children must have "a love of nature and nature's things" instilled in their minds and hearts. Although the Bird Day Book offered no formal program to be followed, it provided biographical information on the famous Southern ornithologist and artist John James Audubon, stressed the importance of preserving Alabama's wildlife, and praised the "usefulness" of Alabama's state bird, the Yellowhammer, in ridding crops of insects and grubs.[40] Bird Day was, together with Arbor Day, a means by which the state could inculcate conservation awareness. The two days, which were celebrated across

the country, heralded a broadening of the definition of patriotism from a nar-
row focus on liberty under law to citizenship as community spirit.[41] Bird Day
and Arbor Day both helped to amplify messages that were being conveyed by
other means—for example, by the inclusion of agriculture as a compulsory
subject in the rural school curriculum and the encouragement given to students to form agricultural clubs or to cultivate kitchen gardens.[42]

Contemporary educational journals exhorted teachers all over the country
not only to encourage their pupils to venerate the natural world but also to
revive ancient folkways and festivals. A 1904 article in the *Elementary School
Teacher* written by Percival Chubb said in part: "Surely it is worth bringing back,
through the maypole, the Harvest Home and the Yule mumming, that child-
like overflow of joy in the ceremony and ritual which greeted the days of great
memory or the season's turning—seedtime and harvest, summer and winter—
and lavished upon them such a wealth of happy inventiveness and creative activity."[43] Throughout his long career in education and his position as director
of festivals at New York's Ethical Culture School, Chubb promoted the pedagogical value of festivals. He thought they should be at the center of the school
curriculum because they integrated work and play, provided moral education,
and promoted a deeper civic and national patriotism.[44] His ideas found a re-
ceptive audience at a time when new public holidays and patriotic celebrations
were being created to forge a united community from diverse ethnic and minority groups.[45] Similarly, in 1911, Horace G. Brown, of the Worcester Normal
School in Massachusetts, set out guiding principles for school celebrations in
an article in *Education*. In 1912, Constance D'Arcy MacKay published *Patriotic
Plays and Pageants for Young People* in which she advocated a variety of patriotic
exercises.[46]

The ideas of Chubb, Brown, MacKay, and others may have influenced Alabama's educators. In 1913 the department of education published *Alabama's
Country Schools and their Relation to Country Life,* which contained a section
entitled "School Fairs and Pageants." In this bulletin there is an example of
the way in which both state and county were appropriating local school rituals
such as commencements and then organizing pageants or festivals for their
celebration. For example, because after 1907 there were growing numbers of
white county high schools, it was common to hold a county commencement
ceremony for children who had completed their elementary education and were
proceeding to high school or had passed a county examination and were leaving school forever. At the Calhoun County Commencement in May 1913 many
of the county's schools took part. The program included a "May Day Festival" in which children performed rites of May. A king of the May festival was
chosen and, in turn, he selected his queen. Sometimes in these ceremonies,
the May queen was presented with a scepter and had "royal" attendants repre-

senting spring, summer, autumn, and winter. Children sang folksongs, waltzed around a beribboned maypole, and danced old English measures such as the milk maids' dance and the weaver's dance.[47] The Anglo-historicism of the Calhoun commencement reinforced the racial message that Alabama was a white society and its traditions—faux or otherwise—would not be compromised by ethnic or racial considerations. The state's actual racial history and the interests of nearly half its children were completely ignored.

In 1910 the *State Manual of the Course of Study for the Public Elementary Schools of Alabama* addressed teachers with this statement: "The schools are for the home and the state. Do something that will serve the home and elevate the state."[48] This was quite a novel claim as, despite the enacted changes in the first years of the century, schools were still largely run for their community's benefit alone. The statement in the manual indicated that those responsible for educational policy making were starting to envisage public schools as agencies for amplifying governmental social policy.

One hugely important matter of governmental social policy related to the strict regulation or prohibition of the production and sale of alcohol. A statewide prohibition law became effective on January 1, 1909, but was under challenge by liquor interests. On August 19, 1909, the legislature passed *An Act to educate the Children of Alabama on the Evils of Intemperance.* This required children to be taught the evils of intemperance on a day set aside for that purpose. Temperance Day was initially observed on February 18, 1910. The teacher of a school at Fatama in Wilcox County—"a noble teacher who tries to do all the state requires of her"—arranged a program that included recitations such as "The Price of a Drink" and "Alcohol's Curse."[49]

In *Alabama's Country Schools and their Relation to Country Life* (1913) Henry Jones Willingham, then state superintendent, made the case for special observances. He said: "There are really no school holidays in Alabama unless authorized by the county boards." He implied that because terms were so short, holidays would interfere with the work students had to complete. He hoped county boards would encourage the observance of "Special Days" rather than holidays—aside from Christmas and perhaps Thanksgiving.[50] Willingham suggested New Year's Day as an occasion that should "be pre-eminently a day of good resolutions and far-reaching plans." He then listed the days and dates upon which to observe the birthdays of Jefferson Davis, Thomas Jefferson, Robert E. Lee, and George Washington as well as the birthdays of other "great soldiers, statesmen, authors or benefactors." He further suggested that days for observance could include Columbus Day, Bird Day, Memorial Day, Independence Day, Labor Day, and moveable days such as Mardi Gras, Good Friday, and Thanksgiving. He also mentioned Temperance Day and Mother's Day and days "worthy of some appropriate observance [which] are proclaimed from time to time by the governor or state superintendent."[51] In 1914–15 these would include "Clean-Up and School Improvement Day," "Good Roads Day," "Better Health Day," and "Better Farming Day" but these were something of a departure. They represented an all-out effort "to arouse community interest throughout the state with the rural school as the moving agency."[52] This was in accord with the ideas of John Dewey, the educational philosopher who believed schools should play an active role in community life instead of just being places to learn lessons.[53]

Other states were also creating special days to involve school in Progressive causes. For example, Louisiana had a School Health Day and in some states there was "Good Roads Arbor Day," a hybrid that must have taxed the ingenuity of those planning its celebration.[54] Yet Alabama may have been unique in having a suite of days scheduled for each Friday in successive months.

⌁

William Francis Feagin was a professional educator with experience both as a college president and in the department of education where he had held the position of chief clerk between 1907 and November 1913, at which date he was chosen to fill the unexpired term of Henry Jones Willingham as state superintendent. On January 18, 1915, he entered upon his own (elected) term of four years as state superintendent. In both his time as chief clerk and during his appointive years, Feagin had helped to plan and build strong county or local school improvement associations throughout Alabama.[55]

Feagin was convinced that the prolonged lack of success in real educational reform and modernization in Alabama was because reform arguments were not based on "detailed study and statistics." Thus in 1914, Feagin commissioned a comprehensive survey of educational conditions in three counties in "divergent geographical sections of the state that would typify conditions both fairly and generally." The three counties surveyed were Covington, Morgan, and Macon and the results were later published as *An Educational Survey of Three Counties in Alabama*. The work was undertaken by the state's two rural school supervisors, Norman R. Baker and James L. Sibley, and investigated thoroughly a large number of criteria such as the quality and ownership of schoolhouses, the level of certificates held by teachers and their salaries, the session lengths, the attendance levels, the implications of farm tenancy on educational continuity, the nature of supervision, health and sanitary arrangements, and the differences between white and "colored" schools. The *Educational Survey* was just the first of a number of investigations and published reports initiated by Feagin. He also spoke widely on the need to increase educational revenue, on eliminating systemic inequalities, and on the rights of all children to receive schooling. He informed teachers of his goals and ambitions and sent material to newspaper editors suggesting they might use it to help create a climate of support for reform.[56]

Feagin might have been an experienced professional and an exemplary bureaucrat but his work in the development of school improvement associations had taught him that educational modernization would never succeed if imposed by the state on local communities.[57] Thus when Feagin planned the four special days—"not holidays but *occasions*" he intended that they would attract to local schools not just teachers, students, trustees, parents, and guardians but all who might be interested.[58] At this time only about 60 percent of Alabama's school-aged children were enrolled in schools and only about 63 percent of these were in average attendance.[59] Feagin hoped to "enlarge the sphere of the school" through "community organization."[60]

Feagin believed the special days, which involved black schools as well as white, could provide "unmistakable evidence that teachers, pupils and parents are thinking as never before of the place which the school should fill in the community, and the part that they should have in helping the school to do its work."[61] Rural people had always had a view of the place their schools should fill in the community but Feagin wanted them to adopt a different perspective.

Feagin's programs for his special days were consistent with what is often referred to as "civil religion." This is the nondenominational expression of religious piety in official observances—a piety that rests on the assumption of the overarching guidance of the state by a transcendent deity.[62] The civil religion reflected in the special day observance programs might not have been denominational but it was unambiguously Christianity—and largely a Protestant version thereof. This would have seemed perfectly normal in Alabama, which, in 1900, was 97 percent Protestant. In 1906 a religious census showed that Baptists and Methodists accounted for three of every four adult church members.[63] All the special day programs included Bible readings, hymns, prayers, and the recitation of creeds.

"Clean-up and School Improvement Day" (held first on October 30, 1914, and the following year on December 10) had a merry, jamboree-like quality involving the whole neighborhood in cooperative endeavor. A morning of hymns, community singing, and talks on topics such as "What the school should do for the community" and "What the community should do for the school" was followed by an afternoon of repair and maintenance activities.[64] Yet, according to one newspaper editor the day had a higher purpose: "Clean-up Day has a broad meaning. In a spiritual sense we can 'rise on stepping stones of our dead selves.'"[65]

The bulletin issued for "Good Roads Day" (Friday, January 15, 1915) was part a consciousness-raising document, part information handbook for improving the state's roads, and part an observance program. Each page was headed with a newly minted aphorism such as "Mud roads belong to the log-cabin days, and log-cabin days belong to the past" and "A lesson in civic pride and righteousness can also be taught from good roads." The Good Roads Day program started with a hymn and included devotional exercises to be led by a pastor whose role was to explain the effects of good roads on the school and church life of the community. Children recited poems about the value of good roads to farmers and studied "how to make a split-log drag."[66]

The next two special days were "Better Health Day" (Friday, February 12, 1915) and "Better Farming Day" (Friday, March 12, 1915). As with that issued for Good Roads Day, the bulletins issued for these two days sought to make teachers, pupils, and parents aware that the school existed in an improvable environment and it was their duty to undertake such improvement.

The "Better Health Day" bulletin was instructional—it included information about the causes of typhoid and hookworm disease and how to minimize the risk of contracting them, how to improve sanitation, ventilation, and lighting, and how to secure an uncontaminated water supply. It was part political in that it urged support for health taxes. It included poems and a creed for recitation and also ominously warned: "Our schools are still cursed with the doctrine that teaches people to neglect their bodies and even to mortify the flesh, in order to gain spiritual control and to subdue their passions."[67]

In the Better Farming Day bulletin Feagin explained that he wanted local communities to witness how the school could stimulate farming activities through theoretical and practical instruction and also aid "the social and economic elevation of farm life."[68] The program provided for a reading from the New Testament (the parable of the sower from The Gospel According to St. Matthew), songs, recitations, declamations ("The Ten Commandments of Agriculture" by ten boys), and "The Farmer's Creed." There were to be talks about agricultural clubs or on topics such as "how to build up worn-out soil" or "how I care for my pig." Those attending were assured that better farming methods would allow them to proclaim (in biblical phrasing): "Now abideth Increased Production, Business Methods and Organization; but the GREATEST of these is ORGANIZATION."[69]

～

In the published observance programs for the special days were various creeds for recitation, declamation, memorization, and/or internalization by teachers and students. These included "The School Teacher's Creed," "The Country Boy's Creed," "The Farmer's Creed," "My Civic Creed," "Our Creed," and "My Health Creed."[70] In their incantatory repetition of "I believe" it is possible to discern in these creeds a trace of, for example, the Apostles' Creed and thus, by implication, an integrated set of convictions validating a teacher's vocation or a child's attachment to rural life. Yet Alabama's churches were mostly nonliturgical, even anti-credal, so the inclusion of creeds was not so much a use of familiar ritual for a new purpose as it was the use of an existing formulary upon which to build a new ethos.

There was something of a contemporary vogue for such creeds. The "School Teacher's Creed" (1901) and "The Country Boy's Creed" (1912) were written by Edwin Osgood Grover, a popular poet. They were first published in *Rural Manhood*, a YMCA journal. "The School Teacher's Creed" was reprinted as "A Teacher's Creed" in a number of Alabama's school publications. Some of the invented creeds were a mixed bag. "The Farmer's Creed" appeared in the bulletin issued in 1915 for "Better Farming Day." Children declaimed ten statements of belief, including "I believe in a country school that prepares for country life, and in a country church that teaches its people to love deeply and live honorably." This has a certain psalmodic resonance but the creed also had children stating their belief in the value of dead weeds, the importance of not slacking when working out their road tax, and the superiority of hundred-bushel corn.[71] Similarly, when declaiming "My Health Creed" children asserted "I believe my body and good health are sacred," thus recalling St Paul's counsel that the body is the temple of the Holy Ghost.[72] On the strength of this belief they made a list of promises such as "I will not put pins or money in my mouth" or "I will use a toothbrush—if I can get one."[73] "Our Creed" was written by John Herbert Phillips, the superintendent of Birmingham's school system who may have wanted to make an Alabamian contribution to the accumulating litany. It was so ambitiously metaphysical that it is unlikely to have meant much to young teachers. It expressed beliefs in the PAST, the PRESENT, and the FUTURE: "WE BELIEVE IN THE FUTURE and in the Suns and Stars that are yet to shine upon the Earth, to hasten the realization of the Divine Purpose in the world. We believe in Faith and Hope as the noblest senses of the soul and in Love as the very essence of the Primal Energy whose creative fiat, 'Let there be Light,' is silently through the ages evolving the Eternal Kingdom of the Spirit."[74]

~

When the revised *State Manual of the Course of Study for the Public Elementary Schools of Alabama* was issued in 1913, it included a section entitled "The School As a Socializing Agency" by Norman R. Baker.[75] Prefiguring some of William F. Feagin's ideas and concerns, Baker advised teachers that "the school must forestall the arrest of social development caused by the limitations of the community." He then went on to enumerate a long list of modern developments by which the community might be enlarged. Baker next considered all the "socializing agencies" contributing influence to a community such as libraries and agricultural clubs (direct agencies) and the Church, Sunday School, and Boy Scout groups (indirect agencies). Baker said "play is difficult to classify . . . but is one of the richest and best factors in the socialization of children."[76]

Baker was correct, but when he proceeded to list and codify games, to suggest those to be encouraged, to advise teachers on "games of imitation" and how they might "create interest for boys," and to even suggest a reading list of books such as *What to do at Recess* and *Education by Plays and Games*, he was seeking to impose upon a world of improvisation and invention, a standardized set of games and rules.[77] By so doing he was thus, indirectly, imposing the imprimatur of the state on the games to be played. Some of the games Baker suggested included croquet, baseball, basketball, tennis—all activities that anticipated the gymnasium, the special court, the interschool competition, and the public spectatorship of the later twentieth century.[78]

The informal learning provided by organized games might provide "mental alertness and physical development" but the games themselves were rather different from play as folkway or as rituals confirming local relationships, cultural traditions, and neighborhood differences. Baker's ideas indicated his appreciation of local games but a lack of insight about the implications of their appropriation and standardization.

~

In the history of Alabama's public education system up to 1915, prominence is usually given to the various constraints of the state constitution on school funding, the wretched provisions for black schools, the slowness of reform on matters such as compulsory attendance, and the efforts made to secure an adequate and reliable source of recurring revenue. These factors were, of course, all critically important, but the ceremonial inventions that helped parents and children to broaden their horizons and to develop a new civic consciousness, assisted to create a climate in which fiscal, constitutional, and legislative change were more likely to be supported. This civic consciousness also helped to dilute the strength of localism.

8
Black Schools in a Dual System

Until 1891 Alabama's black public schools were funded, or underfunded, in ways not dissimilar to the ways in which white public schools were funded. Black communities, like white communities, faced difficulties in acquiring land for schoolhouses, often having to rely on sympathetic farmers. They had to build and equip their schoolhouses at their own expense or rely on private funds or donations. Black teachers, like their white counterparts, were answerable to their patrons and neighbors for the ways in which they conducted their schools.

The data collected by Alabama's Department of Education in the nineteenth century are not always reliable, but they show that during the scholastic year ending September 30, 1875, teachers of black public schools were actually paid more than the teachers of white public schools.[1] Fifteen years later at the end of the 1890 scholastic year, the total number of black public schools taught in the state was 2,174 of which 753 (more than a third) were in the Black Belt. In this same year, of all the children enrolled in public schools, slightly more black children actually attended than did white children (61.82 percent versus 58.87 percent). The average length of the black school term approximated that of the white school term (sixty-nine days) and the average monthly pay of teachers of black schools was only a dollar less than the average monthly pay of teachers of white schools. In twenty-nine counties the teachers of black schools were paid more than the teachers of white schools.[2]

However, these data and their implications must be treated with great care, even skepticism. Being part of a racially bifurcated system, claims of similarity between Alabama's black and white schools cannot go very far. Also, while white communities trusted the educational arrangements and cultural traditions of localism and wished to preserve them against the gravitational pull of modernization, black communities merely struggled to be accorded basic racial justice.[3] They wanted schools that would provide their children with the skills needed to pursue educational and social betterment without white circumscription. Their ambitions were an expression of what the black intellectual and writer W.E.B. Du Bois called "the souls of black folk." By this he meant not only the unique culture of black people and their attribution of value to this culture (seen, for example, in their post-emancipation preference for their own churches), but also their struggle for recognition by and/or coexistence with white America.[4] Yet white officialdom was often unsympathetic to the idea of black education and, more frequently still, was hostile on the subject of the source of school funds—taxes paid by white people.

Few county superintendents exhibited much insight into the circumstances of black life or the economic sacrifice necessary to spare children from agricultural labor, particularly cotton production. Fluctuations in cotton prices meant survival itself was precarious. Irregular attendance—even for a three-month term—was inevitable. In 1875 Sumter County's superintendent, Michael C. Kinnard, demonstrated such lack of insight. He reported that "colored" people would not build schoolhouses but, if helped by whites, might acquire a church building for school purposes. Some of these schools had between sixty and a hundred students but only one teacher who was unable to teach so many. He carped that black patrons were unwilling to supplement or "to board the teacher when the state plays the entire tuition."[5]

Kinnard's comments do not suggest he had given much thought to the causes of the circumstances depicted. He may never even have visited a black school. In 1880 Booker T. Washington, principal of the famous Tuskegee Institute, visited a log-cabin school somewhere in Alabama. He saw five pupils trying to study from a single book. "Two of these, on the front seat, were using the book between them; behind these were two others peeping over the shoulder of the first two, and behind the four was a fifth little fellow who was peeping over the shoulders of all four."[6]

The precariousness of survival in the state's agricultural economy and the sacrifice necessary for black children to attend school was recalled by William Holtzclaw. From the age of nine he had to work in the fields taking turns at the plow with his brother. The two boys attended school on alternate days. "What he learned on his school day he taught me at night and I did the same for him. In this way we each got a month of schooling."

White superintendents also seemed blind to the isolation of black teachers and unsympathetic to their special difficulty—their wistful, but largely futile, desire for inclusion. In 1878 Bosun Roughton, a former Georgia slave who was teaching at Choctaw Corner in Clarke County, wrote to the state superintendent requesting a copy of the "revised code of this state." He described the area where he was living as "a backwoods part of the country and to me its quite desolate as I have no relations in this state. There is but little intelligence realised among the colored race in this section of hills and piney woods." He believed the political manipulation of black people would end if they were literate.[7]

Black public schools not only existed within a system administered by sometimes obtuse, sometimes willfully self-deceptive and frequently unsympathetic white superintendents at the township, county, and state levels, but their pupils were taught within a white pedagogical framework and against a background of racial and caste prejudice.[8] Some white people thought their black fellow citizens were "members of a child-race grown-up in body and physical passions, weak in foresight, self-control and character"—characteristics that had been tempered by slavery—who needed the discipline of work rather than schooling. Furthermore, as black people were destined for a lifetime of agricultural labor, then too much schooling would be pointless and might "spoil" them. The more virulent critics of black education implied it would lead to a bloody war between the races. Besides, according to the *Marengo Democrat*, "as whites paid practically all the taxes, so the Negroes had only the right to a pauper's pittance."[9]

After the 1891 apportionment provisions of the school law were implemented, any resemblances between the schooling experiences of black and white children or the circumstances of teachers and school facilities quickly faded. As funds that had previously been allocated to black students were diverted to whites the effects were dramatic, especially in the Black Belt. In the scholastic year ending September 30, 1890, Wilcox County's per capita educational expenditure was $1.02 per white child and $0.92 per black child.[10] In 1907, the respective expenditures were $10.50 per white child but only $0.37 per black child. In 1903, Lowndes County was spending $13.00 on each white child for every $1.00 it spent on a black child. In 1912 this difference had widened even further with $33.40 being spent on each white child for every $1.00 spent per black child.[11] The ratios were similar in adjoining Butler County. One of Butler's former superintendents attacked the injustices that he said were being perpetrated by people from the same churches seeking Christian converts in China and Africa.[12] In Chambers County, where Alabama borders Georgia, black teachers earned 60 percent less than their white counterparts in 1901.

Such egregious discrimination did not go unprotested by those who were its victims. In 1898, Peter Lewis and John Hart, two black men from Bullock County, wrote to the state governor, Joseph Johnston. They drew the governor's attention to the fact that in several townships there were "from 200 to 300 negro children to about 7 or 8 white children. And the negro children don't get 1/2 of the revenue." Johnston did nothing.[13]

In 1908 the total value of all the equipment in Alabama's public schools was only $262,218 but the black share of this was just $21,825 (about 8 percent). This was despite the fact that approximately 45 percent of the school-aged population was black. Of the 383 libraries in public schools, pupils in black schools had access to twenty-five (only just over 6 percent).[14]

What these figures all confirm is that "white people had it hard and black people had it harder because what are the table-scraps of nothing?"[15] Yet, in the face of the precipitous decline in funding for their schools, black communities still did not yield their educational ambitions—nor their pleas for justice.

Charles Octavius Boothe (1845–1924) was a prominent black Baptist preacher, founding pastor of Dexter Avenue Baptist Church, and an apostle of "uplift"— self-directed black social betterment—as a stratagem for white acceptance and political responsibility. In August 1901 Boothe wrote to John William Abercrombie imploring him for "efficient educational facilities for the *masses* of the colored people." Boothe, who had been a public schoolteacher himself, pointed out that common schools were the "center of the bulk of human life" and, though funding them properly would involve "vast expenditures upon the part of the state" the losses incurred from "ignorance, shiftlessness and criminality" would be even greater.[16] Abercrombie was not much interested in equity. In 1906 he said that, because they were inadequate, any available educational funds "should go to the dominant race."[17]

In 1907, the *Colored Alabamian,* a black newspaper published in Montgomery, commented angrily on a just-released report by the superintendent of that city's schools. This bragged that the city had recently provided for its white children ten "large, nicely constructed, brick buildings well equipped for school purposes." This provision was more than twice that made for the city's black children whose schools were smaller and badly equipped. The newspaper asked for help "in the great and heroic effort we are making for our uplift." It said, "We do not ask for any special favors. All we ask for is 'Equal Rights' before the law and common justice in educational affairs."[18]

In 1899—eight years after the changes to funds apportionment—Bullock County's Thomas A. Craven advised: "The colored people are almost destitute of schoolhouses. Many of their schools are carried on in churches."[19] Craven was being condemnatory because he believed too many churches were being built and too few schoolhouses. Although churches were very far from suitable for educational purposes, they were at least closely related to the lives of those who used them. They did not distance children spatially from other aspects of their daily existence. In fact, churches associated black children with their race's greatest consolation—religion. The church was where men and women were able to sustain each other in the face of their misfortunes. A black Alabamian folk song asserted:

If-a 'ligion wuz er thing that money could buy,
The rich would live and the po' would die.
I'm so glad things jes' like dis,
Dere's 'nother good chance for the po' coon yet.[20]

Church and school were often so closely aligned that the functional boundaries were not always clear. In 1893, a visitor to a service held at Tilden in Dallas County noted of the several ministers who were preaching that "their texts were as often taken from Webster's blue-back speller as from the Bible." Sometimes teacher and preacher were one and the same. In Coffee County, the first black man to receive a teaching certificate was a preacher named Charley Larkins.[21] Often the only way to survive as a rural teacher was to combine teaching with another occupation. Black teachers were also farmers, laborers, preachers, and sometimes all of these.[22]

The apportionment law was not the only blow to the overall support for black public schooling. From 1887 the Peabody Education Fund had been providing financial support for teacher training in Alabama by making grants to normal schools, including black normal schools, and funding scholarships to these schools.[23] It also provided funds for week-long teachers' institutes that were matched in part with state funds—for example, in 1888 a Peabody grant of $1,000 was matched with $500 granted by the Alabama assembly.[24] In 1895 the Peabody Fund decided to allocate all of its teacher training funds to normal schools alone. This cut off one important forum black teachers had for developing their professional consciousness.[25]

Black teachers with aspirations for betterment still conscientiously attended the two-day institutes held throughout the year and the longer institutes supported with a state appropriation after 1911. In 1900, Greene County's John G. Apsey reported he had held two teachers' institutes for "colored" teachers and had succeeded better with these than with those for the white teachers whose "interest was hard to keep up" because the white population was so widely scattered.[26] But even well-intentioned and conscientious teachers and parents could not overcome the shortcomings of black schools, which established "a curriculum in low expectations."[27]

In the absence of compulsion, there were black parents, as there were white parents, who did not see the point of attending school at all or could not spare their children's labor. Also the postbellum fervor for schooling had somewhat waned in later generations—at least in rural areas. Verse Lee Johnson, who should have been in school in the 1920s when attendance was supposed to be compulsory, recalled: "Our daddy didn't send us to school, so aint none of us older chilluns can read and write. . . . When us older ones got big enough to work, Papa kept us in the fields. . . . I learned nothing out of a book."[28]

~

In any review of the influences that shaped Alabama's black public schools, the role of black private or denominational schools and state-subsidized secondary or normal schools such as the Tuskegee Institute (which was also heavily subsidized by the John F. Slater [philanthropic] Fund) cannot be overlooked. This is because the nature of their influence was direct. The private schools trained teachers for the public system and, upon the completion of their studies, found them placements. These teachers took up their positions having imbibed a social vision that extended far beyond the schoolhouse. They had been taught the local school could be made an agency for the transformation of rural life and "for the moral, religious and physical status of the people immediately touching it [the school]."[29]

In the late 1880s and 1890s when ambitious but poor black students—whose only education had been in rural public schools—heard about the Tuskegee Institute they seem to have regarded it as a beacon of educational hope. In 1887 William J. Edwards sent for a prospectus after hearing about the institute's work at a revival. Two years later, William H. Holtzclaw came across a copy of the *Tuskegee Student,* which was advertising student vacancies. He felt this was "providential."[30]

Booker T. Washington's legacy is contested and contentious in part because he was a complex and enigmatic person who wore different masks for different publics in a great number of compartmentalized worlds.[31] For much of the twentieth century Washington was regarded as an obedient accommodationist whose views suited white supremacists. Recently, however, his reputation has been reappraised. Robert J. Norrell is one historian who believes Washington's policies were nothing less than an existential necessity in the racial climate of his era.[32]

If not reactionary, Washington's ideas about rural life were highly conservative. They informed the development of what he considered to be an appropriate—practical—curriculum at the Tuskegee Institute. This was largely "non-literary" or anti-intellectual, and involved "industrial training" a somewhat imprecise and malleable term that embraced not just vocational skills but a taught value system of thrift, duty, hard work, and self-discipline. It was based on the curriculum at Virginia's Hampton Institute where Washington had studied.[33]

While the impact of Washington's educational ideas may have helped to circumscribe black occupational options, to confine black people to a separate and inevitably subordinate economic sphere and to perpetuate traditional black roles in rural communities, his own objectives were always projected positively as those of a realist operating in a white-dominated world. Although he had trenchant critics, such as W. E. B. Du Bois, Washington did inspire black ambition in Alabama. In 1882 he organized the first statewide professional group for black teachers—the Alabama State Teachers' Association (ASTA). Also, in his role as a sort of racial statesman, he helped shape the opinions of Alabama's white educationists and the philanthropists of the Southern education movement.[34]

In 1901 one hundred and fourteen graduates of the Tuskegee Institute's normal department were involved in teaching.[35] Some, including Edwards and Holtzclaw, so thoroughly absorbed Washington's ethos and the industrial curriculum he espoused that they started their own "little Tuskegees."[36] As they became established, some of the small private black schools were favorably commented upon by county superintendents—partly because they were offering educational opportunities to black students where few others existed. They thus came to the notice of state officeholders such as John William Abercrombie. In 1900, John Mack Jones, the superintendent of education for Wilcox County and also a farmer, wrote in his annual report to the state superintendent that he "desired to make special mention of three colored schools and their teachers in our county." One of these schools was the Snow Hill Colored Literary and Industrial Institute. Jones described the teachers as "highly educated" and added in a revelatory comment: "They seem to be on the order of Booker Washington, teaching their race politeness, respect for the white race, and not antagonism. We think it not amiss to encourage their schools."[37]

Jones's suggestion that these schools be "encouraged" may have been influenced further by the fact that Ransom O. Simpson—a former Confederate cavalryman, prominent landlord, store owner, and Methodist Sunday School superintendent—had extended major support to Edwards's school by endowing it with more than one hundred acres of land and by providing Edwards with business and other advice.[38] The institute thus had the imprimatur of white approval from someone representing the local power structure in the Furman/Snow Hill area of Wilcox County. Such approval was often a necessary precondition for the survival and growth of black schools even if limiting the sorts of schools they would be.

During the 1890s, the *Wilcox Progress* had an occasional series called "Rambles in Old Wilcox." This covered matters of interest from each of the county's villages and provided a sort of inventory of their socioeconomic vitality. As well, the doings of local people, including teachers, were noted. In October 1896, five years after local discretion was granted to township superintendents in apportioning school funds, the "Rambler" commented that a number of Wilcox's villages had "a nice new two-story schoolhouse." Black schools, including Edwards's private Snow Hill Institute, might be favorably regarded by the county superintendent (Jones) but they did not receive a single comment in this "state of the county" roundup.[39] They were apparently "mere objects in the landscape."[40]

Washington believed this invisibility could be reversed if rural schools were made "the center of Negro rural life" and followed the curriculum he espoused.[41] The Snow Hill Institute's own goals were "to have its graduates influence the people to build schoolhouses where needed, to extend the school term, and by arousing public interest, to assist in bringing about the reforms essential to economic and upright living."[42]

Positively expressed goals and local role models such as Edwards and the teachers he trained were critically important for black parents and children—especially at a time when race relations were reaching a nadir and the whole South was disenfranchising its black citizens. Several historians, including Horace Mann Bond and James D. Anderson, have attributed to disenfranchisement the dramatic worsening of discrimination against black schools in the ensuing era of Progressive social reform. Disenfranchisement increased the incentive for county governments to levy school taxes because they were freer to spend these on their own white schools.[43]

⟿

Alabama's own new constitution adopted in 1901 made it clear that future state responsibility for public education would be almost entirely directed toward white children. Article XIV, Section 256 specified that the public school fund should be "so apportioned to the schools in the districts or townships in the counties as to provide, as nearly as practicable, school terms of equal duration in such school districts or townships."[44] These were weasel words whose intent was the same as that of the 1891 School Law regarding funding apportionments.

After the constitution was adopted, Joseph B. Graham, who had chaired the committee on education at the constitutional convention and in 1902 would become the Southern Education Board's field agent for Alabama, asserted that the new organic law was free from discrimination. He said it "had been framed from a spontaneous philanthropy too generous to take advantage of the poor, and a sense of right and humanity too proud to wrong an inferior race."[45]

Graham seemed quickly to have forgotten the minority report of the education committee he had chaired. This had advocated county superintendents being permitted to set up two kinds of school districts—black and white—in which residents could vote for property taxes to be levied on racial lines. This would have segregated all tax revenues according to the race of the taxpayer.[46]

Since emancipation, the "inferior race"—as Joseph B. Graham termed those of African descent—had believed it would achieve full participation in American society via politics and education. While the new constitution enshrined white supremacy thus blocking black political participation, it did not eliminate black schools from the public education system.

Despite growing discrepancies between white and black schools according to every measure of educational effectiveness, black public schools still somehow managed to survive. In his annual report for 1909, the state superintendent claimed the total number of black schools in Alabama had increased by 6 percent and that the number of unsuitable buildings being used as schoolhouses, such as churches, had decreased by 13 percent. He further stated that the total value of the schoolhouses in which schools were being taught was "$375,000 for the negroes" and that this was "an increase of $71,625 on the value reported previously." This same report revealed that all the indicators of progress given by the state superintendent for black schools—expenditure, schoolhouse numbers and valuations, term lengths, teacher qualifications—were significantly poorer than those given for white schools.[47] This is hardly surprising given only 12 percent of school funds went to black schools and these were in no one's special care. Yet, if only barely perceptible, there were some improvements to report.

While fragile gains can be seen when aggregated in state reports, they were less easy to discern in struggling rural areas. In the early years of the century, Ned Cobb lived in Tallapoosa County and had several children of school age who attended the local black school. They might be there for just two or three or perhaps six weeks when it would abruptly close owing to insufficient funds. Cobb said, "Mighty little we got from the state government. That money was coming here through white hands and they was half concerned with keeping colored children out of school."[48]

Cobb was convinced the distribution of school moneys was calibrated with the shifting needs of white planters for labor. This is consistent with the interpretations of black historians. W. E. B. Du Bois believed that "enforced ignorance" was "one of the inevitable expedients for fastening serfdom on the country Negro." James D. Anderson has argued that the discriminatory funding arrangements were consistent with a white supremacist agenda bent on preserving a racially segmented labor market in which blacks were subordi-

14. One-Teacher "Colored" School, Lowndes County, circa 1910. Courtesy Alabama Department of Archives and History, Montgomery, Alabama.

nate. Certainly, one outcome of the discriminatory funding in Alabama was the preservation of an all-too-familiar socioeconomic rural landscape in which whites exerted control and black farmers and tenants knew their "place" and were obliged to recognize their economic fealty.[49]

∽

In 1904, Anna T. Jeanes, an elderly and exceedingly wealthy Quaker woman who lived in Philadelphia, decided she wanted to assist "the poor little Negro cabin one-teacher rural schools." Initial grants of $10,000 were made respectively to Hampton Institute in Virginia and to Tuskegee Institute for extension work in their adjacent localities. In 1905 Miss Jeanes made a further benefaction of $200,000 to the General Education Board stipulating that the interest from this sum be used "on behalf of Negro schools." Two years later in 1907, the year of her death, she set aside $1,000,000 to establish a fund she wished to be known as "The Fund for Rudimentary Schools for Southern Negroes" and the income to be devoted "to the sole purpose of assisting in the Southern United States, community, country and rural schools for the great class of Negroes to whom the small rural and community schools are alone available."[50] Thus was born the Anna T. Jeanes Foundation, which provided a catalyst for change in Alabama's black rural schools.

15. Anna T. Jeanes. Charles W. Dabney, *Universal Education in the South*, vol. 1 (New York: Arno Press and the New York *Times*, 1936), 446.

Dr. James Hardy Dillard, a Virginian patrician and former classics professor, was appointed president of the Jeanes Foundation and its trustees included luminaries such as Andrew Carnegie, William Howard Taft, George Foster Peabody, Booker T. Washington, and the Reverend Dr. Hollis Burke Frissell, the president of Hampton Institute.[51] Some of these men had connections with the Southern education movement that had made the "forgotten" poor white child the priority for philanthropic and educational attention. This might have been ominous but, nonetheless, Miss Jeanes's objectives were largely realized.

Dr. Dillard found a model for the school assistance envisaged by Miss Jeanes in Henrico County, Virginia. One of that county's black teachers, Virginia Estelle Randolph, had formed a school improvement league and then leveraged the interest this aroused to transform thoroughly her "little wayside school." By so doing she had also assisted her local community to "live better, to do their work with more skill and intelligence and to do it in the spirit of neighborliness."[52] Dillard decided the Jeanes Foundation would support the "industrial work of Henrico County" by funding two supervisors. Randolph became the first Jeanes "supervising industrial teacher" or simply "Jeanes teacher."[53]

In 1909 the *Citizen-Examiner* printed in Lowndes County reported: "the negroes of the Clio neighborhood [in Barbour County] have received a large donation from the Jeames [*sic*] Fund for the promotion of education in the common schools."[54] The first official reference to Jeanes teachers in Alabama is in a 1913 report to the state superintendent by James Longstreet Sibley, state supervisor of elementary rural colored schools. This hybrid public/private position was funded by the General Education Board but was answerable to the state superintendent of education. Sibley had attracted the attention of Henry J. Willingham (state superintendent, 1911–1914) when Sibley was a student teacher at the State Normal College at Jacksonville. Sibley was said to have "broad views on the training of primitive peoples" and to know how to overcome interracial prejudices and conflict.[55]

By 1913 there were sixteen Jeanes teachers working in seventeen of Alabama's counties.[56] In the year ending September 30, 1916, there were twenty-seven teachers in twenty-three counties, many of whom had been trained at the Tuskegee Institute. They were selected by the state supervisor of elementary rural colored schools (Sibley) and were under his overall supervision though employed by county boards of education.[57] Eventually the counties where they were located started contributing something toward their salary costs.[58]

Most of Alabama's Jeanes teachers were women. James Sibley's official reports as well as his correspondence indicate he strongly believed that "on the whole, women make better supervising industrial teachers than men." This was "owing to their ability to reach the homes of the children."[59] In 1914 he wrote to Dr. Dillard urging him to allocate sufficient funds to ensure the retention of a Mrs. Waterfield, who was the Jeanes teacher in Lowndes County. She had done "such good work this year that she should be kept at a salary of $50.00 per month for at least nine months."[60] Dillard shared Sibley's opinion of women's abilities and claimed "we never had a man on the list that measured up to the work which women accomplish."[61]

Black women brought to the Jeanes teacher's role a self-assurance and authority derived from their domestic status as housekeepers and homemakers. In turn, the role offered black women a number of tangible advantages. The position was adequately paid and fairly secure. As teachers became more experienced they were allowed a degree of latitude as to how they performed their duties, thus allowing opportunities for job enlargement and development. They were a point of contact with a previously indifferent white officialdom whose members, even when well intentioned, were usually cautious not to upset their white constituency. "Our county superintendent is handicapped on account of the intense prejudice against negro schools in this [Dale] county," a white woman wrote to Sibley in 1913.[62]

Since 1891 black schools had not only received a pitiful portion of the school fund, but they were taught by ill-trained and often ignorant teachers who, of necessity, had to adapt for the special needs of their pupils a curriculum designed for white children. Under the county superintendent's general guidance, Jeanes teachers showed the instructors of rural schools how they could make the basic branches of the school curriculum "part of an interested, alert and active response to the whole environment."[63]

The Jeanes teachers generally conducted teaching demonstrations in the winter. In summer they organized "Home-Makers' Clubs" at which girls learned about the necessity of thrift, of how to maintain kitchen gardens in order to achieve food self-sufficiency, of sanitation, of fruit canning methods, of the improvement of homes, of raising crops, and of animal husbandry. Boys were taught manual skills and farming techniques and were encouraged to form agricultural clubs.

Jeanes teachers also assisted with the formation of school improvement associations, which, in turn, enhanced the conditions under which children were taught and made schools a center for black social life. Some of the direct dividends of such aroused interest were that more patrons were willing to pay tuition supplements. This enabled school sessions to be extended. Also, whole communities took part in activities to raise funds for new school buildings and equipment such as patent desks, for acquiring property, for holding adult night schools, and for constructing sanitary lavatories.[64] A Jeanes teacher from Colbert County reported proudly that the community activities she had arranged created more interest "than in anything before—even a funeral." This somewhat arresting comparison suggests not only the benefits to be derived from useful communal enterprise but also the social limitations of quotidian black life.[65]

In 1914 the Jeanes teacher in Mobile County was Miss Olegra Boyd. A glimpse into her role can be gained from a letter that she wrote to James Sibley, who had chided her for the sin of using the term "Canning Club" in her formal reports when the proper term was "Home-makers' Club" and also for spending too much of her time at too few schools.[66] Miss Boyd was defensive, stood her ground, and demonstrated her ambition and application. She said she had successfully supervised all the black schools in the county though this had meant her being away from home for weeks at a time and working on Saturdays and Sundays. She had a conducted a teachers' class each month and had overseen the planting and cultivation of kitchen gardens in which "tomatoes were growing nicely." She told Sibley she was "willing to do anything to make Mobile County schools a success."[67]

In a department of education bulletin published in 1913—*Alabama's Country Schools and their Relation to Country Life*—several pages were devoted to corn and canning clubs and the benefits to be derived from these by students. Instructions were given on how to ship corn to fairs for exhibition purposes.[68] When the work of black students was selected for display at county fairs and when black students took off prizes—as, for example, did Willie Fort when he won $15 at the 1916 Macon County Fair for raising "the best Hampshire boar"—these achievements carried the implicit assertion that children from schools in black communities had just as much right as those from white communities to participate fully in the state's education system. At Dadeville in Tallapoosa County "many [white] ladies and schoolchildren" spoke encouragingly of the high quality of the work "and seemed surprised to know such was being done in the Negro schools of the county."[69]

The items made by black schoolgirls and exhibited at county fairs typically included clothing, intricately patterned quilts, rag rugs, hats made from pine needles and corn shucks, as well as baskets made from split white-oak and willow. Some of the basket-making techniques represented a folk tradition believed to be African in origin.[70] Thus the school craft-work had a double value. It validated black competence and culture to white society and showed black students how to improvise from materials at hand so as to transcend their circumstances. A departmental bulletin reported that two black sisters—Lottie and Daisy Tarver of Russell County—had made enough money from selling hats they had made in Home-makers' Clubs to pay for all their own clothing for a year.[71]

The sorts of improvisations validated by the Jeanes teachers were remembered by Tommie Manley, who grew up in Bullock County at this time. His family slept on mattresses made by stuffing ticks with the crowfoot grass that sprouted in the fields after a frost; other families stuffed theirs with corn shucks. Women made sheets out of flour bags and clothes from guano or feed sacks. This practice continued for as long as there was rural poverty or hardship. During the Great Depression of the 1930s children in school could discern the faint pentimento of a stencilled fertilizer number such as 6-8-4 or 7-10-3 on the backs of their fellow pupils' dyed sacking shirts.[72]

The Anna T. Jeanes Foundation and the teachers whose costs it funded allowed many struggling black communities—gripped by circumstances of poverty and racial prejudice—to shape their educational priorities while remaining within the state system. If any of Alabama's Jeanes teachers in this period encountered resistance to their advice or were resented as outsiders, no evidence survives. Hattie J. Huckabee, the "Special Agent" who coordinated the summer work in twenty-five counties, recalled: "Every house I went into was home to me. I went in not as a guest of honor, but as one of the family circle to serve in whatever way I could and thus I was received and welcomed."[73]

$\sim$

In 1912 Julius Rosenwald, who was president of the retailing giant, Sears Roebuck, decided to do something about remedying the deplorable state of black schoolhouses.[74] The year before, Rosenwald had become a trustee of the Tuskegee Institute and shortly thereafter made a substantial grant of $25,000 to Booker T. Washington to be distributed by him to some of the offshoots of that institute. Upon special request, Washington was authorized to use $2,100 of this sum to build six black rural schoolhouses. Pleased by the results of this building program, on August 1, 1914, Rosenwald agreed to provide a further $30,000 to aid the construction of about one hundred schoolhouses in designated counties of Alabama. Not more than $350 was to be allocated to any one school and these were to be owned and operated by the county as part of the public system. By February 22, 1916, Alabama had seventy-nine new black schoolhouses built as model schools on plans developed at Tuskegee.[75]

Rosenwald was Jewish and his philanthropic strategy was underpinned by the religious injunction to do "tzedakah"—an act of righteousness and justice to those less fortunate than oneself. Yet he was also committed to a philosophy of self-help. He was not interested in just making grants for building schoolhouses but would match funds, either fully or in part, raised from within a community. Rosenwald believed the schools should act as a stimulus for permanent support by the proper authorities. They would engender "enlightened progress."[76]

The first Rosenwald school in Alabama was built in 1914 at Loachapoka in Lee County at a cost of $942. Nearly 30 percent of this amount was contributed by the local black community—Lee's population was about 60 percent black at this time. Local whites donated $360 and Rosenwald contributed $300.[77] All subsequent schools were the result of substantial black contributions—in cash, in land, in materials, and in labor or "sweat equity."[78]

Despite being known ever afterward as "Rosenwald Schools" these schoolhouses were testaments to enterprising black communities and their educational aspirations. The Rosenwald Fund stipulated that the schoolhouses must be built on a lot of at least two acres so there could be a school garden as well as playground space. The buildings themselves had large windows, so as to maximize sunlight and ventilation. Interior walls were painted to reduce glare. Moveable partitions were installed between large classrooms so schools could be used for community gatherings and sometimes a stage or platform was provided. The schoolhouses had heaters and properly constructed privies.[79]

The shacks or improvised accommodation in which black schools had been taught since the end of the Civil War were themselves products of community initiative. The Rosenwald schools showed how, with some well-directed philanthropic assistance, this initiative could result in high-quality buildings equal to, or better than, those in which white schooling was conducted. In this respect they were a taunt to Jim Crow and proved whites did not have a mortgage on the whole of black existence.

Although undoubtedly significant to black educational ambition and enterprise, the Rosenwald schools were unable to effect an overnight transformation in the quality of schoolhouse accommodation and were located in only a few counties. In 1919 a comprehensive report on public education in Alabama pointed out the poor condition and unsuitability of most black school buildings, which, it said, was due in part to a large percentage of them being privately owned."[80] Black communities could not always be persuaded that, having invested so much effort in buying land and erecting a schoolhouse, this should then be deeded to the "state"—a nebulous notion anyway.[81]

~

By 1910, there were substantial and growing black communities in many of Alabama's larger cities such as Birmingham, Mobile, and Montgomery. Birmingham's population in 1910 was 132,685 of which 39 percent was black. The city was sharply segregated along racial lines and the caste system of white supremacy governed all interpersonal relations. Black people were generally assigned to low-status, low-skilled, and low-paying occupations though there was an emergent middle class.[82] Yet the members of this community had a number of advantages not available to those living in rural isolation. They were able to use these to their educational advantage.

In 1874 Birmingham had two public schools—one for each race. In his annual report to the state superintendent, Birmingham's then city superintendent, L. H. Mathews, advised: "The black school is dependent entirely on the school fund and has been kept running nearly five months. The teacher is a colored woman and the pupils are but little advanced all being primary in the strictest sense."[83] Nine years later in 1883 there were two schools for each race. Each school had its own trustees, decided on its own curriculum, and determined classroom procedures. The schools received some public funding but were mostly supported by patron tuition fees. That same year, as a result of action by Birmingham's mayor, Judge Alexander O. Lane, the position of "Superintendent of Education" was established in order to create a system of city schools for Birmingham. John Herbert Phillips was appointed soon afterward and he would hold the position continuously for thirty-eight years until his death in 1921.

John Herbert Phillips was a member of the new breed of professional, reform-minded, modernizing educators. He was an energetic champion of centralized, bureaucratic school systems staffed by properly trained and paid professional teachers and administrators. He was also enthusiastically supported by the Birmingham Board of Education.[84] Like many people of the day who regarded themselves as well informed, Phillips believed black people were behind whites in their cultural evolution.[85] Yet, unlike many others, Phillips had faith that education had the capacity to make black people "an asset instead of a burden to the South." He was convinced white Southerners would invest resources in black education from "enlightened selfishness."[86]

Upon taking charge of Birmingham's schools, Phillips organized them all—including the struggling and largely ignored black schools—into a single system that was centrally operated under the authority of the city. He then devised common standards for all areas of educational policy and administration.

Once Phillips's professional approach had been sanctioned by Birmingham's governing bodies, his policies became the basis for determining school funding allocations for the long term. The rules acted both as a buffer to drastic racial inequities—such as those produced under the 1891 School Law—and also as a permanent constraint that perpetuated discrimination. Yet, owing to the fact there were rules, black communities found that, if they lobbied the board of education sufficiently for amendments, they could sometimes achieve improvements and/or novel provisions. In this way they were able to obtain funding for an "industrial high school," which commenced in September 1900. This became a cultural center for Birmingham's black middle class whose leaders knew how to appeal to the sorts of people who dominated the board of education.[87] They also had articulate spokesmen such as Ulysses G. Mason of the *Birmingham Reporter*, who, in 1910, highlighted the dreadful sanitary conditions in black schools. His reports were picked up in the white press.[88]

In the Black Belt, white planters considered schooling unnecessary for their black laborers whom they preferred to remain ignorant and dependent.[89] Urban industrialists—the so-called Big Mules—though also self-interested—recognized the value of schooling as a way to upgrade the productivity of their employees. Furthermore, they saw that having good black schools in Birmingham could attract and retain black workers and make them less susceptible to the inducements of recruiters who were actively soliciting workers for jobs in the North.[90] Schooling would also equip black workers to be an alternative labor source in the event of strikes by the white workforce.

Birmingham's black community was thus able to derive an educational dividend from several strands of white self-interest and to wring concessions from the city's educational establishment. However, though the quality of black education in Birmingham was better both in comparison to its rural counterpart and in absolute terms, it was hardly adequate. It did not even approach the standards of the city's white schools. Furthermore, in 1903 Birmingham's black public schools only enrolled as few as 42 percent of black school-age children.[91] In 1911 the city's appropriations per child of school age were $18.86 for whites and $2.81 for blacks, and city expenditure per pupil enrolled was 33 percent less for black pupils than for white. John Herbert Phillips was unable to persuade his board of education to invest in the accommodation needed for quality black schools. After touring black schools in 1913, the editor of the *Birmingham News* noted that only one was in a modern, safe, proper building; the rest were in overcrowded shacks.[92]

The curriculum in Birmingham's black schools reflected the likely occupational choices available to black students and also the fad for industrial education. In the upper elementary grades—the city's schools were all graded—students were taught "cooking, sewing, laundering, manual training, furniture repairing, chair caning, handicrafts, shoe repairing, *et cetera*, besides the basic branches."[93] The curriculum required emphasis to be placed on "the study and singing of the Negro Spirituals." This was thought to have been a stipulation of John Herbert Phillips, who had a liking for spirituals. Many black people believed such enthusiasm was mostly "Old South" nostalgia.[94]

∽

The ability of black rural communities to influence educational policy in respect of their own schools was a victim of the 1891 School Law, of the populist political ructions of the 1890s that resulted in ballot rigging and manipulation of the black vote, of disenfranchisement under the 1901 constitution, and of a reform focus on the needs of white children only. Above these reasons was the all-encompassing environment of fierce racial prejudice and Jim Crow segregation. By the early years of the twentieth century, black people had been virtually banished from the educational stage. Any desires they might have for influencing educational policy were unlikely to receive bureaucratic consideration—let alone support. All professional development activities for teachers such as institutes were segregated and teachers could not even join the AEA. Should black teachers wish to develop contacts and share professional experiences they could join a separate association (ASTA)—though only a tiny fraction did so. Furthermore, black teachers were not permitted to attend educational conventions such as the Conference for Education in the South.

Black communities hoped that schooling would assist in their uplift and eventual recognition by a white society built upon assumptions of racial supremacy. But white society wanted black schooling to be limited and circumscribed. Two such divergent positions were hardly reconcilable and it was not really surprising when, in 1915, black Southerners—including Alabamians—started heading en masse to the North in search of economic and educational opportunities that would serve better their aspirations.

9
1915—A Watershed Year?

In January 1915, almost fifty years after the end of the American Civil War, Alabama's legislature met for its regular quadrennial session. Its principal educational work for the session was to be the consideration of fifteen bills placed before it by the state superintendent, William Francis Feagin. The intent of these was to extend further the reform process begun by John William Abercrombie when he introduced his own bills to the assembly in the 1898–99 session.[1] Despite political differences in 1915 between the legislative and executive branches and the dominance of another reform issue (prohibition), Feagin's bills were all enacted—a testament to his political acuity, his strategic campaigning, and the reputation he had built in a number of major educational organizations.[2]

~

If not the most important in the 1915 reform package, the first bill was at least socially innovative. It authorized women to serve on boards of education in counties, cities, and towns for the first time. By 1915 women all over the state had shown themselves to be shrewd political campaigners on behalf of schools and had demonstrated their ability to get things done. Yet Feagin's bill did not mean he recognized any intrinsic rights owed to women for their sustained and beneficial activism. Feagin explained the bill's purpose by saying: "no tales of yesterday and no romance of today can eclipse in wonder the improvements [women] have wrought in local school conditions." He implied this was because women brought to the school their refining "maternal instinct and mother-love."[3] This was not nascent feminism but the old notion of "true womanhood."[4]

Another of Feagin's bills specified the powers and duties of the (elected) county boards of education on which women would now be able to serve. One of these duties included the appointment of county superintendents (thus making the position nonpolitical).[5] Although for at least a decade the majority of the teaching workforce had been female and county superintendents were increasingly expected to have teaching or other "specialized abilities," there was no intention that superintendents could be women. The hierarchy of the school system relied heavily on male dominance in the wider society including most civic and fraternal organizations through which male superintendents could link schools to their community's power structure.[6] Despite some notable exceptions such as, for example, Julia Strudwick Tutwiler—the longtime president of the Livingston Normal School for Women in Sumter County— the traditional belief that professional executive authority should only be wielded by men remained unchallenged. Women would be administrators.

Feagin's second bill was concerned with the societal context of schooling. Its enactment established the Alabama Illiteracy Commission, whose charter was to reduce the state's alarming rates of adult illiteracy. In 1910, 23 percent of Alabama's population over ten years of age was illiterate. Feagin believed that if adults could be rescued from the "confines of their gross ignorance," there was likely to be a greater citizen interest in education.[7] In his annual report for 1915, Feagin related his firsthand experience of the benefits literacy programs were already producing. In Dale County he had seen people who had been "inspired to go to school although their faces were furrowed and their locks white" and had heard from "scores of old folks of the new joy that has come into their lives" by being able to read.[8]

The Alabama Illiteracy Commission operated on a decentralized model and utilized voluntary labor, which was often the after-hours labor of regular public schoolteachers. In December 1916 a Miss Foster, who was a field agent for the commission in Barbour County, reported that literacy classes had had a "wonderful effect on her community." The classes increased enrollments and attendance at the regular day school and parents were able to see for themselves the need for such items as blackboards.[9] Yet, as with everything else in the state's education system, the commission adopted a whites first policy. Black communities had to find their own funding for literacy classes or rely on philanthropy.[10] In 1920 the black illiteracy rate was 39 percent—quadruple the white rate.[11]

Although Feagin occasionally displayed his enthusiasm or approval in somewhat emotional terms, he was a well-informed, astute, and practical realist when it came to educational change, and his proposals always had some prospect of success. The third bill in his package prescribed a minimum age of seventeen for teachers, which he said was a "check upon the employment of immature persons for the serious work of teaching." Although seventeen might be considered "immature," Feagin knew rural schools frequently employed girls from local families and he was trying initially just to eliminate those "of tender years" who were even younger, such as the fifteen-year-old Clara Hall who was granted a teacher's license in Baldwin County in 1896.[12]

Feagin was also aware that 80 percent of first-time teachers had no occupational training at all, and the only way they were likely to acquire any knowledge of pedagogical theory, curriculum content, and/or instructional skills was by attending teachers' institutes. As a consequence he decided that the standard of the institutes available had better be as high as possible and that attending should provide no hardship. His fifteenth bill was incremental to existing legislation concerning teachers' institutes but provided for professionally conducted institutes and payment of teachers while attending.[13]

The major feature of the 1915 package of reform legislation was the fifth bill. This was to enable a referendum to be held for a constitutional amendment allowing local taxation—conditional upon the subsequent approval of eligible voters. A companion bill—the sixth—provided for the follow-on electoral arrangements should the amendment be adopted.

The public school system was supported by the state with revenue from a number of different sources (perpetual fund, escheats, license fees, supplemental appropriations, and so forth). In total this revenue constituted the "Public School Fund," and it was allocated to the counties on a per capita basis according to an annual enumeration of students though, after 1891, its discretionary distribution at the township level redounded almost entirely to the benefit of white children in predominantly black counties. From 1901 onward the Public School Fund remained the only significant public support available to schools unless counties levied the one-mill tax permitted by the constitution or municipal districts made appropriations from their general town or city funds. However, the tradition of supporting schools with private funds such as parental supplements or tuition fees and/or subscriptions to pay for schoolhouses and their equipment continued throughout the state. As these funds bore a direct relationship to parental capacity to pay, they were inherently inequitable. Such payments increased a community's vested interest in its schools and perpetuated local influence but Feagin described the need to resort to such payments as an "uncertain and antiquated plan."[14]

In 1913 forty-three of the forty-eight states raised more than half of their educational revenues from local taxation. Massachusetts raised nearly all (96.8 percent) of its school funds from this source. Alabama raised only 24.0 percent, which was the lowest proportion of any state in the Union.[15] Being aware of this, the AEA and all those who had been active in promoting educational reform had long sought the constitutional amendment to allow both counties and school districts to levy school taxes. They hoped these would not only provide a more reliable source of revenue but would foster "local initiative, local interest, and a keener regard for the methods and management in each public school."[16] A supplementary bill—the seventh—provided for the state to assist counties that undertook what Feagin believed was a "most desirable educational activity" by paying them an annual bonus for levying the tax.[17]

Once the enabling bill for the constitutional amendment was passed by the legislature, Feagin conducted a vigorous campaign in its favor. He even borrowed a large sum of money ($6,000) on his personal account to finance this campaign because he was determined to ensure the amendment would be ratified when put to a referendum in November 1916.[18] His appeal to voters, which included an illustrated pamphlet of questions and answers, was persuasive. The amendment was ratified by a clear majority with nearly 60 percent in favor. By 1918, fifty counties had been given voter approval to levy a three-mill tax for educational purposes but the district tax was much slower to catch on.[19]

Several years later when the initial caution had passed and electors had given many local school districts the authority to levy taxes, the impact of these on rural schools just increased the inequities within and among local systems. Having a higher tax base, city school systems derived greater revenue from local taxes than county systems. By 1924, Birmingham was receiving $20 per student from the three-mill tax whereas Lamar County was receiving less than $3 per student.[20] After 1916, the total moneys available to Alabama's public schools increased significantly but individual schools and school districts, whether by choice or circumstance, remained mirrors of the community in which they were located. District taxation also gave new legitimacy to local communities wanting to maintain their own schools and resist consolidation.

There could be no better example of the persistence of localism as an influence on educational policy making than the issue of school attendance. There were still many people living a traditional life who failed to accept the notion that schooling would significantly benefit their children. The proposition that the state should have the right to prescribe compulsory attendance had been debated over the years and rejected as being an unwarranted intrusion on parental rights. At the turn of the twentieth century this view was supported by industrialists who employed large numbers of children in cotton mills and did not want their options limited. To their great chagrin a mild child labor bill was passed in 1903 after years of lobbying by activists, including Edgar Gardner Murphy.

The question of the state's right to compel attendance was particularly contested in the Black Belt where, as late as 1914, only about 40 percent of black children attended school at all owing to the labor needs of plantation owners. As there was a correlation between tenancy and a low level of school attendance (tenants being more transitory than landowners), compulsory attendance in high-tenancy areas was regarded as impractical.[21]

In the state superintendent's biennial report for 1907–08 all the county superintendents were asked to comment specifically on their constituents' attitudes to compulsory attendance. As might be expected, the range of opinion varied widely across the state. The superintendents of Calhoun, Clarke, Clay, Crenshaw, Fayette, and Hale counties all felt their people were neither ready for nor would have any use for compulsory education and would not vote for such a radical move.[22] The superintendent for Dallas County (a Black Belt county) said the disadvantages of not having children in school should be borne rather than "distress the people of the Black Belt."[23] Washington County's Richard E. Blunt asserted that his constituents wanted "a compulsory school law and would vote solidly for it, *nigger* or no *nigger*."[24] The superintendents of Bibb and St. Clair counties seemed to believe the best justification for compulsory education was that it might reduce crime rates while those of Butler, Jefferson, and Lamar believed compulsion and penalties were necessary to break down the "fortress of parental disinterest."[25] Others wanted "a mild form" of compulsion or felt there were other more pressing educational priorities or that attendance could be secured by other than legal methods.[26]

In the scholastic year ending September 30, 1912, the number of white children attending school as a percentage of those of school age had actually fallen by one percentage point while the number of black children attending had fallen by three percentage points.[27] At the start of 1915 Alabama was, along with Georgia and Mississippi, one of the last three states in the Union without a compulsory attendance law. In April 1914 Feagin addressed the AEA and put forth his own unequivocal position. He acknowledged there were still people who questioned the state's right to compel school attendance but, he said, if parents had rights, so too did their helpless children. Society also had rights and the state had rights. He said, too, that he had no patience with "that prejudice which would have hundreds of our white children grow up in ignorance lest the aspirations of the negro child be awakened too."[28]

Before the 1915 education bills were actually presented, one member predicted: "the compulsory features especially, will meet determined opposition."[29] The ensuing *Compulsory Attendance Act* was thus a splendid feather in Feagin's cap and a satisfactory outcome for his indefatigable championing of the cause. Yet its provisions were hardly stringent—Feagin himself described it as "mild." The law required that children between the ages of eight and fifteen years (inclusive) must attend school for eighty days annually unless they had completed the work of the seven elementary grades. The county boards of education were given the right to reduce the period of compulsory attendance to sixty days if hardship warranted this. In cases of extreme poverty children could be exempted entirely. The law's enforcement was in the hands of the county boards of education. These offered such poor salaries for potential enforcement agents that few positions were ever filled.[30]

In 1919 Governor Thomas E. Kilby commissioned an investigation into Alabama's public educational system. This showed school enrollments had climbed by only two percentage points since the bill's enactment owing to the belief by some Alabamians that their parental rights were sovereign and supreme—particularly their rights to their children's labor. The authors of *An Educational Study of Alabama* stated (in relation to Chambers County): "As in other sections of the State, farm work has precedence over school work. The immediate income of the farm is tangible, while the value to the child of having his life broadened and enriched by the school is not so near nor so tangible."[31] No one made any attempt to compel the attendance of black children knowing the already overcrowded schools would not be able to accommodate them and their labor was needed. Yet Professor James J. Doster of the University of Alabama said there needed to be "a quickening of public sentiment among Negro parents with reference to regular attendance and punctuality."[32]

Besides compulsory attendance, another article of faith for modernizers was the need for the consolidation of multiple one-teacher schools. William Feagin was only one of many who were certain consolidation would mean "better buildings, better teachers, better instruction, and decidedly better results" and larger schools would make school life more stimulating and interesting for the students. Moreover, instead of small groups of children playing improvised games with homemade equipment, they would be able to participate in organized and competitive sport.[33] The consolidated school—being more like a town or city school—would arrest the rate of teachers leaving for opportunities "offering better salaries and more conveniences" elsewhere.[34] It was an urban-oriented viewpoint. Prior to 1915 there was no evidence to show that rural communities had found arguments in favor of consolidation convincing.

There was some inconsistency between Feagin's eager championing of school consolidation and his genuine interest in community engagement. None of those who promoted consolidation sufficiently considered such factors as transport, or the implications for a small village of the loss of an institution that was a focal point for community activities and in which some community members held a proprietary interest, or the hold-outs of parents who resisted consolidation. Similarly, they did not factor in the social detriment of diminishing the status of community leaders such as well-to-do farmers whose donation of land for a neighborhood schoolhouse might no longer be valued. They thought the benefits of consolidation far outweighed the loss that was involved when a local teacher's knowledge of individual children was replaced with the less personal supervision necessarily involved in a much larger school.[35] Yet in some places consolidation meant irremediable cultural injury. In Lamar County, "most of the communities that lost a school owing to consolidation also lost their heart. Activities once carried on in rural communities took place in the school building. Now most of these activities ceased to exist."[36] One principal sounded resignedly discouraged when he reported: "It is hard to get our people to understand the consolidated school over the little one-room school."[37]

Until the enactment of the new county school board law there was no legal authority for the consolidation of schools, which also meant no authority for the transportation of pupils at public expense—and this could be considerable. The wagons that carried children to the Geiger consolidated school in Sumter County cost $40.00 a month—more than many teachers earned. The aggregated daily journey of these wagons was more than fourteen miles.[38] It is likely that parents were unhappy about such journeys and viewed them as cold and tiring for their children.[39]

The fourteenth bill in Feagin's 1915 package appears to have been an effort to try to reverse the disappointing sentiment regarding consolidation. The bill amended a previous state law (Article 31, Chapter 31 of the Code of Alabama, 1907) and appropriated further state support for the "erection, repair and equipment of schools" because, Feagin said: "the rural school of the future in Alabama is to be a consolidated school usually with three or more teachers, comfortably housed, suitably equipped with ample grounds and a teacherage nearby."[40]

Between 1915 and 1918 approximately 162 consolidations of various types had been effected and by 1922 there were 219 consolidated schools, but the slowness of progress and what appeared to be community recalcitrance was a source of almost palpable frustration to the authors of the 1919 *An Educational Study of Alabama*. For example, in their review of conditions in Pickens County they wrote: "The county school board until recently has been increasing instead of diminishing the number of school districts. . . . . The tendency has been to erect school buildings in every district asking for them. The consolidation of schools has not been seriously considered either by the school officials or by the patrons of the schools. There is in the county only one transportation wagon."[41]

The remaining bills in the 1915 package were essentially administrative. Their enactment indicated the growing role of the department of education as a regulatory authority and the strength of a new type of governance within the state.[42]

~

In 1919, *An Educational Study of Alabama* showed disappointing results against many other familiar measures of school progress. It found that teachers were poorly trained, schoolhouses were frequently inadequate, session lengths varied, and funding was insufficient. The study also pointed out in no uncertain terms that: "One in every three black children who should have been in school for upward of three years, could neither read and write and . . . the state must equalize the investment better between the races than it has done if this unfortunate condition is to be remedied in the near future."[43]

Those who had worked so hard and so long to improve Alabama's public schooling must have been disappointed at the slowness of reform but they remained optimistic—and Feagin was careful not to castigate the very people for whom the reforms were intended. He said he did not detect any "lagging public sentiment or a lack of effort on the part of those engaged in educational work." The culprit was outdated laws and constitutional inhibitions that were now "cumbersome and obstructive."[44] Yet despite his empathy, like other modernizers and those who were collectively being termed "Country Lifers," Feagin was not above considering rural schools in the light of a pathological "rural life problem."

In the early 1890s the National Education Association had formed a "Committee of Twelve on Rural Schools" to investigate the inadequacies of such schools across the nation. This committee reported that what was needed was consolidation and pupil transportation, expert supervision by county superintendents, professionally trained teachers, and the connection of the curriculum to "the everyday life of the community."[45] In 1908, Theodore Roosevelt's *Commission on Country Life* had been predicated on the assumption of national rural dysfunction and it accumulated evidence to support its starting premises and eventual findings. The commission was particularly critical of rural schools, which it held largely responsible for "ineffective farming, lack of ideals and the drift to town."[46] Widely read educationists and sociologists at this time regularly used the term "rural life problem" or "rural school problem" as if the findings of the *Commission on Country Life* were universally agreed upon and not open to question. In 1914, Ellwood Patterson Cubberley published *Rural life and education: a study of the rural-school problem as a phase of the rural-life problem* in which he advocated the "better correlation of rural schooling with socioeconomic forces."[47]

William Feagin may have been influenced by what seems to have been a contemporary consensus that the rural school was responsible for many of the alleged deficiencies of rural life.[48] This was not the most promising position from which to secure cooperation for the overturning of long-standing traditions of school control. It appeared, at face value, to overlook the fact that a well-established, organic culture evolves from within. Yet all of Feagin's actions indicate his full understanding that externally devised educational change had to be perceived as necessary by those whose customs and institutions were thought to be wanting. Moreover, change had to be supported by adequate resources.

When John William Abercrombie was actively prosecuting his reform program from 1898 onward, his focus was on bureaucratic reform. He was distressed that Alabama's public education system demonstrated "no system, no uniformity, no standard of qualification."[49] In 1901 when he reviewed the legislative products of localized decision making, he lamented: "Many, too many, local bills were passed. Each one of them is but another patch upon our patchwork system."[50] At the AEA's annual convention in 1924, Abercrombie—who was then again state superintendent—recited a catalog of twenty-three deficiencies associated with the schooling system from Reconstruction onward and particularly evident to him upon his election as state superintendent in 1898. He told the delegates: "Excepting children alone, we had almost none of the things that go to constitute an efficient school system."[51]

By enumerating the deficiencies of the past, Abercrombie implied that each of these had been remedied—though this was not the case. In addition, despite Abercrombie having received his own elementary education in one-teacher rural schools and having served as superintendent for the schools of Anniston in Calhoun County, he offered no counterbalancing virtues for the localized system.[52]

During Abercrombie's first term as state superintendent (1898–1901), the "department of education" comprised himself and three clerical staff.[53] Yet he was able to develop the concept of a strong, centralized policy-making and administrative authority as the basic requirement for educational modernization. His achievements all reflected his belief in the need for such control and were as much his legacy as the influence he exerted to secure the constitutional changes of 1901 that put public schools on a slightly more secure funding basis and allowed an optional county school tax—a decentralizing policy.

Feagin probably could not have accomplished what he did without the spadework done by Abercrombie and others. Yet, although he always saw his legislative package of 1915 as just a start and was ambitious to achieve more, he had greater success overall with his reform efforts than his predecessors. While Feagin tended occasionally to share the prejudicial notion of the "rural life problem," he appreciated the underlying strengths of rural and small-town culture and approached the modernization task with this awareness rather than resorting to corporate diktats. If notions of efficiency, uniformity, and systematization were the leitmotif of Abercrombie's approach then community consultation and involvement were Feagin's.

Besides his understanding of the dynamics of rural communities, Feagin seems to have appreciated their attachment to their schools as a shared facility and neighborhood symbol. He believed the common school was "the institution nearest to the soil and should be made the apostle of intelligence, of industry and of thrift for the regeneration of our rural life." He wanted Alabama to have its own country life commission whose members would promote the development of similarly constituted county committees to lead district and community uplift with the schoolhouse their base of operation.[54]

~

The reform bills of 1915 were a signal modernization achievement in spite of not fully realizing the hopes that so many—including their sponsor—had held for them. Though some patrons were still unwilling to accept the state's right to compel school attendance and others remained to be convinced about consolidation, resistance to reform had diminished. This was facilitated as much by Feagin's passionate campaigning, his marshalling of community interest, and his involvement of thousands of people throughout Alabama in school-centered activities, as it was by his legislative accomplishments in 1915 and the constitutional amendment of 1916 on local taxation.

10
Conclusion
Then and Since

In 1875, after what it deemed to be an unsatisfactory experience with an imported and unaffordable educational system during Reconstruction, Alabama's government devolved a great deal of the responsibility for public schooling to parents and trustees. This educational localism was in harmony with the way in which most of the state's population actually lived. In fact, the arrangements were not dissimilar to those operating elsewhere in the United States where, in 1900, 60.4 percent of the population was "rural" according to the census definition.

In 1910 nearly 38 percent of the nation's public school students attended 212,380 one-room schools. Nearly all one-room schools were rural and had just one teacher. Some had minuscule enrollments—for example, a quarter of Iowa's rural schools had ten or fewer pupils. These schools were under the governance of their communities and were mostly roughly built and ill equipped. Their teachers were poorly trained and transient but responsible for instructing students in the few subjects they could not learn at home.[1] Yet America was undergoing change at an ever-accelerating pace and Alabama was not immune to what was happening elsewhere.

In 1913 Alabama's department of education advised rural teachers of how their communities were being enlarged by technologies such as telephones and automobiles as well as by railroad expansion, better roads, rural mail routes, the parcel post, and other developments: "Every bridge constructed across a small stream makes it impossible to cut off one small community from another but a few rods away." Teachers were told that they must rise to the challenge of the expanded community.[2]

Such advice was being delivered in the context of a national debate about the need for a revolution in agriculture and rural life using the school as the vehicle. In addition, the advice was framed by changing educational ideas being disseminated by people such as Mabel Carney, Ellwood Cubberley, and John

Dewey.[3] Schools were increasingly becoming subject to central direction by professional education experts and bureaucratic management.

The legislation devised and sponsored by William Francis Feagin and enacted in 1915 made Alabama's schooling system more recognizable in law as the enterprise of a modern state. It was intended to create the conditions for delivering improved educational outcomes and to meet the challenge of the changes that were abroad in the land. Yet, while greater professional control, bureaucratic management, improved funding, and growing standardization may have helped in the development of an effective public schooling system, they were not enough.

The educational provisions of the expanded community were not markedly better than those of the localized community. In 1912, Alabama ranked last of the forty-eight states in "educational efficiency." After World War I discrepancies persisted among rural and urban schools, black and white schools, and the schools of different sections. Illiteracy was one ready gauge of the problems. In 1927 Alabama ranked forty-fifth of forty-eight states in literacy levels. It had the seventh highest level of white illiteracy.[4] On the eve of World War II Alabama was forty-sixth in per capita pupil expenditure and forty-fifth in annual teacher salaries.[5]

State governors such as Thomas E. Kilby (1919–1923) and Bibb Graves (1927–1931) sought to make an impact on school reform with varying degrees of success; some problems seemed intractable. In 1930 Danylu Belser, an educationist, freshly pointed out the inconsistent benefits of local taxation—once so optimistically seen as the solution for educational reform. He said it had brought about "gross inequality of opportunity in Alabama." He explained that richer counties could provide adequate school terms, trained teachers, good buildings, and at least a minimum of the materials and equipment necessary for good teaching. Counties in which property values were low could offer none of these essentials.[6]

Implicit in any state system of schooling is the notion that a public good is involved. But the nature of public good and its price are matters determined politically. Even deciding on which groups comprise "the public" is a political matter. In 1901, Alabama's constitution was devised to protect the vested interests of planters and big mules. Its fiscal articles influenced who would benefit from public schooling. Those without full civil rights received the least benefit; the landless and those whose economic status was insecure, such as tenant farmers, were also at a disadvantage.

In 1936 the writer James Agee stayed for a time with some white sharecroppers in Hale County in the Black Belt. He later described with some anger the wrongs he felt were being done to their children by poor schooling. He believed this would forever cheat the children from enjoying life's fullest plea-sures.[7] While laying the blame on their teachers, Agee recognized that these probably lacked the skills to withstand the pressures of class, state, church, and parents. Agee's observations had a wider application then and today. Ill-trained teachers cannot introduce novel or complex ideas or develop the disci-plines by which such ideas might be savored, questioned, and tested.

The wary suspicion with which, in the first quarter of the twentieth century, many in the school community viewed new ideas such as state teacher exami-nations, compulsory attendance, and consolidation, was but a summer shower compared to the furious tempest of animosity, violent protest, and political ob-struction that occurred in the 1960s over school desegregation and federal in-tervention in Alabama's affairs. When the full implications of the 1954 rul-ing by the United States Supreme Court in *Brown v. the Board of Education of Topeka* became evident, huge numbers of white parents withdrew their chil-dren from public schools so they could continue to be educated in a segregated environment. This exodus, aided by governmental maneuverings, called into question whether the public education system might even survive, though its history offered precedents for the qualified assurance that it would. More than ever, however, issues to do with race and poverty would amplify systemic short-comings, and the social consequences of underinvestment would come into sharper focus.

A century ago, Alabama's educational needs were often framed with refer-ence to the modernizing world of the New South. Today, both state and fed-eral policy makers are concerned that students have equal opportunity when it comes to acquiring the skills and knowledge needed for participation in a post-industrial America and a world made global by technology. In this world, con-cepts such as localism, community, and neighborhood would seem to have no place, yet they continue to be invoked as possible solutions for contemporary educational dysfunction. This may indicate a nostalgia for lost cultural certain-ties and/or a common delusion that the past was a better place than the pres-ent when actually it was merely a different landscape.

Notes

Introduction

1. School Law of 1854 in *Alabama Acts*, 4th Biennial Session, 1853–1854. *Alabama State Constitution of 1819*, Article VI.

2. Edgar W. Knight, *Education in the United States*, 3rd rev. ed. (1929; rpt., New York: Greenwood Press, 1969), 563.

3. Alexis de Tocqueville, *Democracy in America*, vol. 1 (1840; rpt., New York: Vintage Books, 1990), 295.

4. Samuel L. Webb, *Two-Party Politics in the One-Party South: Alabama's Hill Country, 1874–1920* (Tuscaloosa: The University of Alabama Press, 1997), 2.

5. William Warren Rogers, Robert David Ward, Leah Rawls Atkins, and J. Wayne Flynt, *History of a Deep South State* (Tuscaloosa: The University of Alabama Press, 1994), 133, 176–177, and 179. 1860 U.S. Census.

6. Charles Lyell, *A Second Visit to the United States of North America*, vol. 2 (London: John Murray, 1849), 40–41.

7. George Lewis, *Impressions of America and the American Churches: From Journal of the Reverend G. Lewis* (Edinburgh: W. P. Kennedy, 1845), 157.

8. Philip Henry Gosse, *Letters from Alabama (U.S.): Chiefly Relating to Natural History* (London: Morgan and Chase, 1859), 43–44.

9. Roderick Nash, *Wilderness and the American Mind*, 3rd ed. (New Haven, Conn.: Yale University Press, 1982), 75–78.

10. Grady McWhiney, *Cracker Culture: Celtic Ways in the Old South* (Tuscaloosa: The University of Alabama Press, 1988), 210 and 214.

11. *Courier Journal*, January 27, 1880. Reprinted in the *Troy Messenger*, February 12, 1880.

12. Anthony Harkins, *Hillbilly: A Cultural History of an American Icon* (New York: Oxford University Press, 2004), 5–6.

13. Writers' Program of the WPA, *The WPA Guide to 1930s Alabama; introduction by Harvey H. Jackson III* (1941; rpt., Tuscaloosa: The University of Alabama Press, 2000), 122–123.

14. Webb, *Two-Party Politics in the One-Party South*, 2.

15. Gunnar Myrdal, *An American Dilemma: The Negro Problem and Modern Democracy*, vol. 1 (New York: Harper & Bros., 1944), 113.

16. Wayne Flynt, *Poor but Proud: Alabama's Poor Whites* (Tuscaloosa: The University of Alabama Press, 1989), 50.

17. The U.S. Census for 1910 showed that the state's population was 2,318,093, of which 17.3 percent was urban and 82.7 percent was rural.

18. de Tocqueville, *Democracy in America*, vol. 1, 40.

19. U.S. Department of the Interior, *An Educational Study of Alabama* (Washington, D.C.: Bureau of Education, 1919), 205.

20. Rose Marie Smith, *Lamar County: A History to 1900* (Fulton, Ala.: privately published by the author, 1987), 155.

21. Robert McMath Jr., "Community, Region and Hegemony," in *Toward a New South?: Studies in Post-Civil War Southern Communities*, ed. Orville Vernon Burton and Robert C. McMath Jr. (Westport, Conn.: Greenwood Press, 1982), 281–295. J. Mack Lofton, *Voices from Alabama: A Twentieth-Century Mosaic* (Tuscaloosa: The University of Alabama Press, 1993), 198.

22. Charles Johnson and Assocs., *Statistical Atlas of the Southern Counties: Listing and Analysis of Socio-economic Indices of 1104 Southern Counties* (Chapel Hill: University of North Carolina Press, 1941), 1–4.

23. *Mountain Eagle*, November 4, 1903.

24. Ibid., October 13, 1909.

25. Alabama *House Journal*, 4th Biennial session, 1853–1854, 303–312.

26. J. Mills Thornton, *Politics and Power in a Slave Society* (Baton Rouge: Louisiana State University Press, 1978), 300–305.

27. Stephen B. Weeks, *History of Public School Education in Alabama* (1915; rpt., Westport, Conn.: Negro Universities Press, 1971), 59. After 1875 the eligibility age-band was seven to twenty-one.

28. In his *Biennial Report* for 1904, the state superintendent, Isaac W. Hill, used the collective term "State Schools" to describe the University of Alabama, the Alabama Polytechnic Institute, the Normal Schools, the Girls' Industrial School, and the nine District Agricultural Schools.

29. William F. Perry, "The Genesis of Public Education in Alabama," *Transactions of the Alabama Historical Society* 2 (1898): 14–27.

30. C. Vann Woodward, *The Origins of the New South, 1877–1913, A History of the South*, vol. 9 (Baton Rouge: Louisiana State University Press, 1967), 398–399.

31. William A. Link, *A Hard Country and a Lonely Place: Schooling, Society, and Reform in Rural Virginia, 1870–1920* (Chapel Hill: University of North Carolina Press, 1986).

32. James D. Anderson, *The Education of Blacks in the South, 1860–1935* (Chapel Hill: University of North Carolina Press, 1988).

33. James L. Leloudis, *Schooling the New South: Pedagogy, Self, and Society in North Carolina, 1880–1920* (Chapel Hill: University of North Carolina Press, 1996).

34. Wayne E. Fuller, *The Old Country School: The Story of Rural Education in the Middle West* (Chicago: University of Chicago Press, 1982). Paul Theobald, *Call School: Rural Educa-

tion in the Midwest to 1918 (Carbondale: Southern Illinois University Press, 1995). David B. Tyack, "The Tribe and the Common School: Community Control in Rural Education," *American Quarterly* 24 (March 1972): 3–19. David Danbom, *The Resisted Revolution: Urban America and the Industrialization of Agriculture 1900–1930* (Ames: Iowa State University Press, 1979).

Chapter 1

1. Conservatives were not politically unified until 1866 when the Democratic and Conservative Party was formed. This happened after three antebellum factions—Whigs, Know-Nothings, and Unionists—came together. Initially preferring the name "Conservatives," the party was also known as the "Conservative Democrats" and later just as "Democrats." It dropped "Conservative" from its title in 1906.

2. Stephen B. Weeks, *History of Public School Education in Alabama* (1915; rpt., Westport, Conn.: Negro Universities Press, 1971), 84.

3. Estimate derived from figures included in ibid., 197–198.

4. Peter Kolchin, *First Freedom: The Responses of Alabama's Blacks to Emancipation* (Westport, Conn.: Greenwood Press, 1972), 84.

5. Ibid., 175–176.

6. The riots were in Memphis and New Orleans. The first (or Military) *Reconstruction Act*, enacted on March 2 1867, was entitled *An Act to provide for the more efficient Government of the Rebel States.* Three related acts followed.

7. The Fourteenth Amendment was passed by Congress on June 13, 1866. The new state constitutions were to be "in conformity with the Constitution of the United States in all respects, framed by a convention of delegates elected by the male citizens of said State, twenty-one years old and upward, of whatever race, color, or previous condition, who have been resident in said State for one year previous to the day of such election, except such as may be disfranchised for participation in the rebellion or for felony at common law."

8. The second *Reconstruction Act* was enacted on March 23, 1867.

9. Albert B. Moore, *A History of Alabama and Its People in Three Volumes* (Tuscaloosa: The University of Alabama, 1951), 487. Kenneth B. White, "The Alabama Freedmen's Bureau and Black Education: The Myth of Opportunity," *Alabama Review* 34 (April 1981): 107–124.

10. Gene L. Howard, *Death at Cross Plains: An Alabama Reconstruction Tragedy* (Tuscaloosa: The University of Alabama Press, 1984). Henry Lee Swint, *The Northern Teacher in the South, 1862–1870* (New York: Octagon Books, 1967), 102.

11. Kolchin, *First Freedom*, 93.

12. Walter L. Fleming, *Civil War and Reconstruction in Alabama* (1905; rpt., Spartanburg: Reprint Co., 1978), 625–626.

13. Jennifer Spiers, "Educating Blacks in Reconstruction Alabama: John Silsby, the American Missionary Association, and the Freedmen's Bureau" (Master's thesis, Auburn University, 1991), 50.

14. *Alabama Constitution, 1868,* Article XI, Sections 10–13.

15. David Mathews, *Why Public Schools? Whose Public Schools? What Early Communities Have to Tell Us* (Montgomery: New South Books, 2003), 65–66 and 178.

16. Montgomery *Daily Mail*, December 25, 1867, quoted by Malcolm Cook McMillan, *Constitutional Development in Alabama, 1798–1901: A Study in Politics, the Negro, and Sectionalism* (Chapel Hill: University of North Carolina Press, 1978), 160. (Emphasis added.)

17. Jerome A. Gray, Joe L. Reed, and Norman W. Walton, *History of the Alabama State Teachers Association* (Washington, D.C.: National Education Association of the United States, 1987), 17–22.

18. This happened on June 12, 1868. Diane McWhorter, *Chronology and Documentary Handbook of the State of Alabama*, Dobbs Ferry, Oceana Publications, 1972, 43.

19. ADAH, Alabama Department of Education, *Annual, Biennial, and Special Reports: State Publications, 1855–[ongoing]*. SG021047, Box 1, Report of the Superintendent of Public Instruction of the State of Alabama to the Governor for the fiscal Year Ending 30th September, 1869, 6. (Hereinafter this report and other *Annual* [or *Biennial*] and *Special Reports* of state superintendents will be cited simply as ADAH, Dept. of Education, *Annual Report or Biennial Report [year/s]*).

20. Ibid., 9.

21. Ibid., 9 and 10.

22. Ibid., 5. The state superintendent appointed the county superintendents, who, in turn, appointed three trustees in each township so there was a direct line of political influence.

23. Fleming, *Civil War and Reconstruction in Alabama*, 609. James F. Clanahan, *The History of Pickens County, Alabama, 1540–1920* (Decatur: Decatur Printing Company, 1964), 272.

24. ADAH, Dept. of Education, *Correspondence files of the State Superintendent of Education*, SG015974-SG015981, Alabama Dept. of Archives and History. (Hereinafter cited throughout the entire book as [Series Number], *Superintendent's Correspondence, [years]*), ADAH. Miel S. Ezell, superintendent of education for Clarke County, to John M. McKleroy, March 29, 1875, and D. D. Dawson to John M. McKleroy, March 5, 1875, and June 15, 1875, in SG015978, *Superintendent's Correspondence, 1867–1907*, ADAH. This box contains eighteen other letters about this matter.

25. C.J.L. Cunningham to Noah B. Cloud, February 20, 1869, in SG015979, *Superintendent's Correspondence, 1868–1913*, ADAH.

26. T. G. Fowler to Noah B. Cloud, May 4, 1869, in SG015979, *Superintendent's Correspondence, 1868–1913*, ADAH.

27. ADAH, Dept. of Education, *Annual Report, 1868–69*, 4.

28. Ibid.

29. ADAH, Dept. of Education, *Annual Report, 1871*, 58, 57.

30. Ibid., 56 and 77.

31. Ibid., 61.

32. Ibid., 44. Italics original.

33. Ibid., 49, 52, 60, 61, 51–52, and 78.

34. ADAH, Dept. of Education, *Annual Report, 1871*, 59.

35. Ibid., 60–61 and 59.

36. ADAH, Dept. of Education, *Annual Report, 1872*, 8–15.

37. Weeks, *History of Public School Education in Alabama*, 101. Letter from Joseph Speed dated July 7, 1873, to W. H. Lawrence, Editor, *Clarke County Democrat* and published in that paper's edition of July 29, 1873.

38. ADAH, Alabama Board of Education, SG13206, *Journal of the Board of Education of the state of Alabama, Session Commencing November, 1873*, 20–22.

39. Lucille Griffith, ed., *Alabama: A Documentary History to 1900* (Tuscaloosa: The University of Alabama Press, 1968), 570. Letter dated October 29, 1874, from H. C. Calhoun (self-described as "colored") of Bluffton, Alabama, to Hon. Mr. Bingham (probably Daniel H. Bingham). (Spelling original.)

40. Oliver H. Farnham to Joseph Speed, June 13, 1873, in SG015979, *Superintendent's Correspondence, 1868–1913*, ADAH. (Spelling original.)

41. ADAH, Dept. of Education, *Annual Report, 1874*, 5.

42. Ibid., 7–10.

43. ADAH, Dept. of Education, *Annual Report, 1875*, 106.

44. Ibid., 48 and 85.

45. Glenn Sisk, "Denominational Schools and Colleges for White Students in the Prairie Section of Mid Alabama, 1875–1900," *Peabody Journal of Education* 35 (July 1957): 27.

46. *Union Springs Herald*, April 30, 1890.

47. Moore, *A History of Alabama and Its People in Three Volumes*, 543.

48. Allen Johnston Going, *Bourbon Democracy in Alabama, 1874–1890*, 2nd ed. (1951; rpt., Tuscaloosa: The University of Alabama Press, 1992), 148.

49. McMillan, *Constitutional Development in Alabama, 1798–1901*, 206. Daniel Savage Gray, in collaboration with J. Barton Starr, *Alabama: A Place, A People, A Point of View* (Dubuque, Iowa: Kendall/Hunt Publishing Company, 1977), 181.

50. *Alabama State Journal* for October 28, 1875, quoted by McMillan, *Constitutional Development in Alabama, 1798–1901*, 213 (footnote 22).

51. *Mobile Register* for October 2 and 26, 1875, quoted by McMillan, *Constitutional Development in Alabama, 1798–1901*, 207 (footnote 122).

52. *Alabama State Journal* of October 27, 1875, quoted by McMillan, *Constitutional Development in Alabama, 1798–1901*, 213 (footnote 26).

53. McMillan, *Constitutional Development in Alabama, 1798–1901*, 216.

54. *Montgomery Advertiser*, September 2, 1877.

55. ADAH, Dept. of Education, *Annual Report, 1875*, 106–107.

56. The Bourbons were nicknamed for French aristocrats who tried to resurrect the *ancien régime* after the defeat of Napoleon.

57. Weeks, *History of Public School Education in Alabama*, 118.

58. Albert Moore, *A History of Alabama and Its People in Three Volumes* (Tuscaloosa: The University of Alabama Press, 1951), 543.

59. *Montgomery Daily Advertiser*, Tuesday, December 4, 1888. Many whites, such as the editor of the *Marengo Democrat*, thought "negroes had only the right to a pauper's pittance."

60. J. Mills Thornton, "Fiscal Policy and the Failure of Radical Reconstruction in the

Lower South," in *Region, Race, and Reconstruction: Essays in Honor of C. Vann Woodward*, ed. J. Morgan Kousser and James M. McPherson (New York: Oxford University Press, 1982), 351–352 and 367–377.

61. J. Wayne Flynt, *Poor but Proud*, 60.

62. Thornton in Kousser and McPherson, *Region, Race, and Reconstruction*, 377.

63. ADAH, Dept. of Education, *Annual Report, 1871*, 52.

64. Horace Mann Bond, *Negro Education in Alabama: A Study in Cotton and Steel* (1939; rpt., Tuscaloosa: The University of Alabama Press, 1994), 149–150.

65. *Public School Laws of Alabama, 1891*, Chapter II, 19.

66. *Wilcox Progress*, February 15, 1888. Going, *Bourbon Democracy in Alabama, 1874–1890*, 157.

67. William. C. Oates to Solomon Palmer, May 27, 1886, in SG015980, Folder 11, *Superintendent's Correspondence, 1889–1953*, ADAH.

68. Going, *Bourbon Democracy in Alabama, 1874–1890*, 168. Wayne Flynt, *Alabama in the Twentieth Century: The Modern South* (Tuscaloosa: The University of Alabama Press, 2004), 222.

69. *Montgomery Advertiser*, November 18, 1888, July 8, 1893.

70. Moore, *A History of Alabama and Its People*, 552.

71. *Mountain Eagle*, August 2, 1893. Alabama Dept. of Education, *Biennial Report, 1894*, 8–13.

72. ADAH, Dept. of Education, *Biennial Report, 1894*, 11.

73. This version of Reconstruction was established by the historian Walter Lynwood Fleming of the pro-South "Dunningite School."

74. Eric Foner, *A Short History of Reconstruction, 1863–1877* (New York: Harper and Row, 1988), xi–xv and 232–234.

75. Federal troops were actually withdrawn from Alabama in 1876.

76. J. Morgan Kousser, "Separate but Not Equal: The Supreme Court's First Decision on Racial Discrimination in Schools," *Journal of Southern History* 46 (February 1980): 42, 43.

77. Wayne Flynt, *Alabama in the Twentieth Century*, 318.

78. The Fifteenth Amendment to the U.S. Constitution was ratified in 1870. It was designed to ensure that color could not be used to bar that person from voting. J. W. Abercrombie is quoted in Robert J. Norrell, *Up from History: The Life of Booker T. Washington* (Cambridge, Mass.: Belknap Press of Harvard University Press, 2009), 203.

Chapter 2

1. Austin R. Meadows, *History of the State Department of Education of Alabama, 1854–1966* (Montgomery: Austin R. Meadows, 1968), 34.

2. ADAH, *Alabama School Laws and Codes, 1858–1901*. Laws Relating to the Public School System of Alabama, 1876–1879, with an Appendix of Forms. Prepared by LeRoy F. Box, state superintendent of education. Chapter II, Article II, Sections 5–11 (particularly Section 7), 8–11.

3. ADAH, Dept. of Education, *Annual Report, 1878*, xviii. *Annual Report, 1891*, 6.

4. Albert Burton Moore, *A History of Alabama and Its People in Three Volumes* (Tuscaloosa: The University of Alabama Press, 1951), 553.

5. Multiple letters on the DeKalb dispute in SG015978, *Superintendent's Correspondence, 1867–1907*, ADAH. Also in SG015974, Folder 3, *Superintendent's Correspondence, 1867–1916*, ADAH.

6. H. J. Martin to Henry Clay Armstrong, August 11, 1883, in SG015978, *Superintendent's Correspondence, 1867–1907*, ADAH.

7. ADAH, *Alabama School Laws and Codes, 1858–1901*. Chapter II, Article III, Sections 12–26, 11–15. Also Chapter II, Article VI, Section 47, paragraphs 1–10, 20–21.

8. Wilbur J. Cash, *The Mind of the South* (1941; rpt., New York: Vintage Books, 1991), 112–113. Grady McWhiney, "Revolution in Nineteenth-Century Agriculture," *From Civil War to Civil Rights—Alabama, 1860–1960: An Anthology from the Alabama Review*, ed. Sarah W. Wiggins (Tuscaloosa: The University of Alabama Press, 1987), 120.

9. Comment made regarding P. Brown Frazier in an undated letter from James C. Sizemore (probably written in August 1877) and enclosed in a letter from Colonel S.K.M. Spadden to LeRoy F. Box, in SG015974, Folder 3, *Superintendent's Correspondence, 1867–1916*, ADAH.

10. Occupations determined from multiple pieces of correspondence in SG015979, *Superintendent's Correspondence, 1868–1913*, ADAH. Also, V. C. Sizemore to John M. McKleroy, August 1877, in SG015974, Folder 3, *Superintendent's Correspondence, 1867–1916*, ADAH. Shelby County Heritage Book Committee, *The Heritage of Shelby County, Alabama* (Clanton, Ala.: Heritage Publishing Consultants, 1999), 400.

11. By Act of the Alabama Assembly in 1888–89 a provision was made for the election of county superintendents in all counties except Autauga, Barbour, Chambers, Choctaw, Cleburne, Dallas, Greene, Hale, Jefferson, Lowndes, Macon, Madison, Montgomery, Mobile, Perry, Pickens, Randolph, Sumter, Talladega, Washington, and Wilcox.

12. Petitions from 138 citizens of Tallapoosa County to LeRoy F. Box in SG15978, Folder 5, *Superintendent's Correspondence, 1877–1878*, ADAH. Also James T. Jones to Solomon Palmer, October 6, 1885, in SG015974, *Superintendent's Correspondence, 1867–1916*, Folder 13, ADAH.

13. Regarding reluctance to secure petitions, see A. S. Stockdale to John M. McKleroy, January 12, 1875, in SG15979, *Superintendent's Correspondence, 1868–1913*, ADAH. Sam C. Cook to John M. McKleroy, January 3, 1875, in SG015974, Folder 2, *Superintendent's Correspondence, 1867–1916*, ADAH.

14. *Troy Messenger,* March 9, 1871, reported that Barbour County had elected a black preacher named Smith as superintendent.

15. John C. Robertson to John M. McKleroy, January 4, 1874, in SG015974, Folder 1, *Superintendent's Correspondence, 1867–1916*, ADAH. N. L. White to John William Abercrombie, September 4, 1899, in SG015975, Folder 2, *Superintendent's Correspondence, 1899–1904*, ADAH. J. L. Davis to John William Abercrombie, February 27, 1899, in SG15979, Folder 1, *Superintendent's Correspondence, 1899–1904*, ADAH.

16. Felix Tait of Wilcox County to John M. McKleroy, December 4, 1874, in SG015978,

Folder 3, *Superintendent's Correspondence, 1873–1874,* ADAH. R. H. Dawson to John M. McKleroy, December 24, 1874, in SG015974, Folder 1, *Superintendent's Correspondence, 1867–1916,* ADAH; Sam C. Cook to John M. McKleroy, January 3, 1875, and D. C. White to John M. McKleroy, January 26, 1875, in SG015974, Folder 2, *Superintendent's Correspondence, 1867–1916,* ADAH. S. T. Frazer of Bullock County to Henry Clay Armstrong, regarding Professor W. P. Stott, September 6, 1883, in SG015978, Folder 10, *Superintendent's Correspondence, 1883–1884,* ADAH. Amos L. Moody to Solomon Palmer, September 5, 1887, in SG015980, Folder 4, *Superintendent's Correspondence, 1886–1887,* ADAH. Unnamed correspondent to LeRoy F. Box, November 1879, regarding J. W. Ferguson in SG015974, Folder 3, *Superintendent's Correspondence, 1867–1916,* ADAH.

17. Allegation made against E. J. Oden of Morgan County in letter from M. F. Patterson to Solomon Palmer, November 30, 1885, in SG015974, Folder 13, *Superintendent's Correspondence, 1867–1916,* ADAH. H. J. Martin to Henry Clay Armstrong, August 11, 1883, in SG15978, *Superintendent's Correspondence, 1867–1907,* ADAH. Joseph E. Acker to John William Abercrombie, August 12, 1899, in SG015975, Folder 2, *Superintendent's Correspondence, 1899–1904,* ADAH.

18. Margaret P. Farmer, *History of Pike County Alabama, 1821–1971* (Anniston, Ala.: Higginbotham, 1973), 213. Farmer is quoting from the *Troy Enquirer* of April 1, 1886.

19. Annie Crook Waters, *History of Escambia County, Alabama* (Huntsville, Ala.: Strode Publishers, 1983), 318.

20. The state superintendent's promotional obligations are stipulated in ADAH, *Alabama School Laws and Codes, 1858–1901,* Chapter II, Article II, 9. The articles setting out the obligations of county and township superintendents did not actually repeat the requirement to promote public education.

21. Patricia Graham, *Community and Class in American Education, 1865–1918* (New York: John Wiley and Sons, 1974), 130–131.

22. ADAH, *Alabama School Laws and Codes, 1858–1901.* Chapter II, Article VI, 20–21.

23. A. M. Nuckols to LeRoy F. Box, February 2, 1880, in SG015974, Folder 6, *Superintendent's Correspondence, 1867–1916,* ADAH.

24. Circular to "The Trustees and Teachers of Public Schools in Russell County" issued in 1882 and located in SG015974, Folder 8, *Superintendent's Correspondence, 1867–1916,* ADAH.

25. Watson, *Coffee Grounds: A History of Coffee County, Alabama, 1841–1970* (Anniston, Ala.: Higginbotham, 1970), 194–195.

26. ADAH, Dept. of Education, *Biennial Report, 1899–1900,* xii.

27. ADAH, *Alabama School Laws and Codes, 1858–1901.* Chapter II, Article VI, 21. Dept. of Education, *Annual Report, 1875,* 104.

28. Letters and petitions of various dates in 1887 to Solomon Palmer, state superintendent, particularly letter from James M. Jordan, probate judge for Franklin County to Solomon Palmer, August 31, 1887, in SG015980, Folder 4, *Superintendent's Correspondence, 1886–1887,* ADAH.

29. Instances of embezzlement or questionable financial transactions occurred in Baldwin, Blount, Clarke, Colbert, Covington, Escambia, Etowah, Lauderdale, and Pike counties.

30. I. J. Loyd to LeRoy F. Box, June 3, 1880, in SG015978, *Superintendent's Correspondence, 1867–1907*, ADAH.

31. ADAH, *Alabama School Laws and Codes, 1858–1901*, Chapter II, Article IV, Sections 27–44, 16–20. Chapter 5, pages 170–171.

32. Jesse S. Sampley to state superintendent of education, February 5, 1880, in SG015974, Folder 5, *Superintendent's Correspondence, 1868–1916*, ADAH. (Spelling original.)

33. M. C. Byrd of Colbert County to Joseph H. Speed, September 12, 1873, in SG015979, *Superintendent's Correspondence, 1868-1913*. ADAH, Dept. of Education, *Annual Report, 1875*, 82 and 98.

34. John J. Steele of Lowndes County to LeRoy F. Box, February 5, 1877, in SG015979, Folder 8, *Superintendent's Correspondence, 1865–1875*, ADAH.

35. Circular addressed to county superintendents from John William Abercrombie, September 26, 1900, in SG015978, *Superintendent's Correspondence, 1867–1907*, ADAH.

36. F. M. Oliver of DeKalb County to LeRoy F. Box, July 10, 1877, in SG015978, Folder 7, *Superintendent's Correspondence, 1867–1907*, ADAH.

37. Richard D. Bounds of Washington County to LeRoy F. Box, August 28, 1880, in SG015978, Folder 7, *Superintendent's Correspondence, 1867–1907*, ADAH.

38. Levi W. Reeves of Marengo County to Henry Clay Armstrong, October 10, 1884, in SG015974, Folder 12, *Superintendent's Correspondence, 1867–1916*, ADAH. (Emphasis original.)

39. J. B. Espy of Henry County to John William Abercrombie, November 28, 1899, in SG015975, Folder 2, *Superintendent's Correspondence, 1899–1904*, ADAH.

40. David B. Tyack, "The Tribe and the Common School: Community Control in Rural Education," *American Quarterly* 24 (March 1972): 5. Mitchell B. Garrett, *Horse and Buggy Days on Hatchet Creek* (Tuscaloosa: The University of Alabama Press, 1957), 148–149. Joe G. Acee, *Lamar County History* (Vernon: *Lamar Democrat*, 1976), 68. Blount County Heritage Book Committee, *The Heritage of Blount County, Alabama* (Clanton, Ala.: Heritage Publishing Consultants, 1999), 60–61. Lawrence County Heritage Book Committee, *The Heritage of Lawrence County, Alabama* (Clanton, Ala.: Heritage Publishing Consultants, 1998), 12.

41. Lawrence S. Knight of Crenshaw County to LeRoy F. Box, February 20, 1880, in SG015979, Folder 6, *Superintendent's Correspondence, 1867–1916*, ADAH.

42. Levi Reeves to Henry Clay Armstrong, October 10, 1884, in SG015979, Folder 12, *Superintendent's Correspondence, 1867–1916*, ADAH.

43. William Warren Rogers, *One-Gallused Rebellion: Agrarianism in Alabama, 1865–1896* (Tuscaloosa: The University of Alabama Press, 2001), xx–xxi.

44. A. S. Stockdale of Clay County to John M. McKleroy, February 6, 1875, in SG015979, *Superintendent's Correspondence, 1868–1913*, ADAH. Petition from eleven citizens of Chilton County to John M. McKleroy, June 23, 1875, in SG015978, Folder 4, *Superintendent's Correspondence, 1867–1907*, ADAH. J. B. Steadham of *The Southern Idea* to Solomon Palmer, September 5, 1887, in SG015979, *Superintendent's Correspondence, 1868–1913*, ADAH. Frank Justice to John William Abercrombie, January 14, 1902, in SG015980, Folder 9, *Superintendent's Correspondence, 1889–1953*, ADAH.

45. Virginia Van der Veer Hamilton, *Alabama: A Bicentennial History* (New York: Norton, 1977), 174.

46. Henry H. Swatos Jr., "Beyond Denominationalism: Community and Culture in American Religion," *Journal for the Scientific Study of Religion* 20 (September 1981): 217–227.

47. ADAH, Dept. of Education, *Biennial Report, 1907–1908,* 74.

48. P. H. Kinney of Bremen, Cullman County, to Henry Clay Armstrong, August 27, 1884, in SG015974, Folder 12, *Superintendent's Correspondence, 1867–1916,* ADAH.

49. Farmer, *History of Pike County Alabama, 1821–1971,* 206.

50. ADAH, Dept. of Education, SG011916, *Annual Historical Reports on Condition of Education for each County/City Board, Annual Report, 1871–1905.*

51. George W. Stewart to Harry C. Gunnels, March 17, 1910, in SG015440, Folder 8, *Superintendent's Correspondence,* ADAH.

52. Alabama State Constitution, 1875. Article XIII, Section 6.

53. ADAH, Dept. of Education, *Annual Report, 1871,* 78.

54. ADAH, Dept. of Education, *Annual Report, 1875,* 101, 105. Ronald Dykes, *Growing Up Hard: Memories of Jackson County, Alabama in the Early Twentieth Century* (Paint Rock, Ala.: Paint Rock River Press, 2003), 36. Baldwin County Heritage Book Committee, *The Heritage of Baldwin County, Alabama* (Clanton, Ala.: Heritage Publishing Consultants, 2001), 67.

55. Winston County Heritage Book Committee, *The Heritage of Winston County, Alabama* (Clanton, Ala.: Heritage Publishing Consultants, 1998), 23. Barbour County Heritage Book Committee, *The Heritage of Barbour County, Alabama* (Clanton, Ala.: Heritage Publishing Consultants, 2001), 127. Blount County Heritage Book Committee, *The Heritage of Blount County, Alabama* (Clanton, Ala.: Heritage Publishing Consultants, 1999), 56–59.

56. ADAH, Dept. of Education, *Annual Report, 1875,* 103 and 106. Alvin M. Spessard of Perry County to John William Abercrombie, December 12, 1899, in SG015975, Folder 2, *Superintendent's Correspondence, 1899–1904,* ADAH.

57. Margaret J. Jones, *Combing Cullman County* (Cullman, Ala.: Modernistic Printers, 1972), 90. *The Heritage of Baldwin County,* 65. Hoyt M. Warren, *Henry's Heritage: A History of Henry County, Alabama* (Abbeville, Ala.: Henry County Historical Society, 1978), 353.

58. ADAH, Dept. of Education, *Annual Report, 1875,* 108.

59. Theodore Rosengarten, *All God's Dangers: The Life of Nate Shaw* (Chicago: University of Chicago Press, 2000), 25.

60. ADAH, Dept. of Education, *Annual Report, 1875,* 91.

61. C. J. Tapscott of Cullman County to Alex Garber, state attorney general, January 20, 1910, in SG015440, Folder 8, *Superintendent's Correspondence,* ADAH.

62. The school law specified a student age range of 7–21 years.

63. ADAH, Dept. of Education, *Annual Report, 1890,* Table IV, cxciii.

64. Garrett, *Horse and Buggy Days on Hatchet Creek,* 167. Linda Jolly Hallmark of Blount County Historical Society in *Heritage of Blount County,* 63. Wade Hall, *Conecuh People: Words from the Alabama Black Belt* (Montgomery: New South Books, 2004), 109–110.

65. Stephen B. Weeks, *History of Public School Education in Alabama* (1915; rpt. Westport, Conn.: Negro Universities Press, 1971), 196.

66. Trudier Harris, *Summer Snow: Reflections from a Black Daughter of the South* (Boston;

Beacon Press, 2003), 23. Farm workers in some parts of the country used the phrase "can see to can't see."

67. Garrett, *Horse and Buggy Days on Hatchet Creek,* 157 and 166.

68. Dykes, *Growing Up Hard,* 106.

69. William J. Edwards, 1918, *Twenty-five Years in the Black Belt,* Repr., Tuscaloosa, The University of Alabama Press, 1993, 5. Charles Johnson, *The Shadow of the Plantation* (Chicago: University of Chicago Press, 1934), 129–132.

70. David B. Tyack, *The One Best System: A History of American Urban Education* (Cambridge, Mass.: Harvard University Press, 1974), 6.

71. Glenn N. Sisk, "Negro Education in the Alabama Black Belt, 1875–1900," *Journal of Negro Education* 22 (Spring 1953): 131.

72. Carl V. Harris, *Political Power in Birmingham, 1871–1921* (Knoxville: University of Tennessee Press, 1977), 168–169.

73. Marshall Fred Phillips, "A History of the Public Schools in Birmingham, Alabama" (Master's thesis, University of Alabama, 1939), 2.

74. Writers' Program of the WPA, *The WPA Guide to 1930s Alabama; introduction by Harvey H. Jackson III* (1941; rpt., Tuscaloosa: The University of Alabama Press, 2000), 113.

75. The Alabama Press Association was consistently pro-reform.

76. The *Wilcox Progress* was founded in 1887, but through later mergers it became the *Wilcox Progressive Era* in 1900.

77. *Wilcox Progress,* May 30, 1888, and July 17, 1889.

78. *Mountain Eagle,* July 12, 1893.

79. Ibid., September 7, 1898.

80. Edward P. Thompson, "Time, Work-Discipline, and Industrial Capitalism," *Past and Present* 38 (December 1967): 84, 89.

81. *Mountain Eagle,* December 9, 1894, June 3, 1896, and September 9, 1896. *Wilcox Progress,* January 1, 1896, November 11, 1896.

82. W. J. Cash, *The Mind of the South,* 86.

83. *Bullock County Breeze,* April 11, 1905, April 18, 1905.

84. U.S. Census reports for 1890 and 1900. Alabama's total population in 1890 was 1,513,401 and in 1900 it was 1,828,697. In 1900 the population was 88.15 percent rural.

85. John D. Humphrey of Madison County to Joseph B. Graham, May 1901, in SG015976, Folder 8, *Superintendent's Correspondence, 1899–1906,* ADAH.

86. *Mountain Eagle,* February 23, 1898.

Chapter 3

1. In the 1868–69 scholastic year there were 2,902 public schools teachers in Alabama. By 1876–77 the number was 4,225. By 1901 the number was 6,302. Stephen B. Weeks, *History of Public School Education in Alabama* (1915; rpt., Westport, Conn.: Negro Universities Press, 1971), 197.

2. Walter L. Fleming, *Civil War and Reconstruction in Alabama* (1905; rpt., Spartanburg: Reprint Co., 1978), 625. 625.

3. *Montgomery Advertiser,* July 30, 1866, and *Selma Times,* June 30, 1866.

4. ADAH, Dept. of Education, *Annual Report, 1871*, 77. ADAH, Dept. of Education, *Annual Report, 1875*, 105. Levi W. Reeves to Henry Clay Armstrong, October 10, 1884, in SG015974, Folder 12, *Superintendent's Correspondence, 1867–1916*, ADAH.

5. ADAH, Dept. of Education, *Annual Report, 1871*, 75.

6. Thomas Wyatt, *History of Chilton County and Her People: History of Chilton County, Alabama* (Montevallo: Times Printing Company, 1976), 42–43.

7. M. H. Savage of Delevan, Wisconsin, to state superintendent of education, August 7, 1873, in SG015978, Folder 3, *Superintendent's Correspondence, 1873–1874*, ADAH.

8. S. P. Lindsay of Evergreen, Conecuh County, to state superintendent, n.d. enclosing letter addressed "To Whom It May Concern," in SG015974, Folder 17, *Superintendent's Correspondence, 1867–1916*, ADAH.

9. Circular from North West Teachers Agency to state superintendent, n.d., in SG015974, Folder 10, *Superintendent's Correspondence, 1867–1916*, ADAH. *Colored Alabamian*, November 30, 1911.

10. Weeks, *History of Public School Education in Alabama*, 155. The term "normal school" (thus "normal" classes) originated with the French *école normale*—a model school. The first public normal school in the United States was established in 1839 in Massachusetts.

11. Ibid., 155.

12. Taken from a speech given by Solomon Palmer to Alabama Educational Association in 1889 and quoted in Don Eddins, *AEA: Head of the Class in Alabama Politics: A History of the Alabama Education Association* (Montgomery: Compos-it Inc., 1997), 232.

13. Curriculum included in SG015978, Folder 11, *Superintendent's Correspondence, 1885–1886*, ADAH.

14. Christine A. Ogren, *The American State Normal School* (New York: Palgrave Macmillan, 2005), 35–36 and 131–132.

15. ADAH, Dept. of Education, *Annual Report, 1890*, xxxviii–xxxix.

16. ADAH, Dept. of Education, *Annual Report, 1889*, 23.

17. William B. Paterson to Henry Clay Armstrong, September 4, 1883, in SG015974, Folder 11, *Superintendent's Correspondence, 1867–1916*, ADAH.

18. Mitchell B. Garrett, *Horse and Buggy Days on Hatchet Creek* (Tuscaloosa: The University of Alabama Press, 1957), 151, 157, 163, and 165.

19. Lorene LeCroy, *Old Schools of Chilton County, Alabama* (Maplesville, Ala.: Chilton County Historical Society, 1997), 6.

20. Margaret J. Jones, *Combing Cullman County* (Cullman, Ala.: Modernistic Printers, 1972), 90; *Standard Gauge*, March 24, 1904. J. Mack Lofton, *Voices from Alabama: A Twentieth-Century Mosaic* (Tuscaloosa: The University of Alabama Press, 1993), 186; Baldwin County Heritage Book Committee, *The Heritage of Baldwin County, Alabama* (Clanton, Ala.: Heritage Publishing Consultants, 2001), 71–72.

21. Adam Fairclough, *A Class of Their Own: Black Teachers in the Segregated South* (Cambridge, Mass.: The Belknap Press of Harvard University Press, 2007), 112–113.

22. Garrett, *Horse and Buggy Days on Hatchet Creek*, 141.

23. Ellwood Patterson Cubberley, *Rural life and education: A study of the rural-school problem as a phase of the rural-life problem* (Boston: Houghton Mifflin, 1914), 105.

24. William Warren Rogers, Robert David Ward, Leah Rawls Atkins, and Wayne Flynt, *Alabama: The History of a Deep South State* (Tuscaloosa: The University of Alabama Press, 1994), 228.

25. LeCroy, *Old Schools of Chilton County, Alabama*, 6.

26. ADAH, Dept. of Education, *Annual Report, 1874*, 6.

27. T.V.R. Matthews to state superintendent, September 5, 1874, and Statement of Claim, March 31, 1875, in SG015974, Folder 1, *Superintendent's Correspondence, 1867–1916*, ADAH.

28. ADAH, Dept. of Education, *Annual Report, 1875*, 90.

29. Amory Dwight Mayo, "Building for the Children of the South," *Education* 5 (1884): 10–11, and "The Women's Movement in the South," *New England Magazine* 5 (1891): 258. Both articles quoted in the introduction to Mayo, *Southern Women in the Recent Educational Movement in the South* (1892; rpt., Baton Rouge: Louisiana State University Press, 1978), xiii and xxi. Pages 242–243 for second quotation.

30. Myra H. Strober and Audri Gordon Lanford, "The Feminization of Public School Teaching: Cross Sectional Analysis, 1850–1880," *Signs* 11 (Winter 1986): 218–219. Barbara Welter, "The Cult of True Womanhood," *American Quarterly* 18 (Summer 1966): 152.

31. Karen L. Cox, *Dixie's Daughters: The United Daughters of the Confederacy and the Preservation of Confederate Culture* (Gainesville: University Press of Florida, 2003), 87–91.

32. Across the South as a whole, women made up 51.2 percent of the teaching workforce by 1880. In 1890 the figure was 58.9 percent. Alabama was actually behind the trend.

33. Calculated from tables appended to ADAH, Dept. of Education, *Biennial Report, 1901–1902*, and ADAH, Dept. of Education, *Biennial Report, 1905–1906*.

34. Calculated from tables appended to ADAH, Dept. of Education, *Biennial Report, 1907–1908*. By 1911, 65 percent of white teachers were female and 69 percent of black teachers were female. ADAH, Dept. of Education, *Annual Report, 1911*.

35. Sumter County Heritage Book Committee, *The Heritage of Sumter County, Alabama* (Clanton, Ala.: Heritage Publishing Consultants, 2005), 94; David Mathews, *Why Public Schools? Whose Public Schools? What Early Communities Have to Tell Us* (Montgomery: New South Books, 2003), 206; *Mountain Eagle*, January 27, 1909; Frank Ross Stewart, *The History of Education in Cherokee County, Alabama* (Center: Stewart University Press, 1981), 86; Wilcox County Heritage Book Committee, *The Heritage of Wilcox County, Alabama* (Clanton, Ala.: Heritage Publishing Consultants, 2002), 51. William H. Holtzclaw, *The Black Man's Burden* (New York: Haskell House Publishers, 1971), 27.

36. LeCroy, *Old Schools of Chilton County, Alabama*, 6.

37. Rose Marie Smith, *Lamar County—A History to 1900* (Fulton: privately published by the author, 1987), 155.

38. Wyatt, *History of Chilton County and Her People*, 78. *The Heritage of Baldwin County*, 68.

39. ADAH, Dept. of Education, *Annual Report, 1889*, 18–19.

40. Cubberley, *Rural life and education*, 283.

41. Smith, *Lamar County—A History to 1900*, 157. Supplemental information obtained from the 1900 census and Alabama marriage records via www.ancestry.com.

42. *The Heritage of Baldwin County*, 68.

43. William Edward Burghardt Du Bois, *The Souls of Black Folk* (1903; rpt., New York: Barnes and Noble Classics, 2003), 49.

44. Garrett, *Horse and Buggy Days on Hatchet Creek,* 136–137. Also Jones, *Combing Cullman County,* 89.

45. Miss Sarah A. Marshall of Elmore County to state superintendent of education, March 10, 1880, in SG015974, Folder 6, *Superintendent's Correspondence, 1867–1907,* ADAH.

46. C. J. Tapscott of Cullman County to Alex Garber, state attorney general, January 20, 1910, in SG015440, Folder 8, *Superintendent's Correspondence,* ADAH.

47. Up to 1879 the report was prepared monthly and teachers were supposed to be paid monthly. Between 1879 and 1903 the report was made quarterly and teachers were paid quarterly. After 1903 the report had again to be prepared monthly and teachers were also again paid monthly.

48. *Public School Law, 1879,* Article IV, Paragraphs 43 and 44. The reporting requirements for teachers were carried over into later versions of the school law—e.g., *Public School Law, 1891,* Chapter 3, Article 1, Section 2, Paragraphs 986 and 987. *Public School Law, 1905,* Article VI, Paragraphs 3580 and 3581. *Public School Law, 1911,* Paragraphs 1748 and 1749, and so on. Before 1879 the Teacher's Report was prepared monthly, teachers had to list the number of visits by the county superintendent as well as the trustees and also indicate pupil "grading."

49. ADAH, Dept. of Education, *Annual Report, 1891,* 23, and *Biennial Report, 1899–1900,* 142.

50. ADAH, Dept. of Education, *Annual Report, 1875,* 115.

51. ADAH, Dept. of Education, *Annual Report, 1871,* 60 and 75.

52. Shelley Sallee, *The Whiteness of Child Labor Reform in the New South* (Athens: University of Georgia Press, 2004), 28–30.

53. Report from J. M. Atkinson for scholastic year ending September 30, 1905, in ADAH, Dept. of Education, SG011916, *County/City Board Annual Report, 1871–1905.*

54. *Weekly Hot Blast,* February 4, 1887 and September 30, 1887. Charles C. Pittman of Randolph County to LeRoy Box, September 6, 1880, in SG015978, Folder 6, *Superintendent's Correspondence, 1878–79,* ADAH.

55. ADAH, Dept. of Education, *Annual Report, 1875,* 82.

56. John W. Abercrombie to Isaac W. McAdory, superintendent of education for Jefferson County, February 22, 1901, in SG015976, Folder 7, *Superintendent's Correspondence, 1899–1906,* ADAH.

57. Eddins, *AEA: Head of the Class in Alabama Politics: Association,* 232–233.

58. *The Public School Law of 1879,* Article VI, Section 47, Paragraphs 7–10. The *Public School Law of 1891,* Article II, Sections 995, 996, 997, and 998. The *Public School Law of 1905,* Article VII, Sections 3590, 3591, 3592, and 3593.

59. ADAH, Dept. of Education, *Annual Report, 1891,* 19–20.

60. ADAH, Dept. of Education, *Annual Report, 1875,* 88.

61. Jesse Monroe Richardson, *The Contribution of John William Abercrombie to Public Education* (Nashville: George Peabody College for Teachers, 1949), 3. ADAH, Dept. of Education, *Biennial Report, 1901–1902,* 40.

62. Superintendent of Chambers County to Henry Clay Armstrong, state superintendent, February 3, 1883, in SG015974, Folder 9, *Superintendent's Correspondence, 1867–1916,* ADAH.

63. Alabama Dept. of Education, *Annual Report, 1885,* 19. *Annual Report, 1874,* 12.

64. ADAH, Dept. of Education, *Annual Report, 1891,* 32.

65. ADAH, Dept. of Education, *Annual Report, 1882,* 8.

66. ADAH, Dept. of Education, *Annual Report, 1889,* 22.

67. ADAH, Dept. of Education, *Annual Report, 1891,* 26, 34.

68. ADAH, Dept. of Education, *Biennial Report, 1899–1900,* 175–176.

69. ADAH, Dept. of Education, *Annual Report, 1891,* 21.

70. *Wilcox Progress,* August 7, 1895.

71. *Troy Messenger,* September 9, 1886.

72. Holtzclaw, *The Black Man's Burden,* 14.

73. Garrett, *Horse and Buggy Days on Hatchet Creek,* 164.

74. John W. Abercrombie, "Official Announcements of State Department of Education," *Educational Exchange* 16, no. 9 (1901): 22–25.

75. *Mountain Eagle,* September 20, 1899.

76. ADAH, Dept. of Education, *Biennial Report, 1899–1900,* xv.

77. Ibid., xii–xv.

78. Ibid., 169.

79. J. J. Williams to John W. Abercrombie, February 23, 1899, in SG015975, Folder 1, *Superintendent's Correspondence, 1899–1904,* ADAH.

80. John Jackson Mitchell of Lauderdale County to John W. Abercrombie, March 3, 1899, in SG015975, Folder 1, *Superintendent's Correspondence, 1899–1904,* ADAH.

81. Henry C. Gilbert to John W. Abercrombie, March 11, 1899, in SG015975, Folder 1, *Superintendent's Correspondence, 1899–1904,* ADAH.

82. L. J. Sherill to John L. Dodson, August 5, 1899, in SG015975, Folder 2, *Superintendent's Correspondence, 1899–1904,* ADAH.

83. *Florence Herald,* January 19, 1905.

84. *Fort Payne Journal,* June 14, 1905.

85. ADAH, Dept. of Education, *Biennial Report, 1899–1900,* xv. *Birmingham Age-Herald,* February 28, 1900 and March 22, 1901 quoted by George W. Prewett, "The Struggle for School Reform in Alabama, 1896-1939." PhD diss., University of Alabama, 1993, 22.

86. J. H. Nunnelee to John W. Abercrombie, November 11, 1899, in SG015975, Folder 2, *Superintendent's Correspondence, 1899–1904,* ADAH.

87. George W. Prewett, "The Struggle for School Reform in Alabama, 1896–1939," (Ph.D. diss., University of Alabama, 1993), 22.

88. George Jones to John W. Abercrombie, October 6, 1899, in SG015975, Folder 2, *Superintendent's Correspondence, 1899–1904,* ADAH.

89. B. W. Collins to John W. Abercrombie, n.d., in SG015975, Folder 14, *Superintendent's Correspondence, 1899–1904,* ADAH.

90. Charles McDowell of Eufala, Barbour County, June 7, 1899; J.M. Sanders of Union Springs, Bullock County, June 19, 1899; P.B. Mize of Brompton in St Clair County, No-

vember 13, 1899; to John W. Abercrombie, in SG015975, Folder 2, *Superintendent's Correspondence, 1899–1904,* ADAH.

91. G. W. Brock to John W. Abercrombie, August 4, 1899. C. L. Cargile to John W. Abercrombie, August 30, 1899, in SG015975, Folder 2, *Superintendent's Correspondence, 1899–1904,* ADAH.

92. John W. Abercrombie to Charles McDowell, August 29, 1899, in SG015975, Folder 2, *Superintendent's Correspondence, 1899–1904,* ADAH.

93. G. W. Brock to John Dodson, August 11, 1899, in SG015975, Folder 2, *Superintendent's Correspondence, 1899–1904,* ADAH.

94. Ibid.

95. John Dodson to John W. Abercrombie, August 9, 1899, in SG015975, Folder 2, *Superintendent's Correspondence, 1899–1904,* ADAH.

96. *General School Laws of Alabama, 1905,* Section 8, 44.

97. F. J. Milligan to John W. Abercrombie, March 6, 1902. Frank M. Justice to Abercrombie, February 10, 1902, in SG015980, Folder 9, *Superintendent's Correspondence, 1902,* ADAH.

98. ADAH, Dept. of Education, *Biennial Report, 1899–1900,* 153.

99. Reports from O. A. Steele, J. N. Word, and L. T. Steele, in ADAH, Dept. of Education, SG011916, *County/City Boards Annual Report, 1905.*

100. E. N. and P. E. Jones, to Hon. William Clarence Jones, September 26, 1903, in SPR184, *William Clarence Jones Letters,* ADAH.

101. Report for Wilcox County by William M. Cook, October 4, 1910, in SG21050, ADAH, Dept. of Education, *Annual Report, 1910.*

102. *General Public School Laws of Alabama, 1905,* 75.

103. Prewett, "The Struggle for School Reform in Alabama, 1896–1939," 53–54.

104. ADAH, Dept. of Education, *Annual Report, 1914,* 52.

105. The pedagogical ideas of Johan Friedrich Herbart (1776–1841) became known in the United States in the 1890s.

106. *State Manual of the Course of Study for the Public Elementary Schools of Alabama* (Montgomery: Brown Printing Company, 1910). *State Manual of the Course of Study for the Public Elementary Schools of Alabama,* Bulletin No. 35, rev. ed. (Montgomery: Brown Printing Company, 1913). *Alabama's Country Schools and their Relation to Country Life,* Bulletin No. 33 (Montgomery: Brown Printing Company, 1913).

107. David B. Tyack, "The Tribe and the Common School: Community Control in Rural Education," 15.

108. Eddins, *AEA: Head of the Class in Alabama Politics,* 233.

109. ADAH, Dept. of Education, *Annual Report, 1915,* 37.

110. Ibid., 21.

Chapter 4

1. Stephen B. Weeks, *History of Public School Education in Alabama* (1915; rpt., Westport, Conn.: Negro Universities Press, 1971), 65–66.

2. Mitchell B. Garrett, *Horse and Buggy Days on Hatchet Creek* (Tuscaloosa: The University of Alabama Press, 1957), 141.

3. Charles Johnson, *The Shadow of the Plantation* (Chicago: University of Chicago Press, 1934), 132.

4. James Agee and Walker Evans, *Let Us Now Praise Famous Men: Three Tenant Families* (Boston: Houghton Mifflin, 1988), 295.

5. Wording is from *Boyd v. State* (1890) decided by Alabama's supreme court. Included in *Public School Laws of the State of Alabama, 1891*, 142–148.

6. ADAH, Dept. of Education, *Annual Report, 1879*, Appended Forms [9]. Lucille Griffith, ed., *Alabama: A Documentary History to 1900* (Tuscaloosa: The University of Alabama Press, 1968), 556.

7. Hoyt M. Warren, *Henry's Heritage: A History of Henry County, Alabama* (Abbeville, Ala.: Henry County Historical Society, 1978), 354.

8. *Alabama State Constitution of 1875*, Article XIII, Section 1. A similar provision was included in the *Alabama State Constitution of 1901*, Article XIV, Section 256.

9. Henry A. Giroux, *Ideology, Culture and the Process of Schooling* (Philadelphia: Temple University Press, 1981), 3. Michael W. Apple, ed. *Cultural and Economic Reproduction in Education: Essays on Class, Ideology and the State* (Boston: Routledge and Kegan Paul, 1982), 4.

10. *Public School Laws of the State of Alabama, 1891*, Chapter II, Article IV, Section 974, 21 and 28.

11. Ronald Dykes, *Growing Up Hard: Memories of Jackson County, Alabama in the Early Twentieth Century* (Paint Rock, Ala.: Paint Rock River Press, 2003), 36. Pike County Heritage Book Committee, *The Heritage of Pike County, Alabama* (Clanton, Ala.: Heritage Publishing Consultants, 2001), 69. Rick Bragg, *Redbirds: Memories from the South* (London: Harvill Press, 1998), 55.

12. ADAH, Dept. of Education, *Annual Report, 1913*, 34. A further 16 percent of schools had just two teachers.

13. Details of inadequate schoolhouses (i) Margaret J. Jones, *Combing Cullman County* (Cullman, Ala.: Modernistic Printers, 1972), 88; (ii) Baldwin County Heritage Book Committee, *The Heritage of Baldwin County, Alabama* (Clanton, Ala.: Heritage Publishing Consultants, 2001), 72; (iii) James Thomason, *General History of Marshall County, Alabama* (Albertville, Ala.: Creative Printers, 1989), 3; (iv) Warren, *Henry's Heritage*, 341; (v) Blount County Heritage Book Committee, *The Heritage of Blount County, Alabama* (Clanton, Ala.: Heritage Publishing Consultants, 1999), 61 and 63: (vi) Garrett, *Horse and Buggy Days on Hatchet Creek*, 152 and 162–163. ADAH, Dept. of Education, *Annual Report, 1875*.

14. ADAH, Dept. of Education, *Annual Report, 1875*, 85.

15. ADAH, Dept. of Education, *Biennial Report, 1901–1902*, 36–37.

16. William H. Holtzclaw, *The Black Man's Burden* (1915; rpt., New York: Haskell House Publishers, 1971), 26.

17. Jones, *Combing Cullman County*, 95. *The Heritage of Baldwin County, Alabama*, 75. Greene County Heritage Book Committee, *The Heritage of Greene County, Alabama*, 28.

18. Garrett, *Horse and Buggy Days on Hatchet Creek*, 157–159. Wesley S. Thompson, "*The Free State of Winston*": *A History of Winston County, Alabama* (Winfield, Ala.: Pareil Press, 1968), 198.

19. The offspring of a number of Jewish merchant families at Greenville in Butler County dominated the public school's honor roll in the 1890s. Patricia A. Graham, *Community and Class in American Education, 1865–1918* (New York: John Wiley and Sons, 1974), 120. In 1900 the total Jewish population of Alabama was approximately 6,000. In 1906 a religious census showed adult Roman Catholic church members numbered 50,000—about 6 percent of total adult church membership.

20. Lawrence W. Levine, *Black Culture and Black Consciousness* (New York: Oxford University Press, 1978), 157.

21. ADAH, Dept. of Education, *Annual Report, 1889,* 33.

22. Fred S. Watson, *Coffee Grounds: A History of Coffee County, Alabama, 1841–1970* (Anniston, Ala.: Higginbotham, 1970), 191. *Mountain Eagle,* December 1, 1909—address by Professor Charles B. Glenn.

23. *Mountain Eagle,* December 16, 1908.

24. *Standard Gauge,* March 24, 1904.

25. Charles C. Pittman to LeRoy Box, September 6, 1880, SG015978, Folder 6, *Superintendent's Correspondence, 1878–79,* ADAH.

26. Weeks, *History of Public School Education in Alabama,* 198.

27. Calculated from tables included in ADAH, Dept. of Education, *Annual Report, 1890,* Table IV, cxciii.

28. Bobby L. Lindsey, *The Reason for the Tears: A History of Chambers County, Alabama, 1832–1900* (West Point, Ala.: Hester Print. Co., 1971), 215.

29. *The Heritage of Baldwin County, Alabama,* 72. Wade Hall, *Conecuh People: Words from the Alabama Black Belt* (Montgomery: New South Books, 2004), 127.

30. Judgment by Justice Henderson M. Somerville of Alabama's supreme court in *Boyd v. State* (1890). Other schoolmasters were charged with abuse of their authority—e.g., *McCormack v. State* (102 Alabama 156).

31. Garrett, *Horse and Buggy Days on Hatchet Creek,* 153.

32. Charles Johnson, *Shadow of the Plantation* (Chicago: University of Chicago Press, 1934), 131–132.

33. Wayne E. Fuller, *The Old Country School: The Story of Rural Education in the Middle West* (Chicago: University of Chicago Press, 1982), 209–210. Paul Theobald, *Call School: Rural Education in the Midwest to 1918* (Carbondale: Southern Illinois University Press, 1995), 137–139.

34. *Proceedings of the Alabama Teachers' Association for 1884,* 14–16, reprinted in Don Eddins, *AEA: Head of the Class in Alabama Politics: A History of the Alabama Education Association* (Montgomery: Compos-it Inc., 1997), 227–229.

35. *The Heritage of Baldwin County,* 79. Glenn N. Sisk, "Churches in the Alabama Black Belt 1875–1917," *Church History* 23 (June 1954): 163.

36. *Troy Messenger,* March 12, 1874.

37. Weeks, *History of Public School Education in Alabama,* 66–67.

38. *Acts of the Board of Education passed at the Session Commencing July 23, 1868,* 21. ADAH, Alabama State Dept. of Education, *Journals and Acts of the Board of Education and Board of Regents of the University or State of Alabama, 1869–1874.* ADAH SG013206, Folder 1, Session commencing November 25, 1872, 62 and 79–80. Act No. 9 of this session adopted Goold

Brown's *The First Lines of English Grammar* (1851) and *The Institutes of English Grammar* (1850) both published by William Wood and Co. of New York.

39. John A. Nietz, *Old Textbooks* (Pittsburgh: University of Pittsburgh Press, 1961), 1.

40. *Standard Gauge,* March 24, 1904.

41. Weeks, *History of Public School Education in Alabama,* 66–67. Rose Marie Smith, *Lamar County—A History to 1900* (Fulton, Ala.: privately published by the author, 1987), 157.

42. E. Jennifer Monaghan, *A Common Heritage: Noah Webster's Blue-Back Speller* (Hampden, Conn.: Archon Books, 1983), 208–210, 219.

43. Henry Steele Commager, ed., *Noah Webster's American Spelling Book* (New York: Columbia University, 1962), 10–11. (Italics original.)

44. Elliott J. Gorn, ed., *McGuffey's First-Sixth Eclectic Reader: Selections from the 1879 Edition* (Boston: Bedford Books, 1998), 11–12.

45. Richard Mosier, *Making the American Mind: Social and Moral Ideas in the McGuffey Readers* (New York: Russell and Russell, 1965), 167–170.

46. Garrett, *Horse and Buggy Days on Hatchet Creek,* 140.

47. John A. Nietz, "Why the Longevity of the McGuffey Readers?" *History of Education Quarterly* 4 (June 1964): 123–124.

48. *Mountain Eagle,* February 5, 1896.

49. Neal C. Gillespie, "The Spiritual Odyssey of George Frederick Holmes: A Study of Religious Conservatism in the Old South," *Journal of Southern History* 32 (August 1966): 305 and 307.

50. *The Heritage of Blount County,* 67. Thomason, *General History of Marshall County, Alabama,* 9.

51. Noah Webster, *The elementary spelling book: Being an improvement on "The American Spelling Book"* (New York: D. Appleton and Co., 1857), 132.

52. Jones, *Combing Cullman County,* 90. Garrett, *Horse and Buggy Days on Hatchet Creek,* 140.

53. William J. Edwards, *Twenty-five Years in the Black Belt* (1918; rpt., Tuscaloosa: The University of Alabama Press, 1993), 15.

54. Watson, *Coffee Grounds,* 201.

55. Garrett, *Horse and Buggy Days on Hatchet Creek,* 140.

56. Watson, *Coffee Grounds,* 57. Griffith, *Alabama: A Documentary History to 1900,* 564.

57. Walter L. Fleming, *Civil War and Reconstruction in Alabama* (1905; rpt., Spartanburg, S.C.: Reprint Co., 1978), 623.

58. Horace Mann Bond, *Negro Education in Alabama: A Study in Cotton and Steel* (1939; rpt., Tuscaloosa: The University of Alabama Press, 1994), 115–116.

59. Robert C. Morris, ed., *Freedmen's Schools and Textbooks,* Vol. 2 *[The Freedmen's Spelling Book, The Freedmen's Second Reader, The Freedmen's Third Reader]* (New York: An AMS Reprint Series, AMS Press, 1980).

60. *Alabama Educational Magazine* 1, no. 3 (June 1871): 191 and 197–198.

61. *Wilcox Progress,* December 18, 1889. *Mountain Eagle,* December 7, 1898.

62. ADAH, Dept. of Education, *Circular from John G. Harris,* dated September 11, 1891.

63. Marie Carpenter, *The treatment of the Negro in American history school textbooks; a comparison of changing textbook content, 1826 to 1939, with developing scholarship in the history of the*

Negro in the United States (Menasha, Wisc.: George Banta Publishing Company, 1941), 9. In an article entitled "Home Education at the South" by Rev. C. K. Marshall in *De Bow's Review* of May 1855 options relating to the Southern production of textbooks were canvassed, including legislative action.

64. Stephen B. Weeks, *Confederate Text-books* (Washington, D.C.: Government Printing Office, 1900), 1143–1147.

65. Laura Hein and Mark Selden, eds., *Censoring History: Citizenship and Memory in Japan, Germany, and the United States* (New York: M. E. Sharp, 2000), 3–4. Michael W. Apple and Linda K. Christian-Smith, *The Politics of the Textbook* (New York: Routledge, 1991), 5.

66. Joint History Committee of the Confederate Veterans Association of Alabama, *Appeal for Information Respecting Histories in Use in Alabama Schools* (Montgomery, n.p., 1902).

67. *Alabama Educational Magazine* 1, no. 3 (June 1871): 155.

68. *Montgomery Advertiser,* November 11, 1888, November 22, 1888, and December 1, 1892.

69. *Wilcox Progress,* December 18, 1889.

70. ADAH, Dept. of Education, *Biennial Report, 1901–1902,* 13.

71. Ibid., 37.

72. Ibid., 5–6. S. J. Griffin to John William Abercrombie, May 1, 1901, in SG015976, Folder 8, *Superintendent's Correspondence, 1899–1906,* ADAH.

73. Weeks, *History of Public School Education in Alabama,* 136.

74. *Alabama Acts*—Act No. 123 of 1896. Smith, *Lamar County—A History to 1900,* 157.

75. William C. Griggs, president of Spring Lake College, St. Clair County, to John W. Abercrombie, February 25, 1899, in SG015975, Folder 1, *Superintendent's Correspondence, 1899–1904,* ADAH.

76. *Alabama Acts*—Act No. 123 of 1896. Section 2, 285.

77. *Winston Herald,* June 25, 1885, quoted in Thompson, 198.

78. *Alabama Acts*—Act No. 123 of 1896. Section 2, 286.

79. Calculations made from reports included in ADAH, Dept. of Education, *Biennial Report, 1901–1902.*

80. George W. Prewett, "The Struggle for School Reform in Alabama, 1896–1939" (Ph.D. diss., University of Alabama, 1993), 26.

81. *General Public School Laws of Alabama, 1905,* 62–75.

82. Ibid., 63.

83. *Mountain Eagle,* November 25, 1903. Adopted books listed.

84. Matthew Fontaine Maury, *Elementary Geography* (New York: University Publishing Company, 1899), 21–22 and 26.

85. *Mountain Eagle,* January 26, 1898.

86. Ruth Elson, *Guardians of Tradition: American Schoolbooks of the Nineteenth Century* (Lincoln: University of Nebraska Press, 1964), 65.

87. Claude H. Nolen, *The Negro's Image in the South: The Anatomy of White Supremacy* (Lexington: Kentucky University Press, 1967), 125.

88. Robert J. Norrell, *Up from History: The Life of Booker T. Washington* (Cambridge, Mass.: Belknap Press of Harvard University Press, 2009), 336.

89. L. D. Miller, *History of Alabama: adapted to the use of schools, and for general reading* (Birmingham: published by the author, 1901), 147.

90. William Garrott Brown, *A History of Alabama for Use in Schools* (New Orleans: University Publishing Company, 1900), 225–226.

91. Joel DuBose, *Alabama History* (Atlanta: B. F. Johnson Publishing Company, 1908), 215.

92. *Cherokee Harmonizer,* April 19, 1906.

93. ADAH, Dept. of Education, *Annual Report, 1891,* 23–24.

94. Carl V. Harris, *Political Power in Birmingham, 1871–1921* (Knoxville: University of Tennessee Press, 1977), 170.

95. Susie P. Tompkins, *Cotton-patch School-house* (Tuscaloosa: The University of Alabama Press, 1992), 34.

96. Lawrence A. Cremin, *The Transformation of the Schools: Progressivism in American Education, 1876–1957* (New York: Alfred A. Knopf, 1961), 90.

97. Cremin, *The Transformation of the Schools,* 90–91.

98. *These Acts in Public School Laws of the State of Alabama, 1891,* 24–25, and *General Public School Laws of Alabama, 1905,* 78–79.

99. ADAH, Dept. of Education, *Biennial Report, 1905–1906,* 5.

100. This is implicit in all departmental publications such as *State Manual of the Course of Study for the Public Elementary Schools of Alabama,* Bulletin No. 35, rev. ed. (Montgomery: Brown Printing Company, 1913).

101. *Fort Payne Journal,* June 7, 1905.

102. *Opelika Daily News,* June 8, 1905.

103. *Bullock County Breeze,* April 11, 1905.

104. Alabama's educators were not alone seeking to wrest control from local interests. See David Tyack, "The Tribe and the Common School: Community Control in Rural Education," *American Quarterly* 24 (March 1972): 16.

105. Successive publications designed for rural schools were *A Suggestive Course of Study for the Common Schools of Alabama* (Montgomery: Brown Printing Company, 1908); *State Manual of the Course of Study for the Public Elementary Schools of Alabama* (Montgomery: Brown Printing Company, 1910; revised in 1913). *Daily Programs of Recitation and Study Suggestive for Use in the Rural and Village Schools of Alabama* (Montgomery: n.p., 1910). *Alabama's Country Schools and their Relation to Country Life,* Bulletin No. 33 (Montgomery: Brown Printing Company, 1913).

106. ADAH, Dept. of Education, *Annual Report, 1912,* 28. ADAH, Dept. of Education, *Annual Report, 1913,* 36–39.

107. Theodore Roosevelt's *Commission on Country Life* was established in August, 1908 to review and recommend on what was needed for the betterment of rural life.

Chapter 5

1. George W. Prewett, "The Struggle for School Reform in Alabama, 1896–1939" (PhD diss., University of Alabama, 1993), 6.

2. Stephen B. Weeks, *History of Public School Education in Alabama* (1915; rpt., West-

port, Conn.: Negro Universities Press, 1971), 26–29. ADAH, Dept. of Education, *Annual Report, 1878,* xii.

3. Weeks, *History of Public School Education in Alabama,* 28 and 35–41. The liquidation was completed in 1853. Ira Harvey, *A History of Educational Finance in Alabama, 1819-1970,* Auburn, Truman Pierce Institute for the Advancement of Teacher Education, 1989, 51-56.

4. Weeks, *History of Public School Education in Alabama,* 53, 60–61.

5. Ibid., 39.

6. William D. Wilson to LeRoy F. Box, October 28, 1880, in SG015974, Folder 6, *Superintendent's Correspondence, 1867–1916,* ADAH.

7. ADAH, Dept. of Education, *Biennial Report, 1899–1900,* 150.

8. *Alabama Acts,* 1875–76, 1877–78, 1878–79.

9. In Bullock County in 1901 a teacher taught a nine-month school for $100.00 per month. The state paid $500, and the balance was provided in the form of a credit note at a local store. The merchant collected the $400 from patrons.

10. William H. Holtzclaw, *The Black Man's Burden* (1915; rpt., New York: Haskell House Publishers, 1971), 25–26.

11. J. Mack Lofton, *Voices from Alabama: A Twentieth-Century Mosaic* (Tuscaloosa: The University of Alabama Press, 1993), 176.

12. *An Act to Establish, Organize and Regulate a System of Public Instruction for the State of Alabama approved February 7, 1879.* Article IV, Section 34.

13. Russell Stompler, "A History of the Financing of Public Schools in Alabama from Earliest Times," 331–332. There is no accurate way of converting salaries of the past into modern equivalents but the 1890 purchasing power of $25.00 was roughly equivalent to the 2006 purchasing power of $571.43.

14. John M. McKleroy to LeRoy Box, August 16, 1877, in SG015978, *Superintendent's Correspondence, 1867–1907,* ADAH.

15. Jill Knight Garrett, *A History of Lauderdale County, Alabama* (Columbia: Jill Knight Garrett, 1964), 148.

16. Malcolm Cook McMillan, *Constitutional Development in Alabama, 1798–1901: A Study in Politics, the Negro, and Sectionalism* (Chapel Hill: University of North Carolina Press, 1978), 241–242.

17. *Mountain Eagle,* November 7, 1894.

18. Ibid., November 14, 1894.

19. Ibid., November 21, 1894. *Alabama Acts,* 1895, Number 275.

20. *Mountain Eagle,* September 9, 1896, October 6, 1896, and November 11, 1896.

21. Ibid., August 25, 1897.

22. Ibid., September 1, 1897.

23. Ibid., June 10, 1908, July 1, 1908, and July 29, 1908.

24. Ibid., April 14, 1909, April 21, 1909, and October 7, 1909.

25. Thomas Jefferson to Pierre Samuel Dupont de Nemours, April 24, 1816. Thomas Jefferson, *The Correspondence of Jefferson and Dupont de Nemours—with an Introduction on Jefferson and the Physiocrats by Gilbert Chinard, Baltimore* (Baltimore: Johns Hopkins University Press, 1931), 256–257.

26. Besides the accounts provided here, see also the *Troy Messenger* of June 16, 1881, and the *Fort Payne Journal* of July 5, 1905. The *Troy Messenger* was published in Pike County and the *Fort Payne Journal* in DeKalb County.

27. *Wilcox Progress*, June 22, 1887, June 29, 1887, July 6, 1887, and July 20, 1887.

28. *Gadsden Times*, July 6, 1877.

29. Theodore Rosengarten, *All God's Dangers: The Life of Nate Shaw* (Chicago: University of Chicago Press, 2000), 218. Nate Shaw's true name was Ned Cobb.

30. *Act to organize and regulate a system of public instruction for the State of Alabama, approved February 7, 1879*, Section 1, Paragraph 8.

31. For example, a special school district was established in the city of Eufala in Barbour County on February 14, 1891, and specified that it would receive "all license moneys from liquor sales in beat 5 in Barbour County."

32. Under Section 52 of the 1881 *Revised Code of Laws for the City of Troy*, it was unlawful to carry on a business or occupation for which a license was required without having paid the scheduled license fee to the city clerk and treasurer. *Troy Messenger*, January 13, 1881.

33. *Alabama Acts* (Act 499, S. 333, approved February 21, 1893). Quoted in Stompler, "A History of the Financing of Public Schools in Alabama from Earliest Times," 294.

34. F. L. McCoy to John W. Abercrombie, August 24, 1899, in SG015975, Folder 2, *Superintendent's Correspondence, 1899–1904*, ADAH.

35. *Acts of Alabama, 1883*. Enacted on February 10, 1883. Quoted in Stompler, "A History of the Financing of Public Schools in Alabama from Earliest Times," 303.

36. *Russell Register*, May 3, 1883.

37. Ibid., June 14, 1883.

38. The *Union Springs Herald* item was reprinted in the *Troy Messenger* in its edition of May 5, 1881.

39. The *Wetumpka Times* item was reprinted in the *Troy Messenger* in its edition of May 21, 1885.

40. *Alabama Acts, 1887*. The act was amended on February 18, 1891.

41. *Acts of Alabama*, Number 163 of 1907. Enacted March 2, 1907.

42. *Bullock County Breeze*, February 14, 1905.

43. Report for Carrollton District in Pickens County for 1904–05 by R. T. Clayton, superintendent of education, in Alabama Dept. of Education, SG011916, *County/City Board Annual Report, 1871–1905*.

44. James B. Sellers, *The Prohibition Movement in Alabama, 1702–1943* (Chapel Hill: University of North Carolina Press, 1943), 86–93.

45. *Troy Messenger*—item reprinted in the *Standard Gauge*, January 15, 1903.

46. *Mountain Eagle*, January 11, 1905, and January 18, 1905.

47. *Cherokee Harmonizer*, May 10, 1906.

48. Sellers, *The Prohibition Movement in Alabama, 1702–1943*, 100.

49. *Standard Gauge*, April 27, 1905.

50. *Mountain Eagle*, July 1, 1903.

51. Ibid., January 11, 1905.

52. Ibid., October 30, 1907.

53. Liquor sales in Alabama were outlawed from January 1909.

54. *Mountain Eagle,* September 30, 1908.

55. *Columbia Breeze* item was reprinted in the *Opelika Daily News* of July 15, 1905.

56. Stompler, "A History of the Financing of Public Schools in Alabama from Earliest Times," 308–309.

57. Weeks, *History of Public School Education in Alabama,* 122.

58. Ibid., 123.

59. Ibid., 122.

60. Ibid., 123.

61. The 1875 constitution limited state property taxes to seven and one-half mills. The "Bulger tax" passed in the 1898–99 legislative session earmarked one mill of this for schools.

62. ADAH, Dept. of Education, *Biennial Report, 1899–1900,* v, vii.

63. *Alabama State Constitution, 1901,* Article XIV, Section 269.

64. Charles W. Dabney, *Universal Education in the South,* vol. 2 (Chapel Hill: University of North Carolina Press, 1936), 280.

65. *Mountain Eagle,* June 8, 1904.

66. *Opelika Daily News,* June 26, 1905.

67. Ibid., September 15, 1905. (Capitalization original.)

68. *Opelika Daily News,* September 19, 1905.

69. Murphy had been a Montgomery clergyman, a child labor activist and, later, a member of the Southern Education Board. Harry Gunnels to Edgar Gardner Murphy, October 27, 1905, in SG07765, Folder 29, *Superintendent's Correspondence, 1904–1905,* ADAH.

70. Hugh C. Bailey, *Edgar Gardner Murphy: Gentle Progressive,* 171, and Weeks, *History of Public School Education in Alabama,* 150–151.

71. *Public School Laws of Alabama, 1891,* Chapter II, Article IV, 19. See chapter 1 for the implications of the 1891 law.

72. Henry J. Willingham to Will M. Cook, August 3, 1912, in SG07765, Folder 23, *Superintendent's Correspondence, 1911–1914,* ADAH.

73. Will M. Cook to Henry J. Willingham, September 5, 1912; William Feagin to Will M. Cook, December 17, 1913; Will M. Cook to William Feagin, December 18, 1913, in SG07765, Folder 23, *Superintendent's Correspondence, 1911–1914,* ADAH.

74. Henry J. Willingham to Charles C. Johnson, April 17, 1912, in SG07765, Folder 23, *Superintendent's Correspondence, 1911–1914,* ADAH. Charles C. Johnson to Henry J. Willingham, April 23, 1912, in same location.

75. William Warren Rogers, Robert David Ward, Leah Rawls Atkins, and Wayne Flynt, *Alabama: The History of a Deep South State* (Tuscaloosa: The University of Alabama Press, 1994), 322.

76. Horace Mann Bond, *Negro Education in Alabama: A Study in Cotton and Steel* (1939; rpt., Tuscaloosa: The University of Alabama Press, 1994), 153. Pamela Barnhouse Walters, David R. James, and Holly J. McCammon, "Citizenship and Public Schools: Accounting for Racial Inequality in Education in the Pre- and Post-Disenfranchisement South," *American Sociological Review* 62 (February 1997): 35.

77. Poll-tax provisions are included in Alabama's state constitutions of 1868 (Article XI, Section 12); 1875 (Article XIII, Section 4); and 1901 (Article XIV, Section 259).

78. *Bullock County Breeze,* April 11, 1905.

79. Carl V. Harris, *Political Power in Birmingham, 1871–1921* (Knoxville: University of Tennessee Press, 1977), 172.

80. Benjamin F. Alvord, M. A. Crosby, and E. G. Schiffman, *Factors Influencing Alabama Agriculture, Its Characteristics, and Farming Areas,* Bulletin 250, Agricultural Experiment Station, Auburn, Alabama Polytechnic Institute, 1941, 45.

81. William J. Edwards, *Twenty-five Years in the Black Belt* (1918; rpt., Tuscaloosa: The University of Alabama Press, 1993), 100.

82. Russell Sage Foundation Division of Education, *A Comparative Study of Public School Systems in the Forty-Eight States* (New York: Russell Sage Foundation, 1912), 33.

83. ADAH, Dept. of Education, *Biennial Report, 1907–1908,* 33.

Chapter 6

1. Dewey W. Grantham, *Southern Progressivism: The Reconciliation of Progress and Tradition* (Knoxville: University of Tennessee Press, 1983), 23.

2. ADAH, Dept. of Education, *Annual Report, 1915,* 23. Lawrence A. Cremin, *The Transformation of the Schools: Progressivism in American Education, 1876–1957* (New York: Alfred A. Knopf, 1961), 82. See also David B. Danbom, "Rural Education Reform and the Country Life Movement, 1900–1920," *Agricultural History* 53 (April 1979): 462–474.

3. This assertion is based on multiple sources. It was the raison d'être for the post–Civil War missions to the people of the Appalachians; it underpinned the assumptions upon which President Theodore Roosevelt's 1908 Commission on Country Life was predicated; and it is the implicit premise of W. F. Feagin's *An Educational Survey of Three Counties* conducted in 1914. Most particularly, see Danbom, "Rural Education Reform and the Country Life Movement, 1900–1920," 474.

4. Mary Martha Thomas, *The New Woman in Alabama: Social Reforms, and Suffrage, 1890–1920* (Tuscaloosa: The University of Alabama Press, 1992), 4.

5. Ibid., 43.

6. Lura Harris Craighead, *History of the Alabama Federation of Women's Clubs, Vol. 1, 1895–1918* (Montgomery: Paragon Press, 1936), 24.

7. Ibid., 27.

8. Ibid., 35–36.

9. *Selma Times,* May 5, 1898.

10. Craighead, *History of the Alabama Federation of Women's Clubs, Vol. 1, 1895–1918,* 43–44.

11. *Birmingham Age-Herald,* May 14, 1901.

12. Karen Blair, *The Clubwoman as Feminist: True Womanhood Redefined, 1868–1914* (New York: Holmes & Meier Publishers, 2000), 103.

13. Craighead, *History of the Alabama Federation of Women's Clubs,* 128 and 303.

14. Ibid., 36.

15. Ibid., 139.

16. School improvement associations, under a number of names, were already being organized in other parts of the South.

17. Craighead, *History of the Alabama Federation of Women's Clubs,* 139.

18. *Mountain Eagle,* April 5, 1905.

19. Joseph F. Kett, "Women and the Progressive Impulse," in *The Web of Southern Social Relations: Women, Family and Education,* ed. Walter J. Fraser, R. Frank Saunders Jr., and Jon L. Wakelyn (Athens: University of Georgia Press, 1985), 172.

20. *Russell Register,* June 14, 1882.

21. ADAH, SPR0106, *Alabama School Improvement Association, Records, 1912–1919.* Constitution in *Proceedings of the Alabama School Improvement Association, March 1913.*

22. Stephen B. Weeks, *History of Public School Education in Alabama* (1915; rpt., Westport, Conn.: Negro Universities Press, 1971), 176. Craighead, *History of the Alabama Federation of Women's Clubs,* 215–216. Alabama Dept. of Education, *Annual Report, 1912,* 25.

23. Blair, *The Clubwoman as Feminist,* 108–110.

24. John William Abercrombie's uncle to Mrs. E. O. Morrisette, 1899, in SG015975, Folder 1, *Superintendent's Correspondence, 1899–1904,* ADAH.

25. Blair, *The Clubwoman as Feminist,* 108–109.

26. *Colored Alabamian,* July 25, 1908.

27. Thomas, *The New Woman in Alabama,* 74–75. Evelyn Brooks, *Righteous Discontent: The Women's Movement in the Black Baptist Church, 1880–1920* (Cambridge, Mass.: Harvard University Press, 1993).

28. Writers' Program of the WPA, *The WPA Guide to 1930s Alabama; introduction by Harvey H. Jackson III* (1941; rpt., Tuscaloosa: The University of Alabama Press, 2000), 124.

29. ADAH. Dept. of Education, SG013232, *Results of Clean-Up and School Improvement Day,* 25 and 28.

30. Ibid., 7–9.

31. Ibid., 23, 40.

32. Ibid., 23.

33. *Opelika Daily News,* June 5, 1905.

34. *Mountain Eagle,* September 11, 1907.

35. *Alabama Acts, 1911.*

36. Craighead, *History of the Alabama Federation of Women's Clubs,* 269.

37. Mitchell B. Garrett, *Horse and Buggy Days on Hatchet Creek* (Tuscaloosa: The University of Alabama Press, 1957), 38.

38. Craighead, *History of the Alabama Federation of Women's Clubs,* 287, 303, 335.

39. ADAH, SPR0106, *Alabama School Improvement Association, Records, 1912–1919.* Reports of meetings held March 1913 and December 19, 1914.

40. Ibid. Report of meeting held December 19, 1914.

41. Russell Sage Foundation Division of Education, *A Comparative Study of Public School Systems in the Forty-eight States* (New York: Russell Sage Foundation, 1912), 33.

42. Craighead, *History of the Alabama Federation of Women's Clubs,* 336.

43. Joseph F. Kett, "Women and the Progressive Impulse," in *The Web of Southern Social Relations: Women, Family and Education* Walter J. Fraser, R. Frank Saunders Jr., and Jon L. Wakelyn, 174 (Athens: University of Georgia Press, 1985).

44. *Mountain Eagle,* December 1, 1909.

45. Leon H. Prather, *Resurgent Politics and Educational Progressivism* (Rutherford: Fairleigh Dickinson University Press, 1979), 208–210.

46. Edwin A. Alderman quoted in Dumas Malone, *Edwin A. Alderman,* 145–146, and requoted in Louis R. Harlan, *Separate and Unequal: Public School Campaigns and Racism in the Southern Seaboard States, 1901–1915* (1958; rpt., New York: Atheneum, 1968), 93.

47. Theodore R. Mitchell, "From Black to White: The Transformation of Educational Reform in the South, 1890–1910," *Educational Theory* 39 (Fall 1989): 345–346.

48. Quoted in Prather, *Resurgent Politics and Educational Progressivism,* 213. Harlan, *Separate and Unequal,* 85, footnote 30. Regarding Page's speech, see also Dabney, *Universal Education in the South,* vol. 2, 46.

49. General Education Board, *The General Education Board: an account of its activities, 1902–1914* (New York: General Education Board, 1914), 15–17.

50. Dabney, *Universal Education in the South,* vol. 2, 153.

51. This phrase (coined by Jefferson) was on the SEB's seal.

52. Harlan, *Separate and Unequal;* Robert Sherer, *Subordination or Liberation? The Development and Conflicting Theories of Black Education in Nineteenth-Century Alabama* (Tuscaloosa: The University of Alabama Press, 1977); William H. Watkins, *The White Architects of Black Education: Ideology and Power in America, 1865–1954* (Teaching for Social Justice, 6) (New York: Teachers College Press, 2001); James D. Anderson, *The Education of Blacks in the South, 1860–1935* (Chapel Hill: University of North Carolina Press, 1988). Theodore R. Mitchell, "From Black to White: The Transformation of Educational Reform in the South, 1890–1910," *Educational Theory* 39 (Fall 1989): 337–350.

53. Dabney, *Universal Education in the South,* vol. 2, 222–223.

54. Joseph B. Graham, "Current Problems in Alabama," *Annals of the American Academy of Political and Social Sciences* 22 (September 1903): 36.

55. Ibid., 37.

56. Ibid. See also *Florence Herald,* July 14, 1905.

57. ADAH, Dept. of Education, *Biennial Report, 1894,* 11 and 9. Hugh C. Bailey, *Edgar Gardner Murphy: Gentle Progressive* (Coral Gables: University of Miami Press, 1968), 158, 159.

58. Ibid., 37–38.

59. *Standard Gauge,* January 15, 1903. *Mountain Eagle,* January 14, 1903.

60. *Standard Gauge,* March 5, 1903.

61. *General Public School Laws in Alabama, 1905* issued by Isaac W. Hill. The numbers of these laws follow: No. 164 of 1903 (Textbook Commission); Act No. 365 of 1903 (Redistricting); No. 391 of 1903 (Teacher summer schools); No. 409 of 1903 (School tax); No. 560 of 1903 (Teaching agriculture).

62. U.S. Census 1910. The state's population was 2,138,093, of which 17.3 percent was urban and 82.7 percent rural.

63. ADAH, Dept. of Education, *Biennial Report, 1899–1900,* 136.

64. Philip Dorf, *Liberty Hyde Bailey: An Informal Biography* (Ithaca, N.Y.: Cornell University Press, 1956), 109–115. Cremin, *The Transformation of the Schools,* 75–76, 78.

65. Dabney, *Universal Education in the South,* vol. 2, 98–99.

66. U.S. Senate, *The Report of the Commission on Country Life* (Reprint of Document No 705, 60th Congress, 2d Session) (Spokane: Spokane Chamber of Commerce, 1911), 9–10 and 41–46. Thomas Jefferson to James Madison on October 28, 1785.

67. Ann M. Keppel, "The Myth of Agrarianism in Rural Education Reform, 1890–1914," *History of Education Quarterly* 2 (June 1962): 105.

68. Theodore Saloutos, "The Grange in the South, 1870–1877," *Journal of Southern History* 19 (November 1953): 485.

69. *Mountain Eagle,* December 2, 1903.

70. The population figures given in the manual were based on the 1900 census when the state was 88.1 percent rural. ADAH, Dept. of Education, *State Manual of the Course of Study for the Public Elementary Schools of Alabama* (Montgomery: Brown Printing Company, 1910), 180 (hereafter cited as *1910 Elementary Schools Manual*). Orville G. Brim, "The Curriculum Problem in Rural Elementary Schools," *Elementary School Journal* 23 (April 1923): 588.

71. ADAH, *1910 Elementary Schools Manual,* 185–187.

72. ADAH, *Alabama's Country Schools and their Relation to Country Life, 1913,* 64–65 (hereafter cited as Alabama's Country Schools). ADAH, Dept. of Education, *Annual Report, 1912,* 36. *Citizen-Examiner,* February 24, 1910 (re Duncan).

73. General Education Board, *The General Education Board: An Account of Its Activities, 1902–1914,* 63.

74. ADAH, SPR0106, *Alabama School Improvement Association, Records,* 1912–1919. Meeting report for December, 1914.

75. ADAH, Dept. of Education, *Annual Report, 1913,* 36–37.

76. ADAH, Dept. of Education, *Annual Report, 1912,* 25.

77. General Education Board, The General Education Board: An Account of Its Activities, 1902–1914, 18-22.

78. Ibid.

79. ADAH, Dept. of Education, *Biennial Report, 1907–1908,* 23.

80. *Opelika Daily News,* June 1, 1905.

81. Bailey, *Edgar Gardner Murphy,* 150–151.

82. Ibid., 150.

83. *Opelika Daily News,* September 19, 1905.

84. *Mountain Eagle,* May 11, 1904.

85. ADAH, Dept. of Education, *Biennial Report, 1899–1900,* 171, 174.

86. ADAH, Dept. of Education, *Biennial Report, 1903–1904,* 78.

87. Report by John D. Forte in Alabama Dept. of Education, SG011916, *County/City Board Annual Reports, 1904–05.*

88. ADAH, Dept. of Education, *Biennial Report, 1903–1904,* 31.

89. Ibid., 67, 45.

90. Ibid., 7.

91. Samuel L. Webb and Margaret E. Armbrester, eds., *Alabama Governors: A Political History of the State* (Tuscaloosa: The University of Alabama Press, 2001), 153.

Chapter 7

1. Based on a definition of culture in Clifford Geertz, *The Interpretation of Cultures: Selected Essays* (New York: Basic Books, 1973), 5.

2. ADAH, Dept. of Education, *State Manual of the Course of Study for the Public Elementary Schools of Alabama* (Montgomery: Brown Printing Company, 1913), 11. This explains the notion of the "expanded community."

3. Michael Kammen, *Mystic Chords of Memory: The Transformation of Tradition in American Culture* (New York: Vintage Books, 1993), 277–279. Ellen M. Litwicki, *America's Public Holidays, 1865–1920* (Washington, D.C.: Smithsonian Institution Press, 2000), 7–8 and 177.

4. Adam Fairclough, *A Class of Their Own: Black Teachers in the Segregated South* (Cambridge, Mass.: Harvard University Press, 2007), 109.

5. Christmas was made an Alabamian public holiday in 1836.

6. Leigh Eric Schmidt, "The Commercialization of the Calendar: American Holidays and the Culture of Consumption, 1870–1930," *Journal of American History* (December 1991): 887–916.

7. Baldwin County Heritage Book Committee, *The Heritage of Baldwin County, Alabama* (Clanton, Ala.: Heritage Publishing Consultants, 2001), 83. Lawrence County Heritage Book Committee, *The Heritage of Lawrence County, Alabama* (Clanton, Ala.: Heritage Publishing Consultants, 1998), 14.

8. Blount County Heritage Book Committee, *The Heritage of Blount County, Alabama* (Clanton, Ala.: Heritage Publishing Consultants, 1999), 67.

9. *Mountain Eagle*, January 9, 1901.

10. Ibid., October 3, 1894.

11. *Wilcox Progress*, September 25, 1889.

12. *Mountain Eagle*, October 5, 1904 (Iron Mountain Public School closing). Susie P. Tompkins, *Cotton-patch School-house* (Tuscaloosa: The University of Alabama Press, 1992), 208.

13. William H. Holtzclaw, *The Black Man's Burden* (1915; rpt., New York: Haskell House Publishers, 1971), 28.

14. *Wilcox Progress*, June 22, 1887.

15. Brian Sutton-Smith, ed., *A Children's Game Anthology: Studies in Folklore and Anthropology* (New York: Arno Press, 1976), 33–42. Alabama Dept. of Education, *An Educational Survey of Three Counties in Alabama*, Montgomery, Alabama, July 1, 1914 (Montgomery: Brown Printing Company, 1914), 140–141.

16. Pike County Heritage Book Committee, *The Heritage of Pike County, Alabama* (Clanton, Ala.: Heritage Publishing Consultants, 2001), 70.

17. ADAH, Dept. of Education, *An Educational Survey of Three Counties in Alabama*, 142. Virginia Pounds Brown and Laurella Owens, *Toting the Lead Row: Ruby Pickens Tartt, Alabama Folklorist* (Tuscaloosa: Alabama Folklorist).

18. Edward N. Clopper, *Child Welfare in Alabama: An Enquiry by the National Child Labor Committee Under the Auspices and with the Cooperation of the University of Alabama* (New York: National Child Labor Committee, 1918), 81–82.

19. Wade Hall, *Conecuh People: Words from the Alabama Black Belt* (Montgomery: New South Books, 2004), 95–96.

20. Ronald Dykes, *Growing Up Hard: Memories of Jackson County, Alabama in the Early Twentieth Century* (Paint Rock, Ala.: Paint Rock River Press, 2003), 37.

21. Margaret J. Jones, *Combing Cullman County* (Cullman, Ala.: Modernistic Printers, 1972), 91.

22. ADAH, Dept. of Education, *Annual Report, 1887,* 29. *Troy Messenger,* January 27, 1887.

23. Leigh Eric Schmidt, "From Arbor Day to the Environmental Sabbath: Nature, Liturgy, and American Protestantism," *Harvard Theological Review* 84 (July 1991): 299–323, 304.

24. *Mountain Eagle,* February 28, 1906.

25. ADAH, Dept. of Education, *Program and Selections for Celebration of the Anniversary of the Day on Which Alabama Was Admitted to the Union: For Use in the Schools of Alabama* (Montgomery: Brown Printing Company, 1903).

26. Karen L. Cox, *Dixie's Daughters: The United Daughters of the Confederacy and the Preservation of Confederate Culture* (Gainesville: University Press of Florida, 2003), 50.

27. *Wilcox Progress,* September 7, 1887 (re Sallie Jones).

28. Mattie Huey, *History of the Alabama Division of the United Daughters of the Confederacy* (1937; rpt., Opelika, Ala.: Post Publishing Company, 2002), 11.

29. Karen L. Cox, *Dixie's Daughters,* 130–131.

30. *Mountain Eagle,* April 28, 1909.

31. ADAH, Dept. of Education, *Programs and Selections for the Celebration January 19, 1907 of the One Hundredth Anniversary of the Birth of General Robert E. Lee* (Montgomery: Brown Printing Company, 1907), 3–8.

32. Richard Pierard and Robert D. Linder, *Civil Religion and the Presidency* (Grand Rapids, Mich.: Acadamie Books, 1988), 22–23. William N. Hutchins, "Moral Values in National Holidays," *Biblical World* 49 (March 1917): 168–170.

33. Charles R. Wilson, *Baptized in Blood: The Religion of the Lost Cause, 1865–1920* (Athens: University of Georgia Press, 1980), 223.

34. W. Lloyd Warner, *The Living and the Dead: A Study of the Symbolic Life of Americans* (New Haven, Conn.: Yale University Press, 1959), 233–234.

35. At the end of the 1906 scholastic year there were 1,548 black schools and 4,100 white schools. Enrollments were 113,121 and 235,275, respectively.

36. *Colored Alabamian,* December 28, 1907.

37. Robert J. Norrell, *Up from History: The Life of Booker T. Washington* (Cambridge, Mass.: Belknap Press of Harvard University Press, 2009), 176.

38. ADAH, Dept. of Education, *Thomas Jefferson's Birthday: Program and Selections for Its Celebration in the Schools of Alabama* (Montgomery: Brown Printing Company, 1909), 2–5.

39. ADAH, Dept. of Education, *Alabama Library Day, Programs and Selections for the Observance of Library Day, November 4th, by the Schools of Alabama* (Montgomery: Brown Printing Company, 1909).

40. ADAH, Dept. of Education, *Bird Day Book, May the Fourth, Nineteen Hundred and Ten* (Montgomery: Brown Printing Company, 1910), 3–13. Ellen M. Litwicki, *America's Public Holidays, 1865–1920,* 197.

41. Litwicki, *America's Public Holidays, 1865–1920,* 196–197, 199.

42. A 1903 bill required rural schools to teach agriculture.

43. Percival Chubb, "The Function of the Festival in School Life," *Elementary School Teacher* 4 (April 1904): 559–565.

44. Percival Chubb (1860–1960) published many books and articles (e.g., *Festivals and Plays in Schools and Elsewhere* [New York: Harper and Brothers, 1912]).

45. Litwicki, *America's Public Holidays, 1865–1920*, 2.

46. Horace G. Brown, "Observances of Historic Days at School," *Education* 32 (November 1911): 147–152. Constance D'Arcy MacKay, *Patriotic Plays and Pageants for Young People* (New York: Henry Holt and Co., 1912), 3, iii, quoted in Litwicki, *America's Public Holidays, 1865–1920*, 181.

47. ADAH, Dept. of Education, *Alabama's Country Schools and their Relation to Country Life*, Bulletin No. 33 (Montgomery: Brown Printing Company, 1913), 24–28. Kimberly O'Dell, *Images of America, Calhoun County* (Charleston: Arcadia Publishing, 1998).

48. ADAH, Dept. of Education, *Elementary Schools Manual, 1910*, 8.

49. *Citizen-Examiner*, January 13, 1910, and February 3, 1910. *Wilcox Progressive Era*, February 24, 1910, and February 23, 1911.

50. ADAH, Dept. of Education, *Alabama's Country Schools and their Relation to Country Life*, 29.

51. Ibid.

52. ADAH, Dept. of Education, *Better Health Day, February 12, 1915*, Bulletin No. 49 (Montgomery: Brown Printing Company, 1915), 3.

53. John Dewey, *The School and Society* (Chicago: Chicago University Press, 1900), 44.

54. Susan Bender Alburtis, *Good Roads Arbor Day: Suggestions for Its Observance* (Washington, D.C.: Government Printing Office, 1913).

55. Thomas M. Owen, *History of Alabama and Dictionary of Alabama Biography in 4 Volumes* (Chicago: S. J. Clarke Publishing Co., 1921), 566. Austin R. Meadows, *History of the State Department of Education of Alabama, 1854–1966* (Montgomery: n.p., 1968), 8.

56. William F. Feagin, "*More Revenue for Education in Alabama*" (Address to AEA, April 9–11, 1914) (Montgomery: Brown Printing Company, 1914). Charles Eugene Millar, "The Contributions of William Francis Feagin to Education in Alabama" (Ed.D. diss., University of Alabama, 1963), 53.

57. Meadows, *History of the State Department of Education of Alabama, 1854–1966*, 8.

58. ADAH, Dept. of Education, SG013206, Box 8, *Minutes of County Boards of Education*, December 1916, Montgomery, Alabama, 13.

59. ADAH, Dept. of Education, *Annual Report, 1915*, 24–25.

60. Ibid., 38.

61. ADAH, Alabama Dept. of Education, SG013232, *Results of Clean-Up and School Improvement Day*, 40. ADAH, Dept. of Education, *Better Health Day, February 12, 1915*, 3.

62. Richard Pierard and Robert D. Linder, *Civil Religion and the Presidency*, 20–25.

63. Based on a 1906 survey. Wayne Flynt, *Alabama in the Twentieth Century* (Tuscaloosa: The University of Alabama Press, 2004), 443–444.

64. ADAH, Alabama Dept. of Education, SG013232, *Results of Clean-Up and School Improvement Day*, 10.

65. *Wilcox Progressive Era,* December 16, 1915. The editor was paraphrasing a stanza from Lord Tennyson's poem *In Memoriam.*

66. ADAH, Dept. of Education, *Good Roads Day, January 15, 1915,* Bulletin No. 47 (Montgomery: Brown Printing Company, 1914), 4–16.

67. ADAH, Dept. of Education, *Better Health Day, February 12, 1915,* 8–16.

68. ADAH, Dept. of Education, *Better Farming Day, March 12, 1915,* Bulletin No. 50 (Montgomery: Brown Printing Company, 1915), 2.

69. Ibid. (Capitalization original.) Wording informed by I Corinthians 13: 13 in the King James Bible.

70. These were "The School Teacher's Creed"—*Elementary Schools Manual, 1910,* 2; "The Country Boy's Creed—*Rural Manhood,* April 1912, 106; "The Farmer's Creed"—*Better Farming Day, March 12, 1915,* 9; "My Civic Creed"—*Elementary Schools Manual, 1910,* 17. "Our Creed"—*Alabama's Country Schools and their Relation to Country Life,* 97; "My Health Creed"—*Better Health Day, February 12, 1915,* 16.

71. ADAH, Dept. of Education, *Better Farming Day, March 12, 1915,* 9.

72. Informed by I Corinthians 6: 19 in the King James Bible.

73. ADAH, Dept. of Education, *Better Health Day, February 12, 1915,* 16.

74. ADAH, Dept. of Education, *Alabama's Country Schools and their Relation to Country Life,* 97.

75. ADAH, Dept. of Education, *Elementary Schools Manual, 1913,* 10.

76. Ibid., 14.

77. George Ellsworth Johnson, *Education by Plays and Games, What to do at Recess* (1907; rpt., Boston: Ginn and Co., 1910).

78. ADAH, Dept. of Education, *Elementary Schools Manual, 1913,* 15.

Chapter 8

1. ADAH, Dept. of Education, *Annual Report, 1875.*

2. ADAH, Dept. of Education, *Annual Report, 1890,* cxc–cxci. James D. Anderson, "Black Rural Education and the Struggle for Education during the Age of Booker T. Washington, 1877–1915," *Peabody Journal of Education* 67 (Summer 1990): 51.

3. *Colored Alabamian,* October 26, 1907.

4. William Edward Burghardt Du Bois, *The Souls of Black Folk* (New York: Barnes and Noble Classics, 2003), 9–14.

5. ADAH, Dept. of Education, *Annual Report, 1875,* 106.

6. Booker T. Washington, *Up from Slavery: An Autobiography* (1900; rpt., Garden City: Doubleday and Company, 1963), 116.

7. William Holtzclaw, *The Black Man's Burden,* New York, Haskell House Publishers Ltd, 1971 [1915], 30-31. Bosun Roughton to state superintendent of education (LeRoy F. Box), May 17, 1878, in SG015978, Folder 5, *Superintendent's Correspondence, 1867–1878,* ADAH.

8. John O. Turner, *Circular of Information from Department of Education authorized by his Excellency Joseph F. Johnston as to Alabama's Educational Status from 1855–1898* (Mont-

gomery: Department of Education, 1898). Turner reported: "One of the marvels of the nineteenth century is the educational progress of the southern negro since the Civil War.... No Southern state has made a better showing in this respect than Alabama."

9. Jacob E. Cooke, "The New South," in *Essays in American Historiography: Papers in honor of Allan Nevins,* ed. Donald Henry Sheehan and Harold C. Syrett, 68 (New York: Columbia University Press, 1960). James L. Leloudis, *Schooling the New South: Pedagogy, Self, and Society in North Carolina, 1880–1920* (Chapel Hill: University of North Carolina Press, 1996), 181. *Marengo Democrat,* July 19, 1901, quoted by Glenn N. Sisk, "Negro Education in the Alabama Black Belt, 1875–1900," *Journal of Negro Education* 22 (Spring 1953): 129.

10. Calculated from table VI in Horace Mann Bond, *Negro Education in Alabama: A Study in Cotton and Steel* (1939; rpt., Tuscaloosa: The University of Alabama Press, 1994), 162.

11. Richard A. Couto, *Ain't Gonna Let Nobody Turn Me Round: The Pursuit of Racial Justice in the Rural South* (Philadelphia: Temple University Press, 1991), 204, and David Nasaw, *Schooled to Order: A Social History of Public Schooling in the United States* (New York: Oxford University Press, 1979), 140.

12. Hugh C. Bailey, *Edgar Gardner Murphy: Gentle Progressive* (Coral Gables: University of Miami Press, 1968), 111.

13. Peter Lewis and John Hart to Governor Joseph Johnston, November 18, 1898. Quoted by George W. Prewett, "The Struggle for School Reform in Alabama, 1896–1939" (Ph.D. diss., University of Alabama, 1993), 89.

14. William Warren Rogers, Robert David Ward, Leah Rawls Atkins, and Wayne Flynt, *Alabama: The History of a Deep South State* (Tuscaloosa: The University of Alabama Press, 1994), 325.

15. The phrase is from Rick Bragg, *Redbirds: Memories from the South* (London: Harvill Press, 1998), 4.

16. Edward R. Crowther, "Charles Octavius Boothe: An Alabama Apostle of Uplift," *Journal of Negro History* 78 (1993): 110–116. Reverend Dr. Charles O. Boothe to John William Abercrombie, state superintendent of education, August 4, 1901, in SG015976, Folder 11, *Superintendent's Correspondence, 1899–1906,* ADAH. (Emphasis original.) Charles Octavius Boothe, *Cyclopedia of the Colored Baptists* (Birmingham: Alabama Publishing Company, 1895), 10–11.

17. Robert J. Norrell, *Up from History: The Life of Booker T. Washington* (Cambridge, Mass.: Belknap Press of Harvard University Press, 2009), 336.

18. *Colored Alabamian,* October 26, 1907.

19. ADAH, Dept. of Education, *Biennial Report, 1899–1900,* 136.

20. Lawrence W. Levine, *Black Culture and Black Consciousness* (Oxford: Oxford University Press, 1977), 160.

21. Edwards, *Twenty-five Years in the Black Belt,* 30. Fred S. Watson, *Coffee Grounds: a History of Coffee County, Alabama, 1841–1970* (Anniston, Ala.: Higginbotham, 1970), 201.

22. Adam Fairclough, *A Class of Their Own: Black Teachers in the Segregated South* (Cambridge, Mass.: Harvard University Press, 2007), 129.

23. J.L.M. Curry, *A Brief Sketch of George Peabody and a History of the Peabody Educational Fund through Thirty Years* (1898; rpt., New York: Negro Universities Press, 1969), 24.

24. Kenneth R. Johnson, "The Peabody Fund: Its Role and Influence in Alabama," *Alabama Review* 27 (April 1974): 122.

25. Robert Sherer, *Subordination or Liberation? The Development and Conflicting Theories of Black Education in Nineteenth-Century Alabama* (Tuscaloosa: The University of Alabama Press, 1977), 19.

26. ADAH, Dept. of Education, *Biennial Report, 1899–1900*, 177 and 130.

27. Richard A. Couto, *Ain't Gonna Let Nobody Turn Me Round: The Pursuit of Racial Justice in the Rural South*, 190.

28. Wade Hall, *Conecuh People*, 19. Oral history recorded from Verse Lee Johnson Manley.

29. For example, see William B. Paterson to Henry Clay Armstrong, state superintendent of education, September 4, 1883, in SG015974, Folder 11, *Superintendent's Correspondence, 1867–1916*, ADAH. Booker T. Washington to John O. Turner, February 20, 1896 in J.L.M. Curry manuscript collection; quoted in Horace Mann Bond, *Negro Education in Alabama*, 218–219. Michael Fultz, "African American Teachers in the South, 1890–1940: Powerlessness and the Ironies of Expectations and Protest," *History of Education Quarterly* 35 (Winter 1995): 406–407.

30. Edwards, *Twenty-five Years in the Black Belt*, 17. Also Holtzclaw, *Black Man's Burden*, 36–37.

31. Louis R. Harlan, *Booker T. Washington in Perspective: Essays of Louis R. Harlan*, ed. Raymond W. Smock (Jackson, University Press of Mississippi, 1988), 199. Louis Harlan, "Booker T. Washington in Biographical Perspective," *American Historical Review* 75 (October 1970): 1581–1586.

32. Robert J. Norrell, "Booker T. Washington: Understanding the Wizard of Tuskegee," *Journal of Blacks in Higher Education* 42 (Winter 2003–2004): 96–109, and Robert J. Norrell, *Up from History: The Life of Booker T. Washington*.

33. Booker T. Washington, *Up from Slavery: An Autobiography*, 109.

34. Harlan, "Booker T. Washington in Biographical Perspective," 1590, 1593, and 1583.

35. ADAH, Dept. of Education, *Biennial Report, 1899–1900*, 57.

36. Sherer, *Subordination or Liberation?*, 147.

37. ADAH, Dept. of Education, *Biennial Report, 1899–1900*, 230. By 1900 there were a number of Presbyterian mission schools in Wilcox County. Jeanette Steele McCall, *The First and Last Bell: A Story of Six Missions for Blacks in Wilcox County, Alabama* (Baltimore: American Literary Press, 2005).

38. Simpson is mentioned in the *Wilcox Progress*, October 28, 1896. Louis R. Harlan, ed., *The Booker T. Washington Papers*, vol. 8 (1972; rpt., Champaign: University of Illinois Press, 1989), 284–286.

39. *Wilcox Progress*, November 4, November 11, November 18, November 25, 1896.

40. Holtzclaw, *Black Man's Burden*, 8–9.

41. Ibid.

42. *Colored Alabamian*, February 26, 1910.

43. Bond, *Negro Education in Alabama*, 153–156.

44. *Public School Laws of Alabama, 1891*, Chapter II, Article IV, p. 19.

45. Joseph B. Graham, "Current Problems in Alabama," *Annals of the American Academy of Political and Social Sciences* 22 (September 1903): 39.

46. Malcolm Cook McMillan, *Constitutional Development in Alabama, 1798–1901: A Study in Politics, the Negro, and Sectionalism* (Chapel Hill: University of North Carolina Press, 1978), 322–323.

47. ADAH, Dept. of Education, *Annual Report, 1909,* 6.

48. Theodore Rosengarten, *All God's Dangers: The Life of Nate Shaw* (Chicago: University of Chicago Press, 2000), 216.

49. Anderson, *Education of Blacks in the South,* 33. W.E.B. Du Bois and Augustus Granville Dill, eds., *The Common School and the American Negro; report of a social study made by Atlanta University under the patronage of the Trustees of the John F. Slater Fund; with the proceedings of the 16th annual Conference for the Study of the Negro Problems, held at Atlanta University, on Tuesday, May 30th, 1911* (Atlanta: Atlanta University Press, 1912), 68–69. Stanley B. Greenberg, *Race and State in Capitalist Development: Comparative Perspectives* (New Haven, Conn.: Yale University Press, 1980), 40.

50. Lance Jones, *The Jeanes Teacher in the United States* (Chapel Hill: University of North Carolina Press, 1937), 18.

51. Ibid.

52. Ibid., 15–16.

53. William A. Link, *A Hard Country and a Lonely Place: Schooling, Society, and Reform in Rural Virginia, 1870–1920* (Chapel Hill: University of North Carolina Press, 1986), 186.

54. *Citizen-Examiner,* January 21, 1909.

55. Dabney, *Universal Education in the South,* vol. 2 (Chapel Hill: University of North Carolina Press, 1936), 521–522.

56. ADAH, Dept. of Education, *Annual Report, 1913,* 44–56.

57. ADAH, Dept. of Education, *The Work of the Jeanes Supervising Industrial Teachers and the Homemakers' Clubs for Negro Girls, Alabama 1916* (Montgomery: Brown Printing Company, Printers and Binders, 1917). Hereafter cited as Dept. of Education, *Work of the Jeanes Teachers,* 6.

58. ADAH, Dept. of Education, SG015442, *Rural School Agent Correspondence, 1913–1914.* Letter dated August 10, 1914, from James Sibley to James H. Dillard.

59. Ibid., letter dated November 10, 1913, from James Sibley to Mrs J. M. Carmichael of Ozark, Alabama. ADAH, Dept. of Education, *Annual Report of state supervisor of colored schools,* dated November 18, 1913, 46.

60. ADAH, Dept. of Education, SG015442, *Rural School Agent Correspondence, 1913–1914,* letter dated August 10, 1914, from James Sibley to James H. Dillard.

61. Leloudis, *Schooling the New South,* 188.

62. ADAH, Dept. of Education, SG015442, *Rural School Agent Correspondence, 1913–1914,* letter dated November 12, 1913, from Mrs. J. M. Carmichael of Ozark, Alabama, to James Sibley.

63. Lance Jones, *The Jeanes Teacher in the United States,* 110–111.

64. ADAH, Dept. of Education, *Work of the Jeanes Teachers,* 16–22.

65. Ibid., 30.

66. ADAH, Dept. of Education, SG015442, *Rural School Agent Correspondence, 1913–1914*, letter dated April 29, 1914, from James Sibley to Miss Olegra Boyd of Plateau, Alabama.

67. Ibid., letter dated April 30, 1914, from Miss Olegra Boyd to James Sibley.

68. ADAH, Dept. of Education, *Alabama's Country Schools and their Relation to Country Life*, Bulletin No. 33, 62–73.

69. ADAH, Dept. of Education, *Work of the Jeanes Teacher*, 10 and 22.

70. Ibid., 8. Howard Marshall, "Basketmaking," in Wilson and Ferris, eds., *The Encyclopedia of Southern Culture* (Chapel Hill: The University of North Carolina Press, 1989), 461.

71. ADAH, Dept. of Education, *Work of the Jeanes Teachers*, 35.

72. Wade Hall, *Conecuh People: Words from the Alabama Black Belt*, 39–40. J. Mack Lofton, *Voices from Alabama: A Twentieth-Century Mosaic* (Tuscaloosa: The University of Alabama Press, 1993), 22.

73. ADAH, Dept. of Education, *Work of the Jeanes Teachers*, 31. Report of Hattie J. Huckabee, Special Agent.

74. J. Scott McCormick, "The Julius Rosenwald Fund," *Journal of Negro Education* 3 (October 1934): 606.

75. Ibid.

76. Ibid., 610.

77. Ibid.

78. Anderson, *The Education of Blacks in the South, 1860–1935*, 154–155.

79. Russell O. Mays, "Julius Rosenwald: Building Partnerships for American Education," *Professional Educator* 28 (Fall 2006): 5–6.

80. United States Department of the Interior, *An Educational Study of Alabama*, Bureau of Education, Bulletin 41 (Washington, D.C., 1919), 181.

81. McCormick, "The Julius Rosenwald Fund," 616.

82. Carl V. Harris, *Political Power in Birmingham, 1871–1921* (Knoxville: University of Tennessee Press, 1977), 34.

83. Report by L. H. Mathews, superintendent of Birmingham schools, in Dept. of Education, SG011916, *County/City Board Annual Report, 1874*, ADAH.

84. Carl V. Harris, "Stability and Change in Discrimination Against Black Public Schools: Birmingham, Alabama, 1871–1931," *Journal of Southern History* 51 (August 1985): 393–394.

85. ADAH, Dept. of Education, SG013240, *State Publications, 1896–1991*, "White Teachers in Colored Schools." Address given to Southern Educational Association at Hot Springs, Arkansas, on January 2, 1896, by Superintendent J. H. Phillips.

86. Harris, "Stability and Change in Discrimination Against Black Public Schools: Birmingham, Alabama, 1871–1931," 396.

87. Ibid., 403–405.

88. Prewett, "The Struggle for School Reform in Alabama, 1896–1939," 100.

89. Anderson, *Education of Blacks in the South*, 33. Du Bois and Augustus Granville Dill, eds., *The Common School and the American Negro; report of a social study made by Atlanta University under the patronage of the Trustees of the John F. Slater Fund; with the proceedings of*

the 16th annual Conference for the Study of the Negro Problems, held at Atlanta University, on Tuesday, May 30th, 1911 (Atlanta: Atlanta University Press, 1912), 68–69.

90. Harris, *Political Power in Birmingham, 1871–1921,* 173.

91. Adam Fairclough, *A Class of Their Own,* 274.

92. Harris, *Political Power in Birmingham, 1871–1921,* 172. Fairclough, *A Class of Their Own,* 273–274.

93. Marshall F. Phillips, "A History of the Public Schools in Birmingham, Alabama" (Master's thesis, University of Alabama, 1939), 109.

94. Ibid. Fairclough, *A Class of Their Own,* 269–270.

Chapter 9

1. Jesse Monroe Richardson, *The Contribution of John William Abercrombie to Public Education* (Nashville: George Peabody College for Teachers, 1949), 32–34.

2. Charles Eugene Millar, "The Contributions of William Francis Feagin to Education in Alabama" (Ed.D. diss., University of Alabama, 1963), 44–45, 40, and 93–94.

3. ADAH, Dept. of Education, *Annual Report, 1915,* 10.

4. Barbara Welter, "The Cult of True Womanhood," *American Quarterly* 18 (Summer 1966): 152.

5. This was Feagin's ninth bill. In 1911 an attempt was made to enact a bill requiring county superintendents to be qualified teachers but this failed. Owen Hunter Draper, "Contributions of Governor Braxton Bragg Comer to Public Education in Alabama, 1907–1911" (Ed.D. diss., University of Alabama, 1970), 204–206.

6. ADAH, Dept. of Education, *Annual Report, 1915,* 10 and 18. David Tyack, "Pilgrim's Progress: Toward a History of the School Superintendency," *History of Education Quarterly* 16 (Autumn 1976): 265.

7. The 1910 U.S. census showed 23 percent of the state's population over ten years was illiterate. ADAH, Dept. of Education, *Annual Report, 1915,* 10.

8. Ibid., 11.

9. ADAH, Dept. of Education, State Publications, SG013206, Box 8, *Minutes of County Boards of Education, December 4 & 5, 1916,* 10.

10. Akenson and Neufeldt, "Alabama's Illiteracy Campaign for Black Adults, 1915–1930: An Analysis," *Journal of Negro Education* 54 (Spring 1985): 189–195.

11. Wayne Flynt, *Alabama in the Twentieth Century: The Modern South* (Tuscaloosa: The University of Alabama Press, 2004), 222.

12. See chapter 3.

13. ADAH, Dept. of Education, *Annual Report, 1915,* 21–22.

14. Don Eddins, *AEA: Head of the Class in Alabama Politics: A History of the Alabama Education Association* (Montgomery: Compos-it Inc., 1997), 249.

15. ADAH, Dept. of Education, *Alabama's Country Schools and their Relation to Country Life,* Bulletin No. 33 (Montgomery: Brown Printing Company, 1913), 105.

16. Edward N. Clopper, *Child Welfare in Alabama: An Enquiry by the National Child Labor Committee under the Auspices and with the Cooperation of the University of Alabama* (New

York: National Child Labor Committee, 1918), 73. ADAH, Dept. of Education, *Annual Report, 1912,* 10–11.

17. ADAH, Dept. of Education, *Annual Report, 1915,* 17.

18. Adelaide Kilgrow and Eugene M. Thomas, *History of Education in Alabama,* Bicentennial Intern Project, Montgomery, Alabama State Department of Education Bulletin, 1975, no. 7, 42.

19. George W. Prewett, "The Struggle for School Reform in Alabama, 1896–1939" (PhD diss., University of Alabama, 1993), 73.

20. Ibid., 125–126 and 134.

21. Eva Joffe, "Rural School Attendance," in Clopper, *Child Welfare in Alabama,* 101–111.

22. ADAH, Dept. of Education, *Biennial Report, 1907–1908,* 19, 31, 29, 41, and 56.

23. Ibid., 47.

24. Ibid., 121. (Italics original.)

25. Ibid., 11, 110, 17, 70, and 73.

26. Ibid., 63, 10 and 45.

27. ADAH, Dept. of Education, *Annual Report, 1912,* 5.

28. William F. Feagin, *More Revenue for Education in Alabama* (Montgomery: Brown Printing Company, 1914), 7–8.

29. *Wilcox Progressive Era,* February 4, 1915.

30. Clopper, *Child Welfare in Alabama,* 83–84.

31. U.S. Department of the Interior, *An Educational Study of Alabama,* Bureau of Education, Bulletin 41, Washington D.C., 1919, 69 and 174.

32. Clopper, *Child Welfare in Alabama,* 97.

33. ADAH, Dept. of Education, *Annual Report, 1915,* 37.

34. Ibid.

35. ADAH, Dept. of Education, SG011916, *County/City Board Annual Reports, 1904–05.* Baldwin County Heritage Book Committee, *The Heritage of Baldwin County, Alabama* (Clanton, Ala.: Heritage Publishing Consultants, 2001), 73. Blount County Heritage Book Committee, *The Heritage of Blount County, Alabama* (Clanton, Ala.: Heritage Publishing Consultants, 1999), 60–61.

36. Joe G. Acee, *Lamar County History* (Vernon, *Lamar Democrat,* 1976), 68.

37. Arthur J. McCray to Dr. James H. Dillard, January 2, 1915, in Alabama Dept. of Education, SG015442, *Rural School Agent Correspondence, 1913–1914,* ADAH.

38. Clopper, *Child Welfare in Alabama,* 79; Eddins, *AEA: Head of the Class in Alabama Politics,* 248.

39. Wayne E. Fuller, *The Old Country School: The Story of Rural Education in the Middle West* (Chicago: University of Chicago Press, 1982), 235–237.

40. ADAH, Dept. of Education, *Annual Report, 1915,* 21.

41. United States Department of the Interior, *An Educational Study of Alabama,* 163.

42. ADAH, Dept. of Education, *Annual Report, 1915,* 13–20.

43. United States Department of the Interior, *An Educational Study of Alabama,* 19.

44. ADAH, Dept. of Education, *Annual Report, 1914,* 7–8.

45. *Report of the Commissioner for Education for the year 1896–97,* quoted in David B.

Tyack, "The Tribe and the Common School: Community Control in Rural Education," *American Quarterly* 24 (March 1972): 15.

46. U.S. Senate, *The Report of the Commission on Country Life* (Reprint of Document No 705, 60th Congress, 2d Session) (Spokane: Spokane Chamber of Commerce, 1911), 121.

47. Ellwood Patterson Cubberley, *Rural life and education: A study of the rural-school problem as a phase of the rural-life problem* (Boston: Houghton Mifflin, 1914).

48. ADAH, Dept. of Education, *Annual Report, 1915*, 23.

49. ADAH, Dept. of Education, *Biennial Report, 1899–1900*, xv.

50. John William Abercrombie, state superintendent, to John D. Humphrey, superintendent of education for Madison County, March 13, 1901, in SG015976, Folder 10, *Superintendent's Correspondence, 1899–1906*, ADAH.

51. Eddins, *AEA: Head of the Class in Alabama Politics*, 349.

52. Richardson, *The Contribution of John William Abercrombie to Public Education*, 3 and 9–11.

53. Austin R. Meadows, *History of the State Department of Education of Alabama, 1854–1966* (Montgomery: Austin R. Meadows, 1968), 34.

54. ADAH, Dept. of Education, *Annual Report, 1914*, 8–9.

Chapter 10

1. David B. Danbom, *The Resisted Revolution: Urban America and the Industrialization of Agriculture, 1900–1930* (Ames: University of Iowa Press, 1979), 13–14.

2. ADAH, Dept. of Education, *State Manual of the Course of Study for the Public Elementary Schools of Alabama* (Montgomery: Brown Printing Company, 1913), 11.

3. Mabel Carney, *Country Life and the Country School* (Chicago: Row, Peterson and Company, 1912). Ellwood P. Cubberley, *Rural life and education: A study of the rural-school problem as a phase of the rural-life problem* (Boston: Houghton Mifflin, 1914). John Dewey, *The School and Society* (Chicago: Chicago University Press, 1900).

4. Wayne Flynt, *Alabama in the Twentieth Century: The Modern South* (Tuscaloosa: The University of Alabama Press, 2004), 223, 225.

5. George W. Prewett, "The Struggle for School Reform in Alabama, 1896–1939" (Ph.D. diss., University of Alabama, 1993), 224.

6. Danylu Belser, *Conditions and Practices Influencing the Elementary Education of White Children in the Public Schools of Alabama* (Birmingham: Birmingham Printing Company, 1930), 33.

7. James Agee and Walker Evans, *Let Us Now Praise Famous Men: Three Tenant Families* (Boston: Houghton Mifflin, 1988), 291.

Bibliographic Essay

This essay is a guide to some of the material I found most useful in researching this book. It does not seek to be comprehensive and omits titles actually named in the text or cited on multiple occasions in the endnotes.

To understand better the concepts of "localism," "culture," and "community" upon which my treatment of the topic rests, I found the following books were a helpful introduction: Anthony P. Cohen's *The Symbolic Construction of Community* (1985); Emile Durkheim's *The Elementary Forms of the Religious Life* (1915); Clifford Geertz's *The Interpretation of Cultures: Selected Essays* (1973); and W. Lloyd Warner's *The Living and the Dead: A Study of the Symbolic Life of Americans* (1959).

In order to research localism in Alabama's educational history I reviewed a large number of county and local histories—both general and educational—and also "heritage book" compilations. A representative county history with educational entries is Margaret P. Farmer's *History of Pike County, Alabama, 1821–1971* (1973). Many local historians have written specifically about schools and/or teachers and/or students of a particular place—Mrs. Frank Ross Stewart's *The History of Education in Cherokee County, Alabama* (1981) being an example. Such histories are written for a vested readership by enthusiasts and are full of anecdotes, which, while they need cautious evaluation, do throw light on schooling experiences (both rural and urban) in the relevant period. I found memoirs and oral history collections such as Wade Hall's *Conecuh People* (2004) and J. Mack Lofton's *Voices from Alabama: A Twentieth-Century Mosaic* (1993) to be similarly enlightening. Patricia Albjerg Graham's *Community and Class in American Education, 1865–1918* (1974) contains a case history of such issues in Butler County. Glenn N. Sisk and Irving Gershenberg have both published scholarly articles in the *Journal of Negro Education* on sectional educational differences.

Stephen B. Weeks's *History of Public Education in Alabama* (1915)—which drew on Willis G. Clark's *History of Education in Alabama, 1702–1889* (1889)—

is still a hugely useful outline of Alabama's early educational history. A doctoral dissertation by George W. Prewett, "The Struggle for School Reform in Alabama, 1896–1939" (1993), is a modern version of the broad systemic inquiry conducted by Weeks. In *Why Public Schools? Whose Public Schools? What Early Communities Have to Tell Us* (2003), David Mathews writes about localism and Alabama's schools—mainly in the antebellum period. His book proposes greater community involvement as an antidote for twenty-first-century problems.

General histories of Alabama usually include sections on public education. Two such histories are *A History of Alabama and Its People* written by Albert Burton Moore in 1927 (but subsequently updated) and the comparatively recent *Alabama: The History of a Deep South State* coauthored in 1994 by four prominent Alabamian scholars, William Warren Rogers, Robert David Ward, Leah Rawls Atkins, and J. Wayne Flynt. Flynt's *Poor but Proud: Alabama's Poor Whites* (1989) is a wide-ranging study of the socioeconomic world inhabited by many students.

Although Alabama was predominantly rural before 1915, its urban dimension was becoming increasingly important. I found Carl V. Harris's *Political Power in Birmingham, 1871–1921* (1977) to be an essential introduction to Birmingham's growth from the 1870s to the 1920s. A master's thesis by Fred Marshall Phillips, "A History of the Public Schools in Birmingham, Alabama" (1939), documents the early years of that city's education system. Lynne B. Feldman's *A Sense of Place: Birmingham's Black Middle-Class Community, 1890–1930* (1999) describes the black experience of living in Birmingham in that period.

I approached the black educational experience with Peter Kolchin's *First Freedom: The Responses of Alabama's Blacks to Emancipation* (1972) and then read Horace Mann Bond's *Negro Education in Alabama: A Study in Cotton and Steel* (1939). Seventy years after it was written, this book remains a masterly examination of the fiscal strangulation of black schools after 1891, of the effects of disenfranchisement on the ability of blacks to influence public education policy, and of the effects of philanthropy. Robert Sherer's *Subordination or Liberation? The Development and Conflicting Theories of Black Education in Nineteenth-Century Alabama* (1977) explores similar issues from a contemporary historian's viewpoint. Henry Allen Bullock's *A History of Negro Education in the South* (1967) and Adam Fairclough's *A Class of Their Own: Black Teachers in the Segregated South* (2007) set black education within a regional context. Having been written closer to the period under review, Lance Jones's *Negro Schools in the Southern States* (1928) and *The Jeanes Teacher in the United States* (1937) were of interest.

Ira Harvey's *A History of Educational Finance in Alabama, 1819–1970* (1989) and a doctoral dissertation by Russell Stompler, "A History of the Financing of Public Schools in Alabama from Earliest Times" (1955), provide details of school funding and tax policies over time and explain clearly the 16th section calamity.

Relevant biographical treatments of Alabama's educational reformers include Hugh C. Bailey's *Edgar Gardner Murphy: Gentle Progressive* (1968), Jessie Pearl Rice's *J.L.M. Curry: Southerner, Statesman and Educator* (1949), Charles Eugene Millar's unpublished dissertation on "The Contributions of William Francis Feagin to Education in Alabama" (1963), and Jesse Monroe Richardson's *The Contribution of John William Abercrombie to Public Education* (1949).

Don Eddins's *AEA: Head of the Class in Alabama Politics: A History of the Alabama Education Association* (1997) and Jerome A. Gray, Joe L. Reed, and Norman W. Walton's *History of the Alabama State Teachers Association* (1987) are organizational histories of the associations that helped shape teaching into a profession. A self-published monograph by Austin R. Meadows, *History of the State Department of Education of Alabama* (1968), assisted me to track bureaucratic changes in that department.

To consider fully the broad context of public schooling I consulted a range of relevant histories, including Edward L. Ayers's *The Promise of the New South: Life after Reconstruction* (1992); Allen J. Going's *Bourbon Democracy in Alabama, 1874–1890* (1951); Sheldon Hackney's *Populism to Progressivism in Alabama* (1969); Malcolm Cook McMillan's *Constitutional Development in Alabama, 1798–1901: A Study in Politics, the Negro, and Sectionalism* (1955); William Warren Rogers's *One-Gallused Rebellion: Agrarianism in Alabama, 1865–1896* (2001); Samuel L. Webb's *Two-Party Politics in the One-Party South: Alabama's Hill Country, 1874–1920* (1997); Jonathan M. Wiener's *Social Origins of the New South: Alabama, 1860–1885* (1978); and C. Vann Woodward's *The Origins of the New South, 1877–1913*.

Many of the issues that beset the development of public schooling in Alabama were common to other Southern states and I mention several studies of state and regional experiences in the introduction. Wayne E. Fuller's *The Old Country School: The Story of Rural Education in the Middle West* (1982) and Paul Theobald's *Call School: Rural Education in the Midwest to 1918* (1995) allowed me to compare Alabama's schooling arrangements with those in regions outside the South.

There have been many studies of Southern Progressivism which spawned a great deal of educational reform. Hugh C. Bailey's *Liberalism in the New South: Southern Social Reformers and the Progressive Movement* (1969) was my entrée to the topic area, and Dewey W. Grantham's *Southern Progressivism:*

The Reconciliation of Progress and Tradition (1983) extended my appreciation of Progressivism's range and complexity. Mary Thomas's *The New Woman in Alabama: Social Reforms and Suffrage, 1890–1920* (1992) surveys the range of concerns of Alabama's female Progressives, and I gained direct insight into the AFWC from Lura Craighead's *History of the Alabama Federation of Women's Clubs* (1936). Anne Firor Scott's *The Southern Lady: From Pedestal to Politics, 1830–1930* (1970) and Karen J. Blair's *Clubwoman as Feminist* (1980) enlarged my view of female activism. William A. Link's *The Paradox of Southern Progressivism, 1880–1930* (1992) considers the role of localism as a brake on reform.

A critique of the "Southern education movement" is offered in Louis R. Harlan's *Separate and Unequal: Public School Campaigns and Racism in the Southern Seaboard States 1901–1915* (1958). The *General Education Board: An Account of Its Activities, 1902–1914* (1914) is a corporate account of the GEB's involvement in the Southern educational movement.

William Bowers's *The Country Life Movement in America, 1900–1920* (1974) introduced me to this movement and its principals (e.g., Liberty Hyde Bailey) who had such a profound influence on the direction of rural education.

I considered many educational matters that weren't specific to Alabama, such as the role of normal schools—for example, Christine A. Ogren's *The American State Normal School* (2005)—and the feminization of teaching—for example, Myra H. Strober and Audri G. Lanford's "The Feminization of Public School Teaching: Cross Sectional Analysis, 1850–1880," in *Signs* (1986). Besides the textbook studies mentioned in chapter 4, I also consulted John A. Nietz's *Old Textbooks* (1961) and Ruth Elson's *Guardians of Tradition: American Schoolbooks of the Nineteenth Century* (1964).

I found David B. Tyack's many books and articles on American educational history to be invaluable—particularly "The Tribe and the Common School: Community Control in Rural Education" in *American Quarterly* (1972). Lawrence Cremin's *The Transformation of the Schools: Progressivism in American Education, 1876–1957* (1961) was an excellent source for comprehending changing philosophies of education in the early twentieth century.

Ellen Litwicki's *America's Public Holidays, 1865–1920* (2000) helped me to understand school celebrations and their significance. Robert Bellah's "Civil Religion in America" in *Daedalus* 96 (Winter 1967) is the seminal work on this subject.

Most of the primary source material accessed for my research is held by the Alabama Department of Archives and History in Montgomery. I made extensive use of legislative and governmental records (particularly the department of education's), newspapers (both original copies and on microfilm), and manuscripts held by the ADAH.

Index